THE PLACE
OF
KENT

Judith Glover

MERESBOROUGH BOOKS

For my daughters, Sonja and Isobel

Meresborough Books are specialist publishers of books on Kent, including a monthly magazine 'Bygone Kent'. Full list sent on request to 7 Station Road, Rainham, Kent. ME8 7RS.

First published 1976 by B.T. Batsford Ltd.
This edition published 1982 by Meresborough Books

ISBN Hardback 0905270 614
Paperback 0905270 622

Printed by Mackays of Chatham Ltd.

CONTENTS

Page 45 Cobham. derivation refers
to Cobham Survey. Cobba's water meadow.

INTRODUCTION

Kent's history — and therefore that of its place names — begins
with the British, descendants of countless tribal migrations
from the European mainland. The names which they gave to
their settlements have disappeared in all but a few cases, surviving most noticeably among the names of the great headlands
which strike out into the Channel waters, the islands which
fringe the county's coastline, and the rivers which carve deep
valleys through the Kentish countryside.

The Romans took not a few of these names when they colo-
nized south-eastern England in the first century AD; but the
Saxons, who followed hard on the shadow of the departing
Legions, largely ignored the old names, or else turned them
round to suit their own tongue. When the Normans attempted
to do the same thing they failed — the place names of Kent
had by then been too long established for any foreign power
to force a change in pronunciation or spelling.

It has been said of Kent that its history is an epitome of the
history of England; and certainly, the place names of the county
trace the course of that history more than anything else.

Thousands of years ago, at a time when the English Channel
was merely a broad river meandering across the great Northern
European plain, Kent was no more than a faceless feature of
that land mass, and though the area was doubtless known to the
nomadic tribes who wandered this way in prehistoric times, it
was not distinguished by any particular name. Not until the
river deepened and widened, engulfing part of the vast plain
and separating Britain from the Continent, was this south-
eastern corner of the island identified as the "rim, or edge":

iv

cantus.

In 55 and 54 BC Caesar and his Legions penetrated into Kent, and, adopting the old British word, called the area *Cantium.* In this form the name has passed down through the centuries, changing only slightly, and is thus the oldest county name in Britain.

The Romans, despite the great social and cultural effect which they had on the county — as on the country — have not left their mark on Kentish place names, preferring to Latinize the existing British forms they found here. But the Saxons, a marauding race from the European mainland, had exactly the opposite effect: they destroyed, not created; they killed or enslaved, not protected; they were feared, not trusted. Yet paradoxically they did what the Romans failed to do, and have stamped their impression firmly on the map of Kent. And in all fairness, it must be said that once they had settled their conquered territory, they soon set about making it into a rich and well-organized kingdom, their art work being perhaps the most beautiful of that period of English history. It is not the Romans, not the British, nor even the Jutes (who were invited to control the unruly subjects of the British king Vortigern in the mid-fifth century, and having done so, helped themselves to a large slice of his territory), but the Saxons whose names are the true foundation of the place names of Kent.

Everywhere, in towns and villages, hamlets and farms, woods and hills and streams, the Saxons have left their mark. They made their settlements first along the open river valleys, building on the ruins of British villages, reoccupying ancient strongholds and Roman forts. Gradually, as the new kingdom established itself under Æsc, the first of the Saxon kings of Kent, small tribal communities were formed; and as the communities expanded and became large villages there were more and more sons to start their own new settlements by the woods, hills and rivers which still bear their names.

Then, in 1066, came the Normans. After 500 years of growth and development, and conversion to Christianity by St. Augustine in the sixth century, the Kentish Saxons were no longer a warrior race; indeed, they were no longer a separate kingdom. They were English (though they were proud of being descended

INTRODUCTION

from the *Cantware*, or people of Kent, and retained a dim
memory of their bloody beginnings against the Jutes, who had
established themselves to the east of the Medway as "the Men
of Kent", while the Saxons, to the west of the river, retaliated
by calling themselves "the Kentish Men". The rivalry still
existed, though in a friendly fashion, by the time England had
become a united kingdom).

In 1086 a great survey was made for William I of his newly-
conquered country. In that year officials visited each county,
and they made a record of, among many other things, the names
of the hamlets, farmsteads and villages in each Hundred — a
sub-division of the county capable of supporting 100 families.

The Norman officials made what they could of the names
which the English had given to their homes and land, and
recorded in the Domesday Book as near a form as possible.
They were foreigners, hearing words which made little sense to
them; but they did their best, just as the British soldiers serving
in Flanders during the First World War did *their* best, trans-
lating Ypres as Wipers, Sailly-la-Bourse as Sally Booze, Mouquet
Ferme as Moo-cow Farm, and Godewaersvelde as Gertie Wears
Velvet.

The Norman officials departed with their Normanised English
place names quaintly recorded in the Domesday Book, and the
old names' spelling continued to be faithfully reproduced by
English clerics in charters, court rolls and parish registers. Though
Kent was now a county largely under the administration of
William's half-brother, Odo of Bayeux, and divided into Lathes,
or county divisions, life went on in much the same fashion as it
had done before 1066. New places grew up, taking the name of
those who settled them, just as the original Saxon communities
had been named for the man, or tribe, who had founded them
many centuries before.

Parish registers, rentals and surveys and court records dating
from the thirteenth to the seventeenth century have provided
us with the names of those families which are now a part of the
Kentish landscape, to be read on signposts and road maps,
attached to Parks and Hills and Greens, Farms and Lanes and
Woods. (As a guide, and to save monotonous repetition of the
same sources, the years in which these family names are recorded

vi

have been placed in brackets in the entries.)

Though the development still goes on, and the original Saxon place names of the county have altered as succeeding generations, speaking a progressively more modern English, have recorded forms which are almost those of today, there are still clues to be found pointing the way back to the origin of a name: the numerous Kentish places ending in -den were once pastures; those ending in -leigh or -ly were clearings made in thickly wooded areas; while those ending in -ing or -inge were tribal settlements. We can tell from these old names, many of them reaching back over almost a thousand years, the type of land and vegetation those early settlers found in Kent, what trees flourished, what crops were grown, what kind of flowers and birds and animals they found here. And place names also give fascinating detail of those long-dead people themselves: their personal names (Raven, Stallion, Badger, Falcon — even Turnip), their customs and religious beliefs, their domestic life and their recreation.

There are almost three thousand place names in Kent, including those such as Greenwich, Bromley and Deptford which have now become part of the Greater London administrative area, but which are to be found in this book because they were, until this century, Kentish places since their beginning and have played their part in the history and development of this

To those interested in pursuing this fascinating subject further, I would recommend the works of Prof. J. K. Wallenberg, author of the standard study of Kentish place names, to which I must acknowledge my indebtedness.

Royal Tunbridge Wells
1975

GLOSSARY

of the most common elements in the place names of Kent

OLD ENGLISH

āc   oak-tree

æcer   cultivated piece of land

æsc   ash-tree

bēce, bōc   beech-tree

beorg   mound, tumulus, barrow

brōc   marshy ground

brycg   bridge

burh   stronghold

burna   stream, bourne

camp   field

clif   cliff, steep slope

cnoll   knoll, hillock

cumb   valley, coombe

dæl   valley, dale

denn   woodland pasture

denu   valley, dene

dūn   hill, down

ēa   river

ēg   island

ersc   stubble field

feld   open land

ford   ford

gāra   gore, wedge-shaped piece of land

geat   gate, cliff-gap

grāf   grove

hæcc   hatch, gate

hǣð   heathland, heather

halh   corner of land

hām   settlement, homestead

hamm   water meadow

OLD ENGLISH

hangra   wooded slope, hanger

hielde   slope

hlinc   rising ground, linch

hōc   hook of land

hōh   spur of land, hoo

hol   hollow

holt   thicket

hrycg   ridge

hyll   hill

hyrst   wooded hill, hurst

ingas   people of, tribe

lǣs   lea, meadow

land   land

lēah   clearing, glade

mǣd   mead, meadow

mere   pool

mersc   marsh

næss   headland, cape

ōra   shore, border, bank

pytt   pit, hollow

scaga   copse, shaw

scylf   shelf, shelving land

snād   detached piece of land

sol   muddy pool

stede   place

strǣt   Roman road, street

tūn   farmstead, manor

weald   forest

wīc   farm

wielle   spring

wudu   wood

Words connecting place name forms

alias   otherwise known as

juxta   next to

A to Z of
The Place Names of Kent

Abbreviations

B	British
OE	Old English
OF	Old French
ME	Middle English
F	French

Note

In entries such as **Abbot's Court** (Hoo St. Werburgh) and **Acton Farm** (Charing), the bracketed name is the parish to which the place name belongs.

Place names set in CAPITALS have their own entries in the A to Z.

Many of the Middle English forms of place names reproduced here end with a single apostrophe: this was a common abbreviation replacing final *e*.

A

Abbey Farm and **Wood** (Higham). The farm stands on the site of Higham Priory, a Benedictine abbey founded in 1148. The wood nearby is also named after the old abbey.

Abbot's Court (Hoo St. Werburgh). So called because the building was once the property of the Abbey of Boxley. Abbott's Court, Burmarsh, similarly takes its name from its early association with St. Augustine's Monastery at Canterbury.

Ackholt (pronounced Ay-colt). Oak thicket (OE *āc holt* → Akholte 1226 → Acolte 1240 → Acholte 1346).

Acol (pronounced Ay-coll). Oak thicket (OE *āc holt* → Acholt' 1270 → Ocholte, Okholte 1292 → Acholte 1343). The name has been abbreviated to its present form perhaps to avoid confusion with ACKHOLT.

Acrise (pronounced Ay-creese). Oak brushwood (OE *āc hrīs* → Acres 1086 → Hacrise 1166 → Ockerise 1215 → Acrise 1226).

Acton Farm (Charing). Acca's farmstead (OE *Accan tūn* → Aketon 1206 → Acketon' 1270 → Acton' 1292).

Acton Farm (Wittersham). Oak pasture: woodland pasture where oaktrees grow (OE *āc denn* → Acdenne 1292 → Acden' 1334 → Akdenn' 1343).

Addington. Eadda's farmstead (OE *Eadding tūn* → Eddintune 1086 → Eadintuna c.1100 → Edingtone, Edintune 1185 → Adington' 1256 → Addington 1610). Eadda also owned a settlement at ENGEHAM.

Adisham (pronounced Addisham). Eade's settlement (OE *Ēades hām* → Adesham 616 → Edesham 1006 → Eadesham c.1100 → Adesham 1254). Eade was the chief of a tribe settled at ITTINGE.

Admers Wood (Meopham). Eadmær's open land (OE *Ēadmæres feld* → Edmeris field 1381). In this name, original 'field' has been superseded by 'wood'.

3

Agney, Upper and **Lower.** Thornbush enclosure island: island with a thornbush enclosure on it (OE *hagan ēg* → Haghne 1240 → Haggehene 1254 → Haghen 1291 → Agene 1293). Agney – once a true island in the Romney Marshes – appears to have been originally distinguished by a hawthorn tree growing on it: in 785 it is recorded as *haganan treæ* – 'tree of the thornbush enclosure'; and in 791, when the place was given by King Offa to Christ Church, it appears in the charter as *Hagenatreou*. Not far from Upper Agney is Hawthorn Corner, which possibly preserves the original name.

Akhurst Farm (Sheldwich). Oak stubble field: stubble field marked by an oak-tree (OE *āc ersc* → to Atersce 993 → Akers 1522). Corruption of final -ers to -hurst is common in place names.

Albans. It is probably associated with the now lost place of Albans in East Peckham, not far away, which derived its name from that of Alban de Wandsworth who became lord of the manor in 1305.

Alderden Manor (Sandhurst). Ealdhere's woodland pasture (OE *Ealdhering denn* → Aldryndenn' 1270 → Aldrindenn' 1278 → Aldryndenne, Altryndenn' 1292).

Aldergate Bridge. Guildhall gate (OE *gildheall geat* → Hyldehallegate 1270 → Ildhallegate 1278 → Ildhalgate 1334). The original gate must have led to a guildhall in LYMPNE.

Aldington. Ealda's farmstead (OE *Ealding tūn* → Aldintone 1086 → Ealdintune, Aldintune c.1100 → Aldyntone 1253 → Aldington 1579). The personal name means 'old man, chieftain': it is also found in connection with ALDINGTON PLACE, ELLINGTON, YALDHAM and YALDING.

Aldington Knoll. Knoll, hillock (OE *cnoll* → Knolle 1292 → Knoll 1431). This is the highest point on the Clay Hills and takes its affix from nearby ALDINGTON.

Aldington Place (Thornham). The name shares the same origin as ALDINGTON and is recorded as Audintone 1086 → Ealdingtun c.1100 → Aldintone 1215.

Aldon. Ælla's hill (OE *Ællan dūn* → Aledon' 1240 → Aldone 1327 → Aldon' 1334). Ælla also owned a farmstead at ALLINGTON and a pool at ALMERY COTTAGE.

Alkerden Manor (Swanscombe). The original name seems to have been simply valley, or coombe (OE *cumb*), since it is found as Combe in 1327 and as Coumbe in 1330. In 1494 the place appears as Combes, and not until 1778 is Alkerden recorded as Alkerdyn, Alchardin *alias* Combes. If the alternative and now present name is an old one, it may possibly be traced back to 'Ealhheard's woodland pasture' (OE *Ealhhearding denn*).

Alkham (pronounced Awkam). Heathen temple settlement: settlement where there is a heathen temple (OE *ealh hām* → Ealhham c.1100 → Aukeham 1204 → Alkam, Alcham 1242 → Alkham 1247). This is the only instance where *ealh* has survived in a place name; other examples of its use are only found in lost names, such as Ealhfleot – 'creek by a heathen temple' – which was an early name given to a channel connecting Faversham with the sea.

Alland Grange. Old land (OE *eald land* → Aldelande 1226 → Ealdelonde, Aldeland c.1250 → Allonde Grang' 1535). A grange was a manor, usually with farm buildings, belonging to a monastery.

Allen's Hill (Cliffe). Together with Allen's Pond here, the name is derived from that of the family of John Aleyn of Cliffe (1327). Allen's House and Allen's Farm at Wrotham are associated with the family of William Aleyn de Mereworth (1352), a native of Mereworth who had settled in Wrotham.

All Hallows. Recorded as Omnium Sanctorum 1253 → Ho All Hallows 1285 → Alhallowes 1610, the place takes its name from its 12th century church of All Saints. It was formerly known as Hoo All Hallows, being in the Hundred of Hoo.

Allington (near Lenham). Æðelnoð's farmstead (OE *Æðelnoðing tūn* → Alnoitone 1086 → Alnodentune c.1100 → Eilnothinton' 1242 → Eylnothynton 1308 → Ailnothintone 1327 → Allington 1610).

Allington (near Maidstone). Ælla's farmstead (OE *Ælling tūn* → Elentun 1086 → Aeilentune c.1100 → Alintone 1210 → Elyngton' 1270 → Allington 1579). Ælla's name is also found in association with ALDON and ALMERY COTTAGE.

Almery Cottage. Ælla's pool (OE *Ællan mere* → Alemere 1327 → Almer' 1334 → Almnery-Green *alias* Almery Green 1782). Amberfield and Amber Green, lying half a mile away from Almery Cottage, are corruptions of the original name and are comparatively late place names.

Amage Farm (Wye). Connected with a water meadow (OE *hamming* → Amyngg', Aminge 1270 → Hamminge 1272 → Ammyng c.1480). The farm lies close to the Great Stour.

Amberfield, Amber Green. See under ALMERY COTTAGE.

Amery Court (Blean). Alms house, almonry (OF *almosnerie* → Aumeneresbleen 1358 → Amycourt in le Bleane 1535). The place once belonged to the almoner of St. Sepulchre's Nunnery in Canterbury.

Amets Hill (Stockbury). It derives its name from that of the family of William Amite (1327), living in the Stockbury area.

Amhurst Hill (Pembury). Meadow hill: wooded hill near a water meadow (OE *hamm hyrst* → Hemhurst 1250 → Hammherst 1348 → Amherst 1489).

Amos Shaw. It is associated with the Wye family of Amos: John, Richard and William Amys are recorded in this area in 1327, and Edmund, Richard and Roger Amys in 1348.

Amsbury Wood (Hunton). Æmbre's stronghold (OE *Æmbres burh* → Ambresbir' 1264 → Ambresbery

1278). The wood, and Amsbury House here, are situated close to an old earthwork which was probably the original stronghold.

Angley Wood (Cranbrook); Angle's clearing (OE *Angling lēah* → Anglingle 1257 → Anglyngley 1267). Alternatively, this may be 'angle's clearing' (OE *angeling lēah*), the angle being formed by a winding tributary of the Beult which rises in the wood. But in the same area is SISSINGHURST, associated with a Saxon, so it seems more probable that Angley Wood, together with Angley Farm and House here, is on land originally belonging to Angles, and was so named to distinguish it from that owned by Saxons nearby.

Ansdore. Ægen's 'door', or pass (OE *Ægenes dor* → Aginsdore 1240 → Agnesdore 1254 → Annysdore 1790). The personal name is also found in connection with EN-BROOK, EYNSFORD, and the now lost place of Eynton in Thornham. OE *dor* — 'door' — was used to mean a pass, or way through a valley, in the same way that *geat* — 'gate' — could also mean a cliff-gap.

Anvil Green. Hagona's open land (OE *Hagonan feld* → Hachenefeud', Haugnefeld' 1240 → Hagkenfeld', Hannefeld' 1254). The present place name is a corruption of the 'Hannefeld' form.

Aperfield Court (Cudham). Apple-tree land: open land on which apple-trees grow (OE *apulder feld* → Apeldrefeld 1242 → Appeldorefeld 1253 → Apeldurfeud 1270).

Appledore. At the apple-tree (OE

æt þæm apuldre → æt Apuldre 893 → Apoldre 1032 → Apeldres 1086 → Appeldere 1226 → Apledowre 1579 → Appledore 1610).

Appleton (pronounced Aypelton). Fruit garden, orchard (OE *æppeltūn* → Apletone 1086 → Appletune c.1100 → Appletone 1253). Appleton Farm, Ickham, has the same original meaning and appears as Appleton' in 1261.

Archer's Court (Whitfield). It is named after the family variously recorded as le Archier, Archer, Archyer, who were in possession of the manor from the 13th century.

Argrove Wood (Hawkinge). Bank grove: grove near a bank (OE *ōra grāf* → Oregraue 1226 → Orgrave 1242 → Oregrove 1263). It stands on the bank of the River Rother.

Arnold's Oak. The place takes its name from Arnold de Bononia, lord of the Manor of Eastling, who is variously recorded as Arnold, Arnald, and (in 1278) as Arnald de Esenyngh' in Eseling' (Eastling).

Arpinge (pronounced Arpinje). Eorpa's people (OE *Eorpingas* → Erping' 1226 → Erpynge 1292 → Erpyng 1362). Alternatively, this tribe may have been nicknamed 'the dusky, or dark-coloured ones' (OE *eorpingas*).

Ash. Ash-tree (OE *æsc* → Eisse 1086 → Æisce c.1100 → Esse 1197). North Ash and South Ash Manor here are recorded as Suthesse in 1240, Northesse in 1275.

Ash-next-Sandwich. Ash-tree (OE

6

æsc → Ece 1086 → Æsce c.1100 → Esse 1262 → Asche 1270 → Esshe, Aysshe 1284).

Ashbank. This appears to be a comparatively late place name, replacing the original Asshelegh which is recorded in 1278 (← OE *æsc lēah*: ash-tree clearing). Probably the name was altered to avoid confusion with ASHLEY.

Ashbourne Mill. Ash-tree stream: stream overhung with ash-trees (OE *æsc burna* → æscburnan, escburna 968 → Assheborne 1570). This was originally the name given to one of the many streams in the Tenterden area.

Ashdown. Ash-tree pasture: woodland pasture marked by an ash-tree (OE *æsc denn* → Esdenne, Esseden' c.1250 → Asshedene, Esden' 1254 → Assheden 1366).

Ashenbank Wood (Cobham). The name is self-explanatory, being recorded as Ashen Bank in 1698.

Ashenden. Æschere's woodland pasture (OE *Æschering denn* → Easserdenne 1253 → Esserinden' 1278 → Asshrendenn' 1313).

Ashenfield Farm (Waltham). Æscmær's open land (OE *Æscmæres feld* → Esmerefel 1086 → Esmeresfeld' 1242 → Asshemerfeld' 1296).

Ashford. Ash-tree corner by a ford (OE *æsc scēat ford* → Essetesford 1086 → Aescedesford c.1100 → Esseteford 1211 → Essheteforde 1262 → Ashford 1610). The town lies within a large bend of the Great Stour and appears to have developed

around a ford or river-crossing at this spot.

Ashley. Ash-tree clearing (OE *æsc lēah* → Eslegh' 1254 → Assele 1270 → Esshele 1313 → Ashley 1489). Ashley House, Sellindge, marks the site of an 'ash-tree hill' (OE *æsc hyll*), the name appearing as Asshell in 1338.

Ashmere. Recorded as Assem'e in 1292, this place name appears to be derived from OE *æsc mere*: 'ash-tree pool'.

Asholt Wood (Newington). Ash-tree thicket (OE *æsc holt* → Esseholte 1240 → Assholt Wood 1539).

Ashour Farm and **Wood** (Leigh). Ash-tree bank: bank marked by an ash-tree (OE *æsc ōra* → Æschore 1044 → Essore 1292 → Asshore 1313).

Ashurst. Ash wooded hill (OE *æsc hyrst* → Æischerste c.1100 → Esserst 1253 → Asshehurst 1261 → Asshurst 1308). Ashurst Lodge Farm, Chart Sutton, shares the same origin, appearing as Esehurst 1253 → Essherst 1344 → Asshehirste 1386.

Austin Lodge, Upper and **Lower.** Ordrīc's valley (OE *Ordrīces dene* → Orchesden 1195 → Orkesdene 1210). The place is situated in a valley.

Avery Farm (All Hallows). Hēahburh's island (OE *Hēahburge ēg* → Heabureahg 686 → Euery 1518 → Aviary Farm 1801). The farm lies at the tip of a promontory which was once a true island belonging to a Saxon lady, Hēahburh. She may

7

have been an abbess, since her property was part of the lands granted to the monastery at Peterborough by Cædwalla in the 7th century.

Aycliff. High cliff (OE *hēah clif*). There are no forms to show how the present name evolved, but Aycliff, which is near Dover, is found as the home of Juliana Heghclyues in 1348.

Aydhurst. Hawthorn wooded hill (OE *hagu-porn hyrst* → Edherst' 1232 → Hetherst 1274 → Heythhurst 1278).

Aylesford (pronounced Aylesfud). Ægel's ford (OE *Ægeles ford* → Ægelesford 455 → Agelesford c. 960 → Ailesford 1086 → Æilesford c.1100 → Aylsforde 1610). The ford would have crossed the Medway at this spot. Ægel's settlement was at AYLESHAM and he was chief of a tribe living at ELLINGE.

Aylesford Green. Ætle's enclosure (OE *Ætles worð* → Atelesworde, Atelesworthe c.1250 → Attlysworthe 1327 → Atlesworthe 1346 → Atelisford 1348 → Adelifford 1502). Change from -worth to -ford is common in place names. The present name is no doubt due to confusion with Aylesford proper.

Aylesham (pronounced Aylesum). Ægel's settlement (OE *Ægeles hām* → Elisham 1367 → Aylysham 1405 → Haylesham 1445). Though the name is old — the personal name is also found in connection with AYLESFORD and ELLINGE — this is a comparatively modern place incorporating Aylesham Corner, Wood and Farm, and was built during the 1920s for the miners of nearby Snowdon Colliery.

Ayleswade. Corner piece of detached woodland (OE *halh snād* → Halsnod' 1224 → Halsnade 1254 → Halesnode 1338). Misreading of *n* as *u* has produced the *w* in this place name.

B

Back Shaw. See under BEX WOOD.

Backtilt Wood (Benenden). 'Back tilth': back, or ridge, which is tilled (OE *bæc tilðe* → Beketilthe 1254). The wood stands on a ridge of land between two streams.

Badlesmere (pronounced Badlesmeere). Bæddel's pool (OE *Bæddeles mere* → Badelesmere 1086 → Bedelesmere 1170 → Badellesmere 1242 → Badlesmer 1610).

Badmonden. Worshippers' woodland pasture (OE *gebedmanning denn* → Bidminden 1213 → Bademinden 1275). OE *gebedmann:* 'man of prayer, worshipper', produced the Middle English word *beodeman,* literally 'bead-man' — or one who used a rosary in prayer. Badmonden was once the property of the Priory of Beaulieu in Normandy.

Badsell. Bēada's miry place (OE *Bēadan syle* → Badeshull 1227 → Badesell 1258 → Badsell 1610). The village is on low-lying ground through which runs a stream.

Bagham. There are no recorded forms for this place name, but it may possibly be associated with the family name of John Bagge of Chilham (1309).

Bagshill Cottages. Rounded, or smooth, water meadow's hill (OE *balg hammes hyll* → **Balgameshull'** 1313 → Balgameshelle 1332 → Balgameshell 1345). The present name is a contraction of these 14th century forms.

Bainden. Bæga's woodland pasture (OE *Bæging denn* → Beginden' 1254 → Beghyndenne 1313). Bæga's name also occurs in connection with a water meadow at BAYHAM, a stronghold at BINBURY, and with the now lost place of Bagden Wood in Throwley.

Baker Lane. It is associated with the family of Thomas Baker of Headcorn (1472). This occupational surname, together with its earlier form of Bakere, is also found in connection with Baker Farm, Lenham; Baker's Close, Elham; Baker's Farm, Egerton; and Baker's Wood, Seal and Stansted.

Baker's Close and **Wood**. See under BAKER LANE.

Baker's Cross. The place is traditionally so called because it was at the cross here that Sir John Baker of Sissinghurst, a notable anti-Protestant during the reign of Mary I, heard of the accession of Queen Elizabeth as he was riding to Cranbrook to preside at a trial of Protestants.

Balcombe (pronounced Bawcum). Bolla's field (OE *Bollan camp* → Bolcompe 1332 → Bolcombe 1334).

Baldock Downs. The name is derived from that of the family of John Ballock' (1357) who lived in the Elham area. Baldock Wood, Lenham, is similarly associated with the family of Bauldocke (1616): there is a memorial to them in Lenham church.

Ballards. It is associated with the family of Richard Ballard of Goudhurst (1642).

Ballsdown. See under BALL'S WOOD.

Ball's Wood (Ashford). It is first recorded in 1636, when it appears as Bales Wood, probably taking its name from that of a local landowner. Ballsdown Farm, Whitstable, derives its name from that of the family variously recorded as Bolle, Balle, between the 14th and 15th centuries.

Balserstreet Farm (Whitstable). It takes its name from a local family who appear between the 13th and 15th centuries as Belsyr, Belsire, Balsier, Balser. The affix 'Street' was added to the name at a later date.

Bapchild (pronounced Bab-child). Bacca's spring (OE *Baccan celde* → Baccancelde 696 → Baccechild 1197 → Bakechild 1219 → Babchilde 1572).

Barden Park. Bære's woodland pasture (OE *Bæring denn* → Barindena c.1100 → Barindenne 1270 → Bardenne 1314). Barden Furnace Farm, three miles away in Bidborough, takes its name from the Park.

Bardingley. Clearing belonging to Bearda's people (OE *Beardinga lēah* → Beardingaleag 814 → Bardingelege c. 1220 → Bardingeleye 1292).

Bardogs. This is a manorial name: John, Nicholas and William Bardehog are recorded in 1313, and John Bardog in 1450.

Baretilt. Barley tilth, or tillage (OE *bere tilðe* → Bertilth 1285 → Beretilthe 1348).

Barfreston. Beornfrið's farmstead (OE *Beornfriðes tūn* → Berfrestone 1086 → Berfredestune c.1100 → Berfreston 1235 → Barfrayston 1610).

Bargrove. Barley grove: grove near which barley is grown (OE *bere grāf* → Beregroue 1327 → Bergroue 1347).

Barham (pronounced Barrum) Beora's settlement (OE *Beoran hām* → Beoraham 805 → Berham 1086 → Barham 1610). Beora's tribe owned land at BELLINGHAM. Barham Court, Teston, was originally an estate which derived its name from the family of Berham, natives of Barham, who owned it from the 12th century onwards.

Barham Court. See under BARHAM.

Barksore. Birch-tree shore: shore near which birch-trees grow (OE *beorc scora* → Berchesores 1177 → Berkesour 1235 → Barkesore 1278 → Barksore 1313). This was once a true shore line before the sea retreated, leaving a belt of marshland known as Barksore Marshes.

Barling Green. It appears to derive its name from BARMING a few miles away, being recorded as Barmlyng 1327 → Barblynge 1334 → Barling 1461. Barling's Hole, Egerton, is probably a manorial name, taken from that of a native of Barming who settled in the 'hole' or hollow here: it appears as Berlynge 1332 → Barlyng' 1334 → Barblyng 1346.

Barling's Hole. See under BARLING GREEN.

Barming, East and **West.** (pronounced Baamin) 'Bramble clearing people': people settled in a clearing rid of brambles (OE *brēmel lēah ingas* → Bermelinge, Bermelie 1086 → Bermeling, Bernuelinges c.1100 → Barmelinges 1186 → Barbling' 1251 → Estbarbling' 1262 → West Barmlynge, West Bramlyng 1308 → Barming 1610).

Barming, Little. See under BARNJET.

Barnden. Recorded in 1292 as Ber-

nesdenn', the name may possibly have had the original meaning of 'Beorn's woodland pasture' (OE *Beornes denn*).

Barnes Cray. It takes its name from the family of Barne who were landowners in this area during the latter half of the 18th century. The affix 'Cray' is from the River Cray, by which the place is situated.

Barnesfield. See under BARNFIELD.

Barnes Street. It derives its name from association with the family of atte Berne (1327): 'dweller by the barn' (OE *bern*).

Barnet's Lane. See under BARNETTS.

Barnetts. Burning: place cleared by burning (OE *bærnet* → Bernette 1283 → Barnette 1381 → Barnettesgrove 1414 → Bernetts 1525). Barnet's Lane in Sturry may share the same original meaning, but there are no records. Barnett's Wood, Shoreham, takes its name from Robert and Roger Burnet (1313) — 'dweller by the burnt place' (OE *bærnet*).

Barnfield. Open land near a barn (OE *bern feld* → Bernefeld 1203). Barnfield Bank, St. Paul's Cray, has the same origin and is recorded in 1598 as Barnefeilde. Barnstreet Farm, St. Mary's Hoo, appears as Bernfeld 1296 → Barnfeld 1482 → Barnstreet 1690. Baron's Place, Mereworth, takes its name from the family of atte Berne (1327) — 'dweller by the barn' (OE *bern*): probably Barnesfield, near Stone, for which there are no records, shares a similar origin, being the open land (OE *feld*) of an owner named atte Berne.

Barnjet. This is the alternative name for Little Barming, the original name being composed of Barming together with the diminutive affix -et. The place is recorded in 1434 as Barmyngett, and in 1535 as Bermynget.

Barnsole. Muddy pool near a barn (OE *bern sol* → Bernesol 1332 → Bernesole 1371).

Barnstreet Farm, Baron's Place. See under BARNFIELD.

Barrett's Green. It takes its name from the family of Robert Barrett of Hawkhurst (1349).

Barrow Green. Mound or barrow (O.E *beorg* — Bergh' 1327 — Berghe 1347). Barrow Hill at Higham is an actual barrow, the name having been given the explanatory addition of 'hill' (OE *hyll*) and appearing in 1492 as Borowhyll. Barrowhill, Sellindge, has the same meaning as Barrow Green and is recorded as Berwe in 1254, Berghe in 1332.

Barrowhill. See under BARROW GREEN.

Bartletts. This is a manorial name taken from the family of John Bertelot de Monketon (1383).

Barton Wood (Crundale). Barley farm (OE *bere tūn* — Bertone 1211 — Berton 1354). The same origin is shared by Barton Court, Canterbury (Bertun 833, Bertone 1210); Wingham Barton Manor, Ashnext-Sandwich (Bertun' 1254, Berton 1313); Bartons, Wrotham (Bertone 1348); Barton's Farm, Hoo St. Werburgh (Berton' 1240, Bertone 1334).

Barty Farm and **House** (Thornham). Stronghold enclosure: enclosure near a stronghold (OE *burh tēag* — Beritege 1214 — Bertegh' 1313). There is an ancient earthwork close by.

Barville Farm (Tilmanstone). Open land near a swine pasture (OE *bær feld* → Barefeld' 1313 → Barfelde 1346 → Barfeild 1479). In this name -field has become -ville through local pronunciation.

Basden Wood (Hawkhurst). Bæddi's woodland pasture (OE *Bæddes denn* → Badisdenne 1253 → Badesden 1270 → Basden denn 1559). The place has given its name to Beston Farm, Benenden, which is recorded as the property of the family of Basden in 1570. The personal name, Bæddi, is also found in connection with BETSHAM.

Bassett's Mill. It takes its name from the family of John Bassett of Chiddingstone (1377). The same surname is found associated with Bassett's Farms at Cowden and Wrotham.

Basted (pronounced Baysted). Mound place: place near a mound or barrow (OE *beorg stede* → Bergstede 1270 → Berstede 1300 → Bersted' 1374).

Baston Farm. See under BAXON

Batchelor's Wood (Edenbridge). Recorded in 1566 as Bachelers, the wood has probably taken the name of a local landowner.

Batfold Wood (Chiddingstone). Fold near a birch-tree (OE *beorc falod* → Berkefaud' 1240 → Bercfold' 1254 → Berckefolde 1338).

Batteries. This seems originally to have been 'Botere's land' (ME *Boteres land*) since it is recorded in 1278 as Boterslond'. Later forms show confusion between the occupational names of 'butler' and 'butcher': the place is found as Boteleslond' in 1332 and as Bochereslonde in 1347. The present name appears to be a corruption of the Butteresfee form recorded in 1563, 'fee', or 'field', having been dropped at some later date to give modern Batteries.

Battle Street. It is associated with Robert Batayll' (1270) and Alexander, John and Matthew Bataille of Cobham (1327), being recorded as Batailleswode in 1375 and as Bataille wood in 1470. Battel Hall, Leeds, received its name from early owners named de la Bataille (1332) and ate Batayle (1338) who originated from Battle in Sussex.

Bavinge (pronounced Bavvinje) Babba's people (OE *Babbingas* → Babinge, Babbynge 1320). Babba himself was owner of a ford at BAYFORD.

Bavins Shaw. The place is connected with the family of Bavent who possessed the Manor of Halling between the 13th and 14th centuries: Roger de Bavent in Haulig' (Halling) is recorded in 1242. The place itself appears as Bavantes maner' in 1392.

Bax. Box-tree (OE *byxe* → Byx 1327 → Bex, Great, Little Backs 1782).

Baxon. At the backstone, or baking stone (OE *aet pǣm bǣcstāne* → Buxston 1331 → Baxtone, Bacston' 1338 → Bexon 1782). Baston Farm, Hayes, shares the same original meaning, being recorded as Bestan, Bicstane in 1254, Bastane in 1368. A backstone was a broad, flat stone which was heated from below and used for cooking or baking.

Baybrooks. 'Bend marsh': marshy ground by a river bend (OE *becge brōc* → Beggebroc 1263 → Beggebroke 1327). The place is low-lying and is situated close to a winding tributary of the Teise.

Bayfield. 'Prickle land': open land on which prickly shrubs grow (OE *bēg feld* → Baifeld 1247 → Bayfelde 1334).

Bayford. Young man's enclosure (ME *boian worthe* → Boywurthe 1442). There are no later forms to show when Boyworth became Bayford, but change from -worth to -ford is quite common in place names.

Bayford Court. (Sittingbourne). Babba's ford (OE *Babban ford* → Babbeford' 1292 → Babeforde 1347). Babba's tribe had their settlement at BAVINGE. His ford appears to have been a shallow crossing on Milton Creek.

Bayhall. 'prickle corner': corner of land where prickly shrubs grow (OE *bēg halh* → Beyhall' 1240 → Bayhale 1292). The corner was

13

probably formed by a bend in the stream here.

Bayham. Bǣga's water meadow (OE *Bǣgan hamm* → Begehā 1208 → Begeham 1228 → Begehamme 1315). Bǣga's name is also found associated with BAINDEN and BINBURY.

Bayley's Hill (Sevenoaks Weald). It takes its name from the family of Robert Bayly (1313) who lived in this area.

Baynards. It is associated with the family of John Baynard (1327).

Beachborough. Rounded, or swollen, mound (OE *bylce beorg* → ME *bilche bergh* → Belcheberche 1262 → Bithborrow 1690). Beachborough lies at the foot of the rounded hill which gave it its name.

Beacon Lane and **Hill** (Woodnesborough). Beacon (OE *bēcon* → the Bekon 1542 → Beaconfield 1689 → Beacon-Lane 1799). The beacon was sited on top of the hill. Beacon Bridge Wood, Herne, was also originally a 'beacon hill', being recorded as Bekynhill 1470 → the Bekyn 1482 → Bekynfield 1529.

Beal's Green. The name is derived from that of the family of Thomas Beale of Hawkhurst (1415).

Bean. Bean, bean-shaped (OE *bēan* → Ben 1240 → Been 1278 → Bean 1347). The name must refer to some hill close by.

Bear's Lane, Bear's Lane Wood (Bethersden). Recorded in 1627 as Bearsland, Bearsland Wood, and as Bearesland in 1632, this must originally have been land belonging to a person surnamed Beare or Bear.

Bearsted (pronounced Bursted). 'Mound homestead': homestead by a mound or barrow (OE *beorg hāmstede* → Berghamstyde c.700 → Bergested', Berhestede 1242 → Bergestede 1285 → Bersted 1610).

Beaute Farm (Staple). (Place) by a thicket (OE *bī holt* → Byholte 1327 → Biholte 1348 → Byholte 1454).

Beaux Aires Farm (Stockbury) (pronounced Bows-airs). Beautiful retreat (F *beau repaire* → Beauerepair c.1450). Probably so called because of its pleasant view.

Beauxfield (pronounced Bowsfield). Bēaw's open land (OE *Bēawes feld* → Bewesfeld c.772 → Bevesfel 1086 → Beausfeld 1215). Bēaw was also the owner of a mound or tumulus at BUESBOROUGH.

Beaver. Beautiful view (F *beau voir* → Beavor c.1165 → Bevere 1272 → Bevyr 1512 → Bever 1616).

Beblets. The name is possibly to be associated with the Chelsfield family of Mabelote, recorded during the 14th century. Assimilation of initial *m* to *b* is not unusual.

Beckenham. Beohha's settlement (OE *Beohhan hām* → Biohhahema mearc 862 → Beohhahammes gemæru 973 → Bacheham 1086 → Bekaham 1141 → Bekenham 1240). The 862 and 973 forms both mean 'boundary of Beohha's settlement'.

Becket's Barn and **House** (Fairfield).

They take their name from Fairfield's parish church, dedicated to St. Thomas à Becket. Becket, or Beckett, a common medieval surname, is found in connection with Becketts Farm, Penshurst; and Beckett's Place, Barming.

Beckley. Beocca's clearing (OE *Beoccan lēah* → Bioccan lea 889 → Bichelei 1086 → Beckele 1242).

Beddlestone. Bætel's farmstead (OE *Bæteles tūn* → Bedestone 1313 → Betlisdon' 1348 → Betleston 1401).

Bedgebury. 'Bend stronghold': stronghold by a river bend (OE *becge burh* → begcgebyra 814 → Bechebyri c.1270 → Beggeberi 1278 → Beggebury 1334 → Bedgbury 1690). The River Teise forms a small lake here which may be the original river bend.

Bedmangore Wood (Lynsted). Worshippers' gore, or wedge-shaped piece of land (OE *gebedmanna gāra* → Bedmangore, Bededmangore 1278 → Bedemanegore 1292 → Bidmongare 1690). The wood once belonged to the Abbey of Boxley and is only five miles east of BEDMONTON: possibly the same group of worshippers, perhaps monks, owned both places.

Bedmonton. Worshippers' farmstead (OE *gebedmanna tūn* → Bedemanton' 1258 → Bedemannetone 1327 → Bedmantone 1332). Worshippers, or men of prayer, are also found associated with BADMONDEN and BEDMANGORE WOOD.

Beechingland. This was probably land owned by the Newenden family of Bechinge (1587), later recorded as Beeching (1609).

Beerforstal Farm (Elham). It derives its name from the family of John le Barbour (barber, surgeon) de Bere de Elham (1313), whose name also appears as de Beer' ate fforstalle (1327) and has the meaning of 'dweller by the swine pasture' (OE *bær*). Forstal is a dialect word used of land in front of farm buildings.

Beesfield. William de Beseville is recorded as living in nearby Eynsford between 1210 and 1212, and the family of de Beseuill' are found in this area in 1254: probably Beesfield is a manorial name, being an anglicised form of this Norman French name.

Bekesbourne. This was originally simply 'stream' (OE *burna*), the name being recorded as Burnes between 1086 and 1200. Sometime during this period it became Lēofing's stream (ME *Lēofinges burne*) and appears as Livingesburn 1206 → Livingeburn 1238 → Lyvyngisbourn 1541. The present place name owes its origin to Willelmus de Beche, or Becco, a native of Bec in Normandy who held the manor between 1198 and 1208; it is recorded as Bekesburn' 1270 → Bekesborne 1280 → Beakesborne 1610.

Belce Wood (Sturry). Rounded, or swollen, wood (OE *bylce wudu* → ME *bilche wode* → Bilechewode 1249 → Bylychewode 1292). Perhaps so called because the wood grew on, or close to, a round hill.

Belgar. Beautiful garden (OF *bel gard* → Belgar' 1307 → Belgarde

15

1381 → Belgar 1535.

Bellevue. Beautiful view (OF *bele vue* → Belavowe 1504 → Bellaviewe 1651). So called from the pleasant view to be seen from this spot.

Bellingham. Water meadow of Beora's people (OE *Beoringa hamm* → Beringahammes gemæru 973 → Beringaham 998 → Belingeham 1198). The 973 form means 'boundary of the water meadow of the *Beoringas*'.

Bell's Forstall. Recorded as Bellhorn in 1782, the name is derived from the family of de Belle (1327). Forstal is a dialect word referring to land in front of farm buildings.

Beltinge (pronounced Beltinje). Belt's people (OE *Beltingas* → Beltinge 1189 → Beltyng 1327 → Beltinge 1468). This tribe appears to have settled at several places in Kent, including BELTRING and BILTING.

Beltring. Belt's people (OE *Beltingas* → Beltringe 1309 → Beltynge 1332 → Beltrynge 1345). The tribe are also found at BELTINGE and BILTING.

Beluncle. Recorded in 1406 as Beleuncle maner', the place takes its name from that of the family of William Beluncle (1240).

Benacre. Bean land: cultivated piece of land on which beans are grown (OE *bēan æcer* → bean eccer c.850 → Beanacr' 1332). Benacre Wood, Whitstable, has the same original meaning, being recorded as Bean acre in 1472.

Benchill Farm (Kenardington). Coarse grass clearing (OE *bēonet lēah* → Benteleye 1301). The present name seems to be a contraction of earlier forms.

Benenden (pronounced Ben-in-dn). Bynna's woodland pasture (OE *Bynning denn* → Benindene 1086 → Binnigdænne, Bennedene c.1100 → Bynindenne 1253 → Benenden 1610). Bynna owned another pasture at BEVENDEN.

Benhill Wood (Bishopsbourne). Beonna's slope (OE *Beonnan hielde* → Bennehelde 1304).

Benover. Bealde's river bank (OE *Bealdan ōfer* → ME *Bealdenoure* → Benhover Street 1801). The place is situated close to the River Beult. The personal name, Bealde, is also found in connection with BEWLBRIDGE.

Bensted. Coarse grass place (OE *bēonet stede* → Benedestede 1086 → Beantesteda c.1100 → Bentestede 1201 → Bentsted 1316).

Bentham Hill (Southborough). Coarse grass meadow (OE *bēonet hamm* → Benthamme 1332 → Bentham 1348 → Bentham brooke 1511). This last form must refer to low-lying marshy ground by the Medway river.

Bere Farm (West Cliffe). Shed, hovel (OE *bȳre* → La Bere 1235 → Bere 1270). The now lost place of Bere in Waltham had the same origin, being recorded as Byere, Biere 1254 → Bere 1278 → Bere 1790.

Berengrave. Recorded in this form

in 1782, the name may possibly be derived from OE *bern græf:* 'barn grave', indicating either a true grave or a pit or trench near some barn here.

Berling Farm (Southborough). It takes its name from that of the family of Henry de la Marche de Berling' (1270): 'Henry of the march, or boundary, of Birling'. The family is further described as living 'in campo de Smocham': in the field of Smockham (now a farm in neighbouring Tunbridge Wells).

Berridge Farm (Woodchurch). Belga's ridge of ground (OE *Belgan hrycg* → Belgeregg' 1278).

Berry's Green. It preserves the name of the lost manor of Bertrey in neighbouring Cudham which became extinct c.1380 and is recorded as Berterebye 1147 → Bertred 1271 → Bertre 1316 → Betrede 1392 → Bertrey 1478.

Berwick. Barley farm (OE *bere wīc* → æt Berwican 1035 → Berwic 1086).

Beston Farm. See under BASDEN WOOD.

Bethel Row. The place possibly derives its name from that of the family of Betyl (1327), also found recorded as Betil (1348). The 'Row' would have been a group of dwellings built on land here.

Bethersden (pronounced Bethersden). Beadurīc's woodland pasture (OE *Beadurīces denn* → Bædericesdænne c.1100 → Bet'ichesden' 1226 → Bederesdene 1270 → Bethersden

1610).

Bethlehem Farm (St. Lawrence). So called because the place once belonged to Bethlem (Bedlam) Hospital in London.

Betsham (pronounced Betsam). Bæddi's settlement (OE *Bæddes hām* → Bedesham 1325 → Bedisham 1338 → Bedsham 1450 → Bettisham 1487 → Betsam 1505). Bæddi owned a pasture at BASDEN WOOD.

Betsom's Hill (Westerham). It takes its name from the family of John Bettesham (1499), who may have been a native of BETSHAM.

Bettenham. Betta's water meadow (OE *Bettan hamm* → Bettenhamme 1240 → Bettenham 1278).

Betteshanger (pronounced Bettsanger). 'House's slope': slope on which there is a house or dwelling (OE *gebytles hangra* → Bedesham 1086 → Betleshangre 1176 → Betlesangre 1242 → Bettleshanger 1254 → Betshanger 1610).

Bettmans Wood Farm (Biddenden). It possibly derives its name from neighbouring BETTENHAM, 'Bettman' being a shortened form.

Beult, River (pronounced Belt). The name first appears in Michael Drayton's *Polyolbion* (1622), where it is recorded as Beule. It is probably derived from OE *belg:* 'belly, bag', and was originally called 'the swollen one', since the river often floods the flat, low-lying lands through which it flows. The River Bewl appears to share the same original meaning as the Beult, being recorded as Bewl 1576 → Beaul 1596 → The Bewle 1782.

Bevenden. Bynna's woodland pasture (OE *Bynning denn* → Benindene 1278 → Benyndenn' 1348 → Bevenden 1635). Bynna had another pasture at BENENDEN.

Beverley Farm (St. Dunstan Without). Bealdfrið's clearing (OE *Bealdfriðing lēah* → **Baluerle 1214** → Balverle 1384 → Balverley 1485 → Bav̄ley 1535).

Bewl, River. See under BEULT.

Bewlbridge. Bealde's bridge (OE *Bealdan brycg* → Beldebrigg', Beldebregg 1313 → Beauldbridge 1576 → Beaulbridge 1596). The place is on the River Bewl, a tributary of the Teise. Bealde's name is also found in connection with BENOVER.

Bewley Farm (Ightham). Beautiful place (F *beau lieu* → Beauley 1521 → Beaulies 1782).

Bewsbury Cross Farm. See under BUESBOROUGH CROSS.

Bexley. Box-tree clearing: clearing marked by a box-tree (OE *byxe lēah* → Bixle 765 → Byxlea 814 → Bixle, Byxle 1240 → Bexle 1314 → Bexley 1610).

Bexleyheath. This is a comparatively recent development. It was originally heathland lying to the south of BEXLEY, from which it takes its name.

Bex Wood (Tunstall). This is a manorial name, derived from that of the 14th century family who are variously recorded as Bak' or Bac. The same family name, derived from OE *bæc* and meaning 'dweller on the ridge', is found in connection with Back Shaw at Throwley.

Bickley. Bicca's clearing (OE *Biccan lēah* → Byckeleye 1279 → Bykeleye 1292). Bicca also owned land at BICKNOR.

Bicknor. Bicca's bank, or border (OE *Biccan ōra* → Bikenora 1185 → Bikenore 1253 → Byknor 1610).

Bidborough. Bitta's mound or tumulus (OE *Bittan beorg* → Bitteberga c.1100 → Betbergh 1219 → Bitteborugh 1367 → Bidborow 1610).

Bid Bridge. Situated on a tributory of the Medway, the place is recorded in 1353 as Bittebregge and is probably, like BIDBOROUGH, named after a Saxon settler, Bitta.

Biddenden (pronounced Biddnden). Bidda's woodland pasture (OE *Bidding denn* → Bidingden 993 → Bidindænne c.1100 → Bidindenne 1204 → Byddenden 1610).

Bigbury Camp. 'Bulge stronghold': stronghold on a bulge, or swelling (OE *bycge burh* → Beggebery 1226 → Beckeberri c.1290 → Bigberry Wood 1790). The 'bulge' must refer to the hill on which the Iron Age fort here was built.

Biggin Hill. Hill by a building or dwelling-place (ME *bigging hill* → Byggunhull 1499). Biggin Street in Dover has the original meaning of 'Roman road running past a building' (ME *bigging strete*) and appears in 1547 as Byggenstrete. It follows the course of one of the old Roman roads into Dover.

Bilham. 'Sword meadow': water meadow shaped like a sword (OE *bill hamm* → Bilham 1272 → Bylhamme 1304 → Bilhame 1346). The place stands on a projection of land above flat marshland bordering the East Stour river. Bill Street near Frindsbury is recorded as Bilstrete in 1372, Byll Streete in 1572, and is probably so called because of the sword-like straightness of a (Roman) road in the area.

Bill Street. See under BILHAM.

Bilsington. Bilswiδ's farmstead (OE *Bilswiδe tūn* → Bilsvitone 1086 → Bilswithetun c.1100 → Bilsintune 1122 → Bylsington 1610). Bilswiδ appears to have been a lady of rank since her name was commonly given to a queen or abbess.

Bilting. Belt's people (OE *Beltingas* → Belting', Beltinge 1272 → Byltyng 1438). The place is also recorded in 1272 as Beltesburne (← OE *Beltes burne:* Belt's stream). He had two other tribal settlements in Kent, at BELTINGE and BELTRING.

Binbury Manor (Thornham). Stronghold of Bæga's people (OE *Bæginga burh* → Bengeberi 1214 → Bengebury 1285 → Byngebury 1319). There is an earthwork close by.

Bingley's Island. Within a river (OE *binnan ēa*). The island, which is enclosed by two arms of the Great Stour, is referred to in a charter of 814 as Binnanea. In 1268 it appears as Binnewiht, but there are no further forms to show how the present name evolved.

Binney Farm (All Hallows). Within a river (OE *binnan ēa* → Bynne 1291 → Bynneye 1292). Binny Cottages at Tonge shares the same origin and appears as Bynee, Bynneye in 1258, Bynney in 1292.

Birches Wood, Birchett Wood. See under BIRCHETTS.

Birchetts. Recorded as Birchettfeld in 1239, and as Birchette in 1313, the original place name seems to have meant 'open land near a birch copse' (OE *bircett feld*). Birches Wood, Cranbrook, takes its name from the family of John Birchett (1647). Birchett Wood, Brenchley, which appears as Byrchletts in 1562, probably derives its name from a landowner surnamed atte Byrchette, or atte Birchet: 'dweller by the birch copse' (OE *bircett*).

Birchington. Birch hill farmstead: farmstead near a hill where birch-trees grow (OE *bierce hyll tūn* → Birchilton' 1240 → Berchinton', Bircheton' 1254 → Bercelton 1264 → Birchinton' 1270 → Byrchington 1610).

Birchley. Birch-tree clearing: clearing marked by a birch-tree (OE *beorc lēah* → Berkelegh' 1327 → Barkelegh' 1334).

Bircholt. Birch thicket (OE *bierce holt* → Brichholt 1087 → Biricholt 1204 → Bircheholt 1219 → Bircholt 1610).

Birling (pronounced Berlin). Bærel's people (OE *Bærelingas* → Boerlingas

19

788 → Bærlingas 964 → Berlinge 1086 → Birlingis c.1100). This tribe were also settled in Sussex, at Birling Gap.

Bishopsbourne. Stream (OE *burna* → æt Burnan 799 → Burnes 1086 → Biscopesburne c.1100 → Bisshopsborn c.1500). From the 11th century the Manor of Bourne belonged to the Archbishops of Canterbury.

Bishopsdale. Bishop's woodland pasture (OE *biscopes denn* → Bissopesden', Biscoppesdenn' 1226 → Bisshopisdenn' 1313). At some later date the place name ending -den was superseded by -dale. Great Bishopsden hamlet nearby has a similar origin, being 'woodland pasture associated with a bishop' (OE *biscoping denn* → bisceopincg dene c.850 → Byssopindenne 1323). Proximity to Bishopsdale has produced the present form.

Bishopsden, Great. See under BISHOPSDALE.

Bishopsden, North and **South.** Bishop's woodland pasture (OE *biscopes denn* → Bischopisden 1286 → Bysshopesdenne 1313).

Bishop's Down (Tunbridge Wells). The place appears in 1292 as Bisshoppesdoun', being originally a hill (ME *dun*) on land belonging to the Tonbridge family of Bisshop. The same family name is found in connection with Bishop's Farm, Cranbrook, where Robert Bisshop' is recorded in 1352 and Joan Bishoppe in 1514.

Bishopstone. Bishop's farmstead, or manor (OE *biscopes tūn* → Bissope-

stoune 1310 → Bisshopeston 1314 → Bishopeston 1348).

Bistock. Young man's place (ME *boian stoc* → Boystack' 1270).

Bitchet Green. Together with neighbouring Bitchet Common and Lower Bitchet, the place derives its name from the family variously recorded as de la Birchette (1240), atte Byrchette (1313) and ate Birchet (1378) – 'dweller by the birch copse' (OE *bircett*).

Blackbrook (near Bromley). Black marshy ground (OE *blæc brōc* → Blakebrok' 1278 → Blakebroke 1332). Blackbrook, near Wittersham, has the same original meaning, being recorded as Blakebrok' in 1240.

Black Charles (Under River). The house takes its name from the family of Blakecherl, or Blaccherl, recorded in the Seal area in the late 13th and early 14th century. This surname is from OE *blæc ceorl*: 'black churl, or peasant', perhaps with reference to dark colouring. The house takes its name from the genitival form 'Blakecherl's'.

Blacketts. Recorded as such in 1782, the name is presumably derived from that of some local family.

Blackfen. The place appears as Blakewæne 1240 → Blakeben Strete, Blakeben Gate 1407, and may possibly have had the original meaning of 'black fen' (OE *blæc fenn*), describing dark marshy ground in this area. Blacklands Wood, Penshurst, certainly has this meaning, being recorded as Blakefenn' 1278 →

Blakeuenne 1301 → Blackfennys 1564.

Blackhall. Hall built of black, or dark-coloured, materials (OE *blæc heall* → Blakehall' 1334 → Blakhall 1479 → Blackhall 1610).

Blackheath. Black heathland (OE *blæc hæð* → Blachehedfeld 1166 → Blakeheth 1275 → Blackheathe 1610). The same meaning, a reference to the dark-coloured soil of the heathland, is also found in the name of Blackhoath Wood, Leigh, recorded as Blackhethe in 1408, Blakhoth in 1438.

Blackhoath Wood. See under BLACKHEATH.

Blackhouse Hill Shaw. Black ooze, or mire (OE *blæc wāse* → Blakewose 1253 → Blakewase 1341 → Blakose *alias* Cayn Court 1537 → Blackose 1581). The 1537 form refers to Canons Court Manor here, a religious house for canons of the Premonstratensian order.

Blackland. Self-explanatory (OE *blæc land* → Blaklond 1392 → Blakelond 1398). Blacklands Shaw, Boxley, has the same original meaning and appears as Blackland in 1553. Black Lane in Eastry is recorded as Blakelond 1407 → Blacklond 1491 → Blackeland Bush 1541.

Blacklands Wood. See under BLACKFEN.

Black Lane. See under BLACKLAND.

Blackman's Lane. It derives its name from that of the Hadlow family of Blakeman, recorded during the latter half of the 13th century.

Blackmanstone. Blæcman's farmstead (OE *Blæcmanes tūn* → Blachemenestone 1086 → Blacemannestune c.1100 → Blakemaneston' 1199 → Blakemanston' 1242). Alternatively, this may have been the farmstead of a man nicknamed 'the black, or dark-visaged one' (OE *blæc mann*).

Blackney Hill (Wingham). The name appears as Upper, Nether Blackney in 1594. Blackney Hill is not far from the Wingham river, and may once have been an island standing in dark, marshy ground which was liable to flooding, giving the place the original meaning of 'at the black island' (OE *æt þǣm blæcan ēge*).

Blackpit Wood. See under COLD-BRIDGE.

Blacksole Farm (Herne). Black muddy pool (OE *blæc sol* → Blaksole 1529). Blacksole Field at Wrotham shares the same original meaning, being recorded as Blacksoll croft in 1442.

Blackwall. Black spring: spring with discoloured water (OE *blæc wielle* → Blakewelle 1313).

Bladbean. Blood beam, or tree (OE *blōd bēam* → Blodbeme 1226 → Blodebeame 1327 → Blodbeine 1471). The name must refer to the red-coloured foliage of a tree which once stood here: Redoak lies only half a mile from Bladbean, taking its name from a red oak, or *Quercus borealis*.

21

Blaxland Farm (Sturry). This was once land belonging to the local medieval family of Blak', or Blake, and is recorded as Blakeslaunde 1226 → Blakeslond' 1292 → Blakislonde 1346.

Blean, Forest of. In the coarse, rough place (OE *in þǣm blēan* → in Blean 786 → to Blean þem wiada 858 → Bleen 1230). The ancient Forest of Blean, which once covered the entire area between the Great Stour and the sea, is now little more than a belt of thick woodland lying roughly two miles inland from Seasalter.

Blean. It takes its name from BLEAN Forest and is properly known as St. Cosmus and St. Damian in the Blean, its 13th century church being dedicated to SS Cosmus and Damian. The village is recorded as Cosmerisblene, Cosmerysblen 1432 → ch. of SS Cosmas and Damian, Blene 1439 → Cosme and Dannyane Le Bleen 1525.

Bleangate. This was formerly the meeting-place of the Blengate Hundred, the origin of the name being 'gate into the Forest of Blean'.

Blendon. Blǣda's hill (OE *Blǣding dūn* → Bladidun, Bladindon' 1240 → Bladindoune 1327 → Bladindon' 1334). The modern place name is a contraction of these forms.

Bletchenden (pronounced Bletchin-dn). Blecca's woodland pasture (OE *Bleccing denn* → bleccingdenn c.750 → Blechinden' 1240 → Blechyndenn' 1292). Blecca also owned land at BLETCHINGLEY; his tribal settlement was at the now lost place of Bletching-Court in Lydd.

Bletchingley. Blecca's clearing (OE *Bleccan lēah* → Blecchelegh' 1334 → Blechelegh' 1338 → Blechingleghe 1347 → Blecchyngle 1417). The personal name is also found in association with BLETCHENDEN.

Blindgrooms. Recorded in 1500 as Blyndegromys, the place appears to have taken its name from a medieval owner nicknamed, or perhaps surnamed, 'blind servant' (ME *blinde grome*).

Bloodden. Bledda's people (OE *Bleddingas* → Bledding, Bledynge 1270 → Bleddyngge 1348). There are no further forms to show how this name evolved to its present one.

Bloodshot Cottages. The name appears in 1527 as Bloodyshot feld (field) and Bloodyshot grove, and is perhaps descriptive of reddish coloured soil in this area.

Bloors Place. See under BLOWERS HILL.

Blowers Hill (Cowden). It takes its name from the family of le Blowere (1278). Blower's Cottage, Brenchley, is similarly associated with Robert le Blowere and Thomas le Blawere (1292). Bloors Place, Rainham, is connected with the 14th century family of le Blowere, also found recorded as le Blore.

Blundells Shaw. The name is derived from that of the family of Blondel (1348), who also appear as Bloundell (1483). The affix 'Shaw' is from OE *scaga:* a copse.

Boardedhouse Farm (Chislet). The name is self-explanatory, being recorded during the 15th century as The Boordehouse, derived from ME *boarden:* boarded, describing the boards, or planking, used in the building.

Boarden. Stream pasture: woodland pasture near a stream (OE *burna denn* → Burdenn' 1254 → Borden', Burdenn' 1278 → Burdenne 1313). The name is descriptive of the site.

Boardfield Church. Burda's open land (OE *Burdan feld* → Berdefeld' 1205 → Burdfeld 1226 → Bourdefeld 1311 → Bourdfield 1610). The affix Church may be due to the proximity of the 18th century Church of St. Lawrence in neighbouring Otterden.

Boarhill. This may originally have been a hill on land belonging to the estate of Bore Place, less than two miles away. The family of Bore, owners of the estate from the time of Henry III, are first referred to in 1313 when their name appears as atte Bore – 'dweller by the bower' (OE *būr*). Bore Place is recorded as such in 1511.

Boarley. Stream clearing: clearing through which runs a stream (OE *burna lēah* → Burnlegh 1240. → Borle, Burle 1278 → Burlee 1313 → Burleghesfeld 1315). This last form means 'land belonging to Boarley'. The place is situated on a tributary of the Medway.

Boatman's Hill (Sandwich). It derives its name from the family of Henry Bateman (1526), the present spelling being the result of associations with the port of Sandwich.

Bobbing (pronounced Bobbin). Bobba's people (OE *Bobbingas* → Bobinge c.1100 → Bobbing' 1205 → Bobbinges 1234 → Bobbing 1610).

Bockham. Bocca's water meadow (OE *Boccan hamm* → Bocceham 993 → Bocham 1278 → Bokham 1313). The place is on low-lying ground near a stream. The personal name, Bocca, is also found in connection with BOCKINGFOLD.

Bockhanger (pronounced Bockhanger). Beech slope: slope covered with beeches (OE *bōc hangra* → Bochangre 1212 → Bockhangr' 1268).

Bockingfold. Fold of Bocca's people (OE *Boccinga falod* → Bokingefold' 1232 → Bockingefaud' 1247 → Bokingfold 1278). Bocca himself owned land at BOCKHAM.

Bodsham Green (pronounced Boddsam). Bodd's settlement (OE *Boddes hām* → Botdesham c.675 → Boddesham 811 → Bodesham 993).

Bodshead Farm (Challock). First mentioned in Hasted's history of Kent (1778-99) as Badsted, the name may originally have been 'Bæddi's place' (OE *Bæddes stede*), but there are no earlier forms to corroborate this. It has been suggested that the name is a corruption of BEARSTED.

Bogden. Bucge's woodland pasture (OE *Bucging denn* → Bugindenn' 1232 → Bugginden' 1254 → Bogyndeñe 1327 → Bogyndenne 1347). This Saxon lady also owned land at

BOUGHURST and BOWLEY.

Boldshaves. The name is the result of connection with the family of William Broadsheafe (1591), the present form resulting from the genitival 'Broadsheafe's'.

Bold Snoad Wood (Woodchurch). Boga's detached piece of woodland (OE *Bogan snād* → Boghesnod' 1240 → Bosnod 1254 → Bowsnode 1313).

Bonnington. Buna's farmstead (OE *Buning tūn* → Bonintone 1086 → Buningtun, Bonintune c.1100 → Boninton 1229 → Bonington 1251). Bonnington Farm, Goodnestone, shares the same origin, being recorded as Boninton' in 1240, Bonington in 1287.

Boormanhatch Farm (Stelling). It takes its name from the family of Brouman (1278), who are also found recorded as Borman (1348): the surname is from OE *būrmann:* cottager.

Bopeep. There are no forms to explain the origin of this name, but like Bopeep in Sussex, it may be associated with the act of peeping out: for instance, it may once have had a turnpike gate, or have been used as a look-out point.

Borden. Elevated woodland pasture (OE *bor denn* → Borden' 1190 → Bordene 1198 → Borden 1208).

Bore Place. See under BOARHILL.

Borough Green. First recorded in 1575, as Borrowe Grene, the name is• probably a reference to the manor, or borough, of Wrotham.

Borstal (pronounced Bawstle). Security place, or place of refuge (OE *borg steall* → Borcstealla, Borcstealle c.975 → Borchetelle, Borcstele 1086 → Borstalle 1107 → Burstalle, Borstalle 1210). Originally a village, this is now a suburb of Rochester: the borstal itself stands between the Maidstone Road and the Medway. Other early places of refuge have produced the names of Borstal Hall, Minster (Borstall' 1240, Borstall 1368); Borstalhill Farm, Whitstable (Borstal 1323, Borstall 1479); and Bostall Wood, Plumstead (Borstall' 1254, Burstall 1397). Borstal is a common dialect word used of steep, narrow paths leading up the sides of hills.

Bossenden. Bōsa's woodland pasture (OE *Bōsing denn* → Bosenden 1204 → Bossyngden', Bosindenne 1278). The personal name is also found in connection with BOSSINGHAM and BOSSINGTON.

Bossingham. Bōsa's field (OE *Bōsing camp* → Bossingcamp 1226 → Bosingkomp 1264 → Bosyncompe 1343). The present name is the result of -camp being corrupted in speech to -cum and later to -ham.

Bossington. Bōsa's farmstead (OE *Bōsing tūn* → Bosingtune 873 → Bosingtun 941 → Bosington' 1227). Bōsa also had land at BOSSENDEN and BOSSINGHAM.

Bostall Wood. See under BORSTAL.

Bough Beech. Bowed or curved beech-tree (OE *bogen bēce* → Boubeche 1396 → Bowbeche 1440). Bough Beech Reservoir now covers much of this old area.

24

Boughton Aluph (pronounced Borton Alluf). Charter farmstead: farmstead or manor granted by charter (OE *bōc tūn* → Boctun c.1020 → Boltune 1086 → Boctune c.1100 → Boctun' Alulphi 1270 → Bocton aluph 1610). Alulphus de Boctune – who is also referred to in 1215 as Alof de Bochtone and Alulfus de Boctone – owned the manor during the first part of the 13th century and gave his name to this Boughton to distinguish it from BOUGHTON-UNDER-BLEAN, BOUGHTON MALHERBE and BOUGHTON MONCHELSEA. OE *bōc tūn*, from which the names of the Kentish Boughtons have originated, literally meant 'beech farmstead' in early Saxon times; but since the Anglo-Saxon runic alphabet was incised on boards made of beech, *bōc* gradually came to mean book, or charter.

Boughton-under-Blean (pronounced Borton). Charter farmstead: farmstead or manor granted by charter (OE *bōc tūn* → Boltune 1086 → Bocton' 1226 → Bocton juxta la Blen 1288 → Boctone juxta Bleen 1292 → Bocton under bleane 1610). In *The Canterbury Tales* (begun in 1386), Chaucer refers to this place as Boghton under Blee. Its affix is due to the fact that it originally lay below, or under, the Forest of Blean. Nearby Boughton Street, recorded as Bocton Street in 1690, was originally a farmstead lying at the end of a road running from Boughton-under-Blean.

Boughton Lees (pronounced Borton). Pasture (OE *lǣs* → Lese 1240 → Lese de Bocton' Alulphi, Boctoneslese 1313). The place is in

BOUGHTON ALUPH and was once a pasture belonging to the parish.

Boughton Malherbe (pronounced Borton Mallaby). Charter farmstead: farmstead or manor granted by charter (OE *bōc tūn* → Boltone 1086 → Boctun c.1100 → Bectone Malherbe 1253 → Boutton' Malerbe 1278 → Bocton malherbs 1610). Robert de Malherb held the manor during the reign of King John (1199-1216): his name has been affixed to this Boughton to distinguish it from the others in the county.

Boughton Monchelsea (pronounced Borton Munchelsey). Charter farmstead: farmstead or manor granted by charter (OE *bōc tūn* → Boltone 1086 → Boctune c.1100 → Bocton' 1242 → Bocton' Monchansy 1278 → Boulton Munchensey 1279 → Bocton Munchelsey 1610). In 1242 the manor was held by Warin de Montchensie, or de Montecanisio, a native of Mont-Canisi in Calvados, Normandy.

Boughton Street. See under BOUGHTON-UNDER-BLEAN.

Boughurst Street. Bucge's wooded hill (OE *Bucgan hyrst* → Buggehurst 1200 → Bukehirst 1254 → Boghurst 1278). The original meaning is shared by Boughurst Down Wood here. Bucge, a Saxon lady, also owned land at BOGDEN and BOWLEY.

Bounds, Great and **Little.** Recorded in 1348 as Bounde, the place was possibly so called because of its position on the boundary of Southborough parish. Alternatively, it may be a manorial name derived from the medieval surname le Bounde or le Bonde.

Bourne, River. The name is derived directly from OE *burna:* stream, or bourne. Bourneside, the name of which is self-explanatory, stands beside it. *Burna* also occurs in Bourne Farm, Sandhurst, recorded as Burne in 1240, Bourne in 1334; Bourne Park, Bishopsbourne; and Bournemill Farm, Tonbridge, which is on the site of a watermill and appears as Bournemell' in 1348.

Boutshole Shaw, Little. See under LITTLE BOUTSHOLE SHAW.

Bow Bridge (New Romney). Bow, or bow-shaped (OE *boga* → Boghe 1348). Bow Bridge, Yalding, spanning the River Beult, has the same original meaning, the reference being to an arched bridge.

Bowerland. See under BOWER WOOD.

Bower Wood (Stelling). Bower, or dwelling (OE *būr* → Bour' 1338). This Old English word is also found in the names of Bower Place, Maidstone (Boure 1327 → Le Boure 1390 → Bowre Wood 1484); Bower Farm, Eynsford (Bor 1292, Boure 1379); Bower Farm, Molash (Bure 1278 → Boure 1294 → Bourhouse 1348); and Bower Wood, Chilham (Bure 1278, Boure 1347). Bowerland at Chilham has the original meaning of 'land by a bower' (OE *būr land*), and appears as Burlonde in 1275, Bourlonde in 1304.

Bowley Farm (Boughton Malherbe). Bucge's clearing (OE *Bucgan lēah* → Bogelei 1086 → Buggele 1177 →

Buggeleye 1270 → Boggelye 1331). Bucge, a Saxon lady, also owned land at BOGDEN and BOUGHURST.

Bowman's Hill (Luddesdown). Recorded in 1572 as Bawmans hill, and in 1698 as Bowmans hill, it probably derives its name from some former landowner in this area.

Bowzell. Beech building: building standing near a beech (OE *bōc (ge) selle* → Buggesell 1272 → Bogeselle 1332 → Bouxsull 1362 → Bokesell *alias* Bowsell 1778).

Boxhurst. Box-tree hill (OE *box hyrst* → Boxhurste 1240 → Boxhurst 1346).

Boxley. Box-tree clearing: clearing marked by a box-tree (OE *box lēah* → Boseleu 1086 → Boxlea, Boxelei c.1100 → Boxle, Buxlee 1197 → Boxley 1610).

Boxted. Beech place: place near a beech (OE *bōc stede* → Boxted 1598). Alternatively, this may originally have been a place granted by charter (see BOUGHTON ALUPH).

Boyce Wood (Great Chart). It probably takes its name from that of the family of Edward Boyse (1664). Boyes Hall, Willesborough, built in 1616, is named after its builder, Thomas Boys. Boys' Firs, Tilmanstone, is similarly named after William Boys, a resident here during the reign of Elizabeth I.

Boy Court (Ulcombe). Young man's cot, or cottage (ME *boian cot* → Boycote 1240 → Boycote, Boicote c.1275).

Boyden Hill (Chislet). Young man's farmstead (ME *boian tone* → Boytune, Boitun 1208 → Boytun' 1275).

Boyes Hall. See under BOYCE WOOD.

Boyington Court (Swingfield). Young men's farmstead (ME *boiena tone* → Bointon 1207 → Boyntone 1253 → Boynton 1431).

Boyke Wood (Elham). Young man's farm (ME *boian wic* → Boiwiche 1122 → Boiwic 1226 → Boywyk' 1292).

Boys' Firs. See under BOYCE WOOD.

Boyton Court (East Sutton). Young man's farmstead (ME *boian tone* → Boitton 1202 → Boytone 1278 → Boyton 1535).

Brabourne (pronounced Bray-burn). Broad stream (OE *brād burna* → Bradeburnan 863 → Bradeburne 1086 → Braburne 1166 → Braborne 1610). This is an early name for the East Stour, flowing close to the village.

Brackenston. Since there are quarries close by, the most likely explanation of this name is 'break stone': the place is recorded as Brekston in 1332. Breakstones, in the neighbouring parish of Speldhurst, obviously shares this meaning.

Bradbourne. Broad stream (OE *brād burna* → Bradeburn' 1292 → Bradebourn 1327 → Bradborne 1610). The name probably refers to a small tributary of the Medway. Bradbourne Hall, Riverhead, has

the same original meaning, appearing as Bradeburn' in 1278, Bradebourne in 1327: it lies close to the River Darent.

Bradfield. Broad open land (OE *brād feld* → Bradefeld 1218 → Bradefelde 1346). Great and Little Bradfield Woods at Ospringe share the same origin, being recorded as Bradefelde in 1247.

Brambles Farm and **Place** (Horsmonden). Bramble building: building near a spot where brambles grow (OE *brēmel (ge)selle* → Brembelselle 1327 → Brembesell' 1338). Bramble's Farm, Wye, derives its name from the family of William Brembil (1324).

Bramling (pronounced Bramlin). Bramble dwellers (OE *brēmelingas* → Bremlinge 1167 → Bramling', Bremlinges 1240 → Bremlyng' 1327). This was the name given to a tribe who chose to make their settlement in a place where brambles grew.

Brampton Place (Bexley). Broom farmstead: farmstead where broom grows (OE *brōm tūn* → Bromton' 1301 → Brompton' 1327). Brandon House, Shoreham, has the same original meaning, being recorded as Bromptone in 1332.

Bramsell's Farm (Hever). 'Bramble miry place': miry place where there are brambles (OE *brēmel syle* → Brembelshulle, Brembelsulle c.1240 → Brembeselle 1301).

Branbridges. Steep bridge (OE *brant brycg* → Brantbrigge 1325 → Brantebrig 1404 → Brandbridge 1610). The name refers to a bridge spann-

27

ing the Medway near East Peckham.

Branden. Bera's woodland pasture (OE *Bering denn* → Berindenne c.1220). The present name is a shortened form of the original.

Brandenbury. Stronghold of the sword people (OE *Brandinga burh* → Brandingebyri 1240 → Brondingebiri 1278 → Brondyngbery 1346). This was obviously a warrior tribe, taking its name from OE *brand*: sword, weapon; fire.

Brandfold. It is variously recorded during the 14th century as Brangilfold, Brangelfold and Brangynfold. The second element in this place name is 'fold' (OE *falod*), but the first cannot with any certainty be interpreted. It has been suggested, however, that the name contains an obsolete English word 'brangle', meaning to totter, or sway to and fro, giving Brandfold an original meaning of 'dilapidated fold'.

Brandon House. See under BRAMPTON PLACE.

Brandred Farm (Acrise). Fire cleared: land cleared of undergrowth by burning (OE *brand rīed* → Terra brandet, Brand 1086 → Brandrede 1203 → Brandered 1270).

Brands Hatch. Brink's gate: gate leading on to a slope, or brink (OE *brances hæcc* → Bronkeshach', Bronkesesch 1292 → Brontyshecche 1334). Brands Hatch is situated on a fairly steep slope.

Brasted (pronounced Braysted). Broad place (OE *brād stede* → Bradesteda c.1100 → Bradested' 1242 →

Brasted 1610).

Brattles. Recorded as Bratillys Hill in 1546, the place derives its name from the family of Bratel, Bratill or Bratyll, who are found from the 14th to the 16th century in the Brenchley area.

Breach (near Newington). Newly cultivated land (OE *bræc* → Breche 1254 → Brek', Brech' 1270 → Little Breach 1598). Breach, near Barham, has the same origin, appearing as Breche in 1226.

Breadland Farms (Sturry). Broad land (OE *brād land* → Bradeland' 1226 → Bradelond 1275 → Brodelonde 1327).

Breakstones. See under BRACKENSTON.

Bredgar (pronounced Bred-gar). Broad gore, or wedge-shaped piece of land (OE *brād gāra* → Bradegare c.1100 → Bradgare 1205 → Bredgar 1610).

Bredhurst. 'Board hill': wooded hill where boards are got (OE *bred hyrst* → Bredehurst 1240 → Bredherst 1270 → Bradherst 1690).

Breeches Wood (Chiddingstone). It derives its name from the family of de la Breche (1270). Breeches Wood, Willesborough, is similarly associated with a 13th century family of de la Breche, the surname being derived from OE *bræc* and meaning 'dweller by the newly cultivated land'.

Brenchley. Brænci's clearing (OE *Brænces lēah* → Bræncesle c.1100 →

28

Brenchesleie 1191 → Brancheslegh 1230 → Brenchelee, Branchelee 1254 → Brenchely 1610).

Brenley Corner. Fire clearing: clearing rid of undergrowth by burning (OE *brand lēah* → Brendlegh' 1254 → Brendle 1278 → Brenle 1292 → Brenleye 1302).

Brent, The. (Land) overgrown with broom (OE *brēmðe* → Bremthe c.1375 → Dartford Brent, The Brent 1778). Brent Lane, Dartford, takes its name from this place. The same original meaning is shared by Brent Cottages, Upchurch, recorded as la Brenithe in 1206; and it is also found in the now lost places of Bremthe in Chislet, and Bremthe in Ash.

Brenzett (pronounced Branzit). Burnt house (OE *bernede sǣte* → Brensete, Brand, Brandet 1086 → Bretseta 1189 → Brensete 1266 → Branzet, Brensete 1278). *Circa* 1100 the place is recorded as Bennedecirce – 'burnt church' (OE *bernede cirice*): perhaps the 'house' in the origin of this place name refers, in fact, to a church here which was destroyed by fire.

Brewer's Bridge. Recorded in 1541 as Brewars bridge over the Delf, the place takes its name from some former landowner in the Worth area. Brewer's Hall, Mereworth, is connected with the family of Brewer who lived in the parish for several generations until they moved to West Farleigh in the time of Henry VI. Brewers Wood, Shorne, appears as Brewer's wood in 1698.

Brickhurst Wood (Bethersden). This was formerly the site of a brick-kiln, or oast, and appears as Brick-hoste 1620 → Brickehost wood 1629 → Brickoast wood 1680.

Bridewell Plantation (Great Chart). It first appears as Bridewell in 1624, the name possibly being derived from OE *bridd wielle*: 'young bird spring'.

Bridge. Self-explanatory (OE *brycg* → Brige 1086 → Brygge c.1100 → Brigge 1235 → Bredge 1610). It lies on the Nailbourne stream.

Brimsdale Farm (Eythorne). Bryni's muddy pool (OE *Brynes sol* → brynessole 944 → Bremesdal' 1254 → Brumisdale 1347).

Brishing Wood and **Court** (Langley). Brēosa's people (OE *Brēosingas* → Bressinges 1242 → Brasinges 1253 → Bresyng 1346 → Brysshyng 1494 → Brising *alias* Brishing 1782). Brēosa himself owned land at BRISSEN-DEN.

Brissenden (near Frittenden). Brēosa's woodland pasture (OE *Brēosing denn* → Bryssendenne 1348 → Bresynden Dene 1394 → Brissenden 1649). Brissenden, near Tenterden, shares the same origin, being recorded as Bresinden', Brusenden' 1254 → Bresyndenne 1327 → Bresindene 1348. Brēosa's tribal settlement was at BRISHING.

Britton Street. It is associated with the Gillingham family of Brutin (1254), who are also recorded as Brutyn (1304). Britton's Farm, Riverhead, which appears as Bretons maner' in 1479, derives its name from the family of Brutone

(1319) or Breton (1348).

Broad Ford. Self-explanatory. The name appears in 1514 both as Brodeford and as Brodeford mylle, showing that there was once a water mill near the 'broad ford' here.

Broader Lane. Broad bank, or border (OE *brād ōra* → Brodore 1270).

Broadfield. Broad, or wide, open land (OE *brād feld* → Brodefelde 1327).

Broadham Cottages. Broad water meadow (OE *brād hamm* → Bradeham 1226 → Brodehamme 1332 → Brodhame 1347).

Broadmead. Broad mead, or meadow (OE *brād mǣd* → Brademed 1216 → Brademede 1327).

Broadoak (near Seal). Broad oaktree (OE *brād āc* → Brodok' 1348). Broadoak Wood, Cobham, is first recorded in 1698, as Broadoak wood.

Broadoak (near Sturry). Broad, or wide, hook of land (OE *brād hōc* → Brodhoc c.1250 → Brodeoke 1479).

Broadstairs. Broad, or wide, stairs (ME *brode steyr* → Brodsteyr Lynch 1434 → Brodestyr 1479 → Broadstayer 1565 → Brod stayrs 1610). The name refers to a broad flight of steps cut into the cliff face here at the beginning of the 15th century.

Broad Street (Hoo St. Werburgh). It appears as Brodestrete in 1478, denoting a broad, or wide, way. Broad Street, Hollingbourne, has the same meaning and is recorded as Brodestret in 1327, Brodestrete in 1338 (← OE *brād strǣt*).

Broadwater Farm (East Malling). Self-explanatory (OE *brād wæter* → Bradewat' 1240 → Brodewatre 1332). The name is probably a reference to a tributary of the Medway.

Broadwaygreen Farm (Petham). Broad way, or track (OE *brād weg* → Bradewey 1240 → Bradeweye 1292 → Broadway 1690).

Brocas (pronounced Brock-ass). It derives its name from the family of Brokeys (1347), also found as Brokas (1383), and is recorded as Hevere Brocas 1397 → Heveresbrokas 1403 → Hevere Brokays 1423. The place is close to HEVER.

Brockhill Park. Marsh hill: hill close to marshy ground (OE *brōc hyll* → Brokhill' 1254 → Brokhille 1299). It is close to a brook called the Brockhill Stream.

Brockhill Wood (Chevening). Marsh corner: corner of land near marshy ground (OE *brōc halh* → Brochal' 1254). Brockhoult Mount near the wood derives its name from the same source.

Brockhoult Mount. See under BROCKHILL WOOD.

Brockley. Marsh clearing: clearing where there is marshy ground (OE' *brōc lēah* → Brocele 1182 → Brocleg', Brockel' 1226 → Brockele 1328 → Brookley 1690).

Brockman's Bushes. It takes its name from the family of Brockman, owners of land in the parish of Newington during the 17th century.

Brockton. Marsh farmstead: farmstead near marshy ground (OE *brōc tūn* → Brokton 1286 → Broctone 1348). The place is not far from a stream. Broughton House, Dunton Green, possibly has the same origin, being recorded as Brogton' in 1365.

Brodnyx. It derives its name from the family of Richard Broadnex (1467).

Brogdale. Marsh dale: dale, or valley, where there is marshy ground (OE *brōc dæl* → Brokedale 1240 → Brokedele 1355). In 1254 the place is referred to as Brokeden' (← OE *brōc denn*: woodland pasture near marshy ground).

Brogden. Marsh pasture: woodland pasture near marshy ground (OE *brōc denn* → Brocden 1285 → Brokedenn 1367). There is a small stream close by.

Broke Cottage (pronounced Bruck). See under BROOK.

Bromley. Broom clearing: clearing where broom grows (OE *brōm lēah* → Bromleah 964 → Bromleage 998 → Bronlei 1086 → Bromlega 1178 → Bromley 1610). Bromley Green, near Shadoxhurst, shares the same original meaning, being found as Brumlegh' in 1254, Bromleye in 1292. There was also a now lost Bromley in the parish of Goudhurst, recorded as Bromlegh' 1254 → Bromle 1281 → Bromleye 1314. Bromley Wood, Barfreston, has the original meaning of 'broom-covered open land' (OE *brōm feld*),

and is recorded as Bromfelde in 1235, Bromley Wood in 1582.

Brompton (pronounced Brumton). Broom farmstead: farmstead where broom grows (OE *brōm tūn* → Bromdone 1270 → Brompton' 1313 → Brampton 1346).

Brook. Marshy ground (OE *brōc* → Broc 1066 → Broke 1226 → Brooke 1610). It lies on a tributary of the Great Stour. *Brōc*, together with the family name atte Broke — 'dweller by the marshy ground' — is also found in connection with Brook at Ospringe; Brook Bridge, Graveney; Brook Cottages, Minster; Brook Farm, Wingham and Yalding; Brook Place, Sundridge; Brooke House, Ash; Brookgate, Hawkhurst; and Broke Cottage, Ditton. Brook Farm near Reculver was originally called 'marshy ground's gate': gate leading on to marshy ground (OE *brōces geat*), and is recorded as Brokesgate, in 1292, Brooksgate in 1790.

Brookgate. See under BROOK.

Brookland. Land by marshy ground (OE *brōc land* → Broklande 1262 → Broclonde 1278 → Brockland 1286 → Brookland 1610). The place lies on the edge of the Romney Marshes.

Brooks End. Self-explanatory (OE *brōces ende* → Brokesend 1205 → Brockesende 1292 → Brokesende 1327).

Broombourne Farm (High Halden). Brown stream (OE *brūn burna* → Bronbourne 1327 → Brombourn' 1347 → Brunbourne 1348). Probably so called because the water of the stream here was discoloured by mud.

Broome. Broom: place where broom grows (OE *brōm* → Brome 1240).

Broomfield. Open land where broom grows (OE *brōm feld* → Brunfelle 1086 → Brumfeld c.1100 → Bromfeld 1278). Broomfield near Throwley has the same origin, appearing as Bromfeld in 1505. Broomfield, Herne, is recorded as Bromefield in 1470, Broomefield in 1647; Broomfield Wood, Kingsdown, is found as Bromfeld in 1306; and Broomfield Shaw, Cobham, appears as Bromefields in 1612.

Broomhills. Broom-covered hill (OE *brōm hyll* → ME *brom helle* → Bromhelle c.1385 → Bromhill 1511).

Broomy Farm (Cooling). Broom hedged enclosure (OE *brōm (ge) hæg* → Bromgehege 778 → Bromhaie 1202 → Brumeheye 1232 → Brumhaye 1254).

Brotherhood Farm (Hackington). It is so called because the farmstead here was once the property of the hospitals of St. Nicholas at Harbledown, and of St. John at Northgate (Canterbury), both of which were monastic establishments.

Broughton House. See under BROCKTON.

Browning Bridge. It lies close to Wye and is probably associated with the lost place of Bronesford in Wye, which was originally *'Brūn's ford'* (OE *Brūnes ford*) and is recorded as æt Brunesforda 993 → Bruneford', Brunnesford' 1240 → Brunesford' 1270. Although there are no recorded forms for Browning Bridge, it seems likely that its original meaning was 'Brūn's bridge' (OE *Brūning brycg*).

Browning's Wood (Frinsted). It derives its name from the Frinsted family variously recorded during the 13th and 14th centuries as Broning, Bruning or Brounyng. Brownings, Chiddingstone, is similarly associated with the family of Brounyng (1362).

Browns, Great and **Little.** The name is associated with that of the 13th century family of le Brun. Brownshill at Chatham was originally a hill on land belonging to the family of Alan and Henry Brun (1327).

Brownshill. See under BROWNS.

Broxhall Farm (Upper Hardres). Badger's hollow (OE *brocces hol* → Brockyshole 1304 → Brokkeshole 1338).

Broxham Manor (Edenbridge). Brocc's settlement (OE *Brocces hām* → Brocces ham 973 → Brockesham 1240 → Brokesham 1304 → Broxham 1610). Brocc also owned land at BURSCOMBE.

Bubhurst. Bubba's wooded hill (OE *Bubban hyrst* → Bubbeherst 1475).

Buckholt Farm (Petham). Beech thicket (OE *bōc holt* → Bocholt 1272 → Bokholt 1278).

Buckhurst. Beech wooded hill (OE *bōc hyrst* → Bokhurst 1292). Buckhurst near Hever has the same original meaning, appearing as Bocherst'

1232 → Bokehirst 1278 → Bokhurst 1338; Buckhurst near Frittenden is Bocherst in 1232, Buckhurst in 1475; and Buckhurst Farm, Cranbrook, is Bochurst in 1226, Bokherst in 1334.

Buckland. Land granted by deed, or charter (OE *bōcland* → Bochelande 1086 → Bocland' 1205 → Boklonde 1253). The same origin is shared by Buckland near Luddesdown (Bocland' 1215, Boklond 1325); Buckland near Cliffe (Boclonde 1327); Buckland near Dover (Bochelande 1086, Bockland 1198); Buckland Farm, Woodnesborough (Bocoland 1086, Bocland c.1100); and Little Buckland near Maidstone (Bocland 1226, Bucland, Bokland' 1254).

Buckmore Wood (Wouldham). Bucks' pool: pool frequented by bucks or deer (OE *bucca mere* → Buckem'e 1240 → Bukkem'e 1254). The last element in these forms is an abbreviation of 'mere'.

Buckwell. Bucks' spring: spring frequented by bucks or deer (OE *bucca wielle* → Bucwell' c.1275 → Bocwelle 1327 → Boukwelle 1332). Buckwell Farm, Boughton Aluph, has the original meaning of 'beech spring: spring where beeches grow' (OE *bōc wielle*), and is recorded as Berchvelle 1086 → Bechewelle 1114 → Bokwell 1270 → Buckwell 1610.

Buddles. It derives its name from the family of Henry and Robert Buthel (c.1275).

Budds, Little. Recorded as Buddys in 1444, the name is a manorial one associated with William Bud, a 15th

century owner. Budd's at Shipbourne is similarly named after the 13th century family of le Bud, or le Boude. The same family name is also found in connection with Budd's Farm, Wittersham; North and South Budge Plantation, Great Mongeham; and Butts Farm, Stelling.

Budge Plantation. See under BUDDS.

Buesborough Cross (pronounced Bewsbury.). This was the meeting-place of the Bewsborough Hundred and was a crossroad in the parish of Whitfield. It was originally 'Bēaw's mound' (OE *Bēawes beorg*) and is recorded as Bevsberge 1086 → Beausberga 1087 → Bawesberg' 1226 → Beawesberghe 1253 → Bewsbroughe 1610. Bewsbury Cross Farm here is a variation of the name's spelling. The personal name, Bēaw, is also found in connection with BEAUXFIELD.

Bugden Farm (Dartford). It is first recorded in the latter part of the 14th century as Bulkeden, and may possibly have had the original meaning of 'bullock pasture' (OE *bulluc denn*).

Bugglesden. Beech thicket's pasture: woodland pasture marked by a beech thicket (OE *bōc holtes denn* → Bocholtesden' 1270 → Buckhurstden 1801).

Bullace Lane. It appears as Baletts Lane in 1471 and as Bulletts Lane in 1535, the name being derived from that of a local landowner.

Bullfinch Corner. The place derives

its name from the family of Bole-fynch (1348).

Bull Green. Recorded as such in 1700, the name is self-explanatory, being given to a village green or common on which a bull was tethered.

Bullingstone. This was originally a farmstead (ME *tone*) belonging to the family of Baluinch, first recorded in 1218. The name is later found variously recorded Bolewynch (1313), Bolefynch (1332), Bulleuynche (1339) and Bolfynch (1348).

Bullockstone. This was originally a farmstead belonging to the family of Boullynge, first recorded in 1348: the present name is derived from the original ME *Boullynges tone*.

Bully Hill (Rochester). Place covered with birch-trees (OF *boulaie* → Boley 1278 → Boleye 1338 → Bully-hill 1442 → The Bullie 1460 → Bully Hill 1595).

Bumpitt. Bone pit: pit in which bones have been found (OE *bān pytt'* → Bomepett' 1254 → Bonput 1278 → Bonipette 1304 → Bony-pette, Bompette 1332). The name may be a reference to an old grave unearthed here.

Bunce's Court (Otterden). It derives its name from John Bunce who is recorded as the owner of Hall in Otterden in 1503. The 'Hall' is now Hall's Place, and appears as Hall *alias* Otterden Place in 1782.

Burford. The name is first recorded in 1616, and may possibly be derived from OE *burh ford*: strong-hold by a ford. There are no earlier forms to corroborate this, but Bur-ford does lie close to the River Beult and there may have been a stronghold guarding a fording place here.

Burgess Wood (Tenterden). It takes its name from that of the family of Burgeys (1292).

Burham (pronounced Burrum). Stronghold settlement: settlement close to a stronghold (OE *burh hām* → Burhham 995 → Burham 1016). The 'stronghold' is a reference to nearby ROCHESTER.

Burleigh (pronounced Burly). Bower clearing: clearing containing a bower, or dwelling (OE *būr lēah* → Burlegh 1327 → Berlee 1348 → Burley 1465).

Burmarsh. Burghers' marsh (OE *burhwara mersc* → Burwaramersce 1016 → Bvrwar maresc 1086 → Burewaremareis 1226 → Borwar-mershe 1240). This was originally marshland belonging to the burgh-ers, or citizens, of Canterbury: from early Christian times, the land here was owned by the Monastery of St. Augustine in Canterbury.

Burnt Barn. It is recorded as such in 1799, the name being self-explanatory.

Burr Farm. See under BURSTED WOOD.

Burr's Hill (Brenchley). The place takes its name from the family of Richard le Borre (1278), also recorded as le Burre (1292), Burr (1327) and Bur (1347).

34

Burscombe Farm (Egerton). Brocc's coombe, or valley (OE *Brocces cumb* → Brockescumbe 1292 → Broxcommbe 1328 → Broscombe 1334). The personal name is also found in connection with BROX-HAM.

Bursted Wood (Bexley). Stream place: place by a stream (OE *burna stede* → burnes stede 814 → Borstede 1301 → Burstede 1347). Burr Farm close by also derives its name from the stream here, the Shuttle. Burr Farm, Warehorne, has a similar origin, being simply 'stream' (OE *burna*) and recorded as Burne in 1254, Bourne in 1332.

Burton, Great and **Little**. Byre farmstead: farmstead with a cattle byre (OE *bȳre tūn* → Burton 1219 → Byerton' c.1250 → Byrton' 1278 → Burton 1421).

Bush, Upper and **Lower**. Barley stubble field (OE *bere ersc* → Beresse 1147 → Berherssc 1243 → Berersshe 1346 → Beresh 1778).

Buston. Burgrīc's farmstead (OE *Burgrīces tūn* → Burricestune, Burgericestune c.1100 → Byrston' 1315 → Burston 1535 → Buston 1610).

Butcher Wood (Bethersden). It derives its name from the family of Walter Bucher (1340). Butcher Wood, Stanford, is similarly associated with the family of John and Walter Bochard, or Bocher (1357).

Butler's Hill (Hernhill). The place takes its name from that of the family of Bottrell (1540). Butler's Court, Blean, passed into the ownership of the Boteler family during the 14th century, and is recorded as Botillers Court in 1486.

Butterfield Wood (High Halden). Butter ford (OE *butere ford* → Boterford 1338 → Boterforde c. 1450). The name may either be suggestive of good pasture-land by this ford, or of slippery, muddy ground on either side of it.

Butts Farm. See under BUDDS.

Buttsole. It appears in 1494 as the Butts, and in 1542 as Buttes, and was probably a place where archery was practised. The affix -sole is a dialect word meaning 'muddy pool' and is directly derived from OE *sol*.

Buxford House (Great Chart). Bucks' ford: ford frequented by bucks or deer (OE *bucca ford* → Bockford 1278 → Buxforde melle 1500 → Buxford mill 1628 → Buckford 1690).

Bybrook. Bee marsh: marshy ground infested with bees (OE *bēo brōc* → Beo broce 940 → Bybrooke 1610). The bees were probably attracted by the marsh flowers growing here.

35

C

Cacket's Farm. See under CAL– COTT.

Cacketshill Wood (Eynsford). The hill stands on land once owned by the family of Roger Cacote de Eynesford (1345).

Cadlocks. It derives its name from the family of John Kedelak' (1327).

Cage Farm (Tonbridge). Recorded as le Cagegate in 1483 and as the Cage in 1533, the farm must stand on the site of a 'cage', a lock-up once used for minor offenders.

Calais Court (Ryarsh). It is referred to in 1782 as 'Carews Court, now commonly called Callis Court': the family of Carew owned the house from 1433 onwards. Care Hill Wood in Ryarsh may once have been part of their property, the name being a corruption of Carew.

Calais Wood. See under CALLIS COURT.

Calcott. Cold cot, or cottage (OE *cald cot* → Kaldecote c.1250 → Caldecote 1357). Cacket's Farm, Chelsfield, has the same origin, being recorded as Caldecote 1198 → Cakote 1240 → Kaldecote 1242 → Cacote 1301. 'Cold cot' was the name given to wayside shelters in which travellers could rest during bad weather.

Calehill. This was the meeting place of the Calehill Hundred, the origin of the name being 'bare hill' (OE *calu hyll* → Cale Helle 1086 → Calehele c.1100 → Calehulle 1178 → Cale hill 1610).

Calfstock. At the bare stock, or stump (OE *æt pǣm calewan stocce* → kalewan stocce 944 → Calovestok' 1344).

Callaways Lane. See under CALLIS COURT.

Calley Well. It derives its name from the family of John Coly (1348).

Callis Court (St. Peters). The place is referred to in 1535 as Caleis Grangia, and in 1624 as Callis Court, or Callis Grange, deriving its name from the family of William Caleys (c.1275). This name, its form a

36

result of the English pronunciation of Calais, from whence the original members of the family came, is also found in connection with Cailaways Lane, Newington, recorded in 1598 as Callis Croft; and in Calais Wood, Great Chart, recorded in 1674 as Callis medow.

Callum Hill (Lower Halstow). It appears in 1598 as Horsham Croft *alias* Callums, the latter name probably being that of a landowner in this area.

Camden Hill (Cranbrook). Valley pasture: woodland pasture in a valley (OE *cumb denn* → Cumbden' 1261 → Cumden' 1278 → Comdenn' 1313). Camden Place, Chislehurst, is named after William Camden (1551-1623), the antiquarian, who retired to live here in 1609.

Camer (pronounced Kaymer). There are no records for this place name, apart from 'Borstalle field' which appears in 1381. The present name seems to have resulted from confusion between the first element Bor- and OE *būr:* bower, the Anglo-French word for which was 'cambre' (← OF *chambre*).

Cane Wood (West Langdon). It is recorded in 1535 as Canewodd and is mentioned together with Capellwod and Holyrode Parke as belonging to the abbey of Langdon. It seems likely, therefore, that the name was originally 'canon wood'.

Cannon Wood (Halling). It derives its name from the family of John Canoun (1327).

Canon Court, Great and **Little** (Wateringbury). During the reign of Henry III the place became the property of the prior and canons of Leeds.

Canterbury. Stronghold of the *Cantware,* or people of Kent (OE *Cantwara burh* → Cantwaraburg 754 → Cantwaraburg, Contwaraburg c. 890 → Canterburie 1086 → Canterbury 1610). The earlier British name for the city appears as Darovernon c.150, Dorovernia in 605, derived from the British words *duro* (fort) and *verno* (swamp). The Romans adopted this name and called Canterbury *Durovernum Cantiacorum.*

Canter Wood (Elham). Cæntwaru's enclosure (OE *Cæntware worð* → Kanteworth' 1240 → Cantreworthe 1313 → Canterworth 1444 → Canterwood 1690). Cæntwaru was a Saxon woman.

Capel (pronounced Kayple). Chapel (ME *capel* → Capella 1226 → La Chapele 1270 → Capel 1293). Capel Farm, Warehorne, has the same origin and is recorded as Capella 1275 → Chapele 1292 → Capele 1346 → Capell 1486.

Capel-le-Ferne (pronounced Kayple-le-furn). The place is named after its 13th century Church of St. Mary, originally a chapel built on a site where ferns (OE *ferne*) grew. It is recorded as villa scē Marie in the Verne 1369 → Capel ate Verne, in seynte Marie in the fferne 1377 → Capell 1431 → Capell' in le Ferne 1535.

Capston. Cybbel's farmstead (OE *Cybbeles tūn* → Kebbeliston' 1254 → Kilbeston' 1292 → Keblistone

1347).

Catford 1254).

Cardens Wood and **Farm** (Cliffe). The name is derived from that of a family variously recorded during the 13th and 14th centuries as Cardon, Kardon' and Cardoun.

Care Hill Wood. See under CALAIS COURT.

Caring. Caru's people (OE *Caringas* → Karynge 1270 → Caringe 1334 → Caryng 1367).

Carpenters Wood (Sellindge). It is associated with the family of Elias le Carpenter (1313).

Casebourne Wood (Hythe). At the hovel-dweller's stream (OE *æt pǣm casing burnan* → Casincburnan 811 → Kasing burnan, Casing burnan 812 → Caseburn' 1203). Casebourne may have been an early name for the Seabrook Stream which flows nearby. OE *casa:* hovel-dweller, was associated with *case*: a hovel, or small dwelling, which in Old French was *case* or *casel*. This word seems to be the origin of the name of Castle Hill, Brenchley, which is recorded as La Case 1316 → Case 1320 → Le Case in Brenchysle 1439.

Castle Hill. See under CASEBOURNE.

Castweazel. Hovel-dweller's fork (OE *casan twisla* → Cassetuisle c. 1100 → Castwysle 1240 → Castwysele 1313). This is a reference to the fork of a stream.

Catford (pronounced Catfud). Cats' ford: ford frequented by wild cats (OE *catta ford* → Catteford' 1240 →

Cattsford (pronounced Catsfud). Cress ford: ford where cress grows (OE *cresse ford* → Crisford 1313 → Kirsforde 1327 → Kersford' 1334). There are no later forms to show how the name developed to Cattsford.

Catt's Place (Brenchley). It derives its name from the family of Jordan le Cat (1240). Catt's Farm, Lower Hardres, is similarly associated with the family of John le Kat (1278).

Cauldham. Cold settlement (OE *cald hām* → Caldham 1235). So called because of its high, exposed position.

Chafford Park. Market ford: ford by which a market is held (OE *cēap ford* → Chafford' 1254 → Chefforde 1327 → Chafford 1690). The place is on a tributary of the Medway, not far from the boundary between Kent and Sussex, and may well have been a trading place for the natives of the two counties.

Chainhurst. It is associated with a family variously recorded in 1278 as Cheyney, de Cheneye and de Cheuenye, the gentival form 'Cheyney's' becoming corrupted to Cheyners, and later to Chainhurst.

Chalk. Self-explanatory (OE *cealc* → cealc c.975 → Celca 1086 → Chalcha 1164 → Chalke 1215). Chalk Wood, North Cray, has the original meaning of 'chalk slope' (OE *cealc hielde*) and is recorded as Chelkchelde, Chelkehelde in 1301. Chalk Wood, Ash, appears as Chalke' in Asch in 1499. The names refer to the chalky soil in these areas.

Chalkcroft. Chalk croft: croft, or small piece of arable land, on chalky soil (OE *cealc croft* → Chalccroft 1217).

Chalkwell. Chalk spring: spring rising in chalky soil (OE *cealc wielle* → Chalkwell' 1334 → Chalkwelle 1343 → Chalkwell 1451).

Challenden (pronounced Chall-in-dn). Ceolla's woodland pasture (OE *Ceolling denn* → Chellyndenn' 1292 → Chillindene 1327 → Chelyngdenn' 1340 → Chilindenn' 1346). The personal name is also found in connection with CHILLENDEN.

Challock (pronounced Cholluck). At the calf enclosure (OE *æt pæm cealf locan* → cealflocan 833 → Chalfeloc 1240 → Chalewelok' 1247 → Chalfloke 1270 → Challok 1610).

Chambers Hill Wood (Cobham). It appears as Chamberlaynes hill wood in 1572, deriving its name from some former landowner. Chambers Wall, St. Peters, is associated with the 14th century family of atte Chambre, or atte Chaumbre.

Champion Wood (Newnham). The family of de Campania, or Champion, were lords of the Manor of Newnham from the latter part of the 12th century.

Chandler's Barn. It derives its name from the family of John Chaundeler (1431).

Chantry Cottages (Bredgar). This is the original chantry house of the College of the Holy Trinity, founded by Robert de Bradgare in 1393. Chantry Farm, Headcorn, appears as Kents Chantry *alias* The Chantry Farm in 1782, and is on the site of a chantry founded in 1466 by John Kent.

Chapman's Wood (Brasted). It is associated with the family of Nicholas le Chapman (1313). Chapman Farm, Staplehurst, is similarly connected with John Chapman (1327).

Charcott. Cot of the churls, or peasants (OE *ceorla cot* → Chercote 1240 → Cherecot 1275 → Cherecote 1301).

Charing (pronounced Chairin) Ceorra's people (OE *Ceorringas* → Cerringes 799 → Cheringes 1086 → Cherringes 1175 → Charringes 1185 → Cherring 1203 → Charing 1610).

Charlton. Farmstead of the churls, or peasants (OE *ceorla tūn* → Cerletone 1086 → Cherleton' 1240 → Cherlton' 1292 → Charlton 1610). Charlton Court, East Sutton, has the same origin, being recorded as Carleton 1227 → Cherletone 1253 → Cherlton' 1338. Charlton Farm, Bishopsbourne, appears as Cherlton' in 1240, Cherltone in 1338. Old Charlton Road in Dover is recorded as Cerlentone 1086 → Cerletune 1087 → Ceorletun c.1100 → Cherleton, Karletone 1290.

Charmans. The original name of this place seems to have been 'wood of the husbandmen' (OE *ceorlmanna wudu*) since it appears in 1316 as Cherlmanewod. The present name is derived from the family of John

Chareman (1320), whose own name was in turn derived from the place name.

Chart, Great. Rough common (OE *cert* → Cert 762 → Certh 1086 → Cert, Eastcert c.1100 → Chert, Estchert 1226 → Est Chart 1254 → Great Chart 1271). In 1042 Great Chart is recorded as East-Cert and oðer Cert, the 'other' Chart referring to Little Chart, which has the same original meaning and appears as Litelcert 1086 → Litlechert 1206 → Little Chert 1242. 'Chart' is still used as a dialect word in Kent to denote a rough common, or commonland overgrown with shrubs and bracken.

Chart, Little. See under CHART, GREAT.

Chart, The. Rough common (OE *cert* → bosco de Chert 1226).

Chartham (pronounced Chartum). Rough common settlement: settlement on rough commonland (OE *cert hām* → Certham c.871 → Certeham 1086 → Certaham, Certeham c.1100 → Chartham 1610).

Charton. It is recorded as Charton in 1464 and as Cheryngton in 1535, taking its name from the family of Ceriton, or Cheriton, natives of Cheriton who owned land in Farningham parish during the 13th century.

Chart Sutton. Rough common (OE *cert* → Cært 814 → Certh 1086 → Cert c.1100 → Chert 1278 → Chert near Sutthon 1280 → Chert by Sutton 1305). The affix Sutton refers to nearby SUTTON VAL-ENCE.

Chartway Street. Rough common way: way, or track, over rough commonland (OE *cert weg* → Cherweye 1226 → Chertewey 1278 → Chartweye 1285).

Chartwell (Westerham). The name of this house, the home of Sir Winston Churchill, appears to be derived from OE *cert wielle:* rough common spring, or spring rising in rough commonland.

Charwell Cottage. Spring of the churls, or peasants (OE *ceorla wielle* → Cherlewell' 1292).

Chatham (pronounced Chattum). Forest settlement (B *cēto* + OE *hām* → Cetham 880 → Cætham c.975 → Ceteham 1086 → Cettaham c.1100 → Chatteham 1194 → Chatham 1226).

Chattenden (pronounced Chatt-in-dn). Forest settlement hill: hill near a forest settlement (B *cēto* + OE *hām dūn* → Chetindunam, Chatendune c.1100 → Chatindone 1281 → Chetyndone 1287 → Chatyndon 1535). Chattenden is close to Chatham, the original forest settlement, and it has been suggested that the whole of this area may have been known to the British as *Cēt:* the forest.

Cheesecourt Gate. See under CHEESE WOOD.

Cheese Wood (Selling). It derives its name from the family of Richard Chese (1327). Cheesecourt Gate, Hackington, is associated with the family of Thomas Chesman (1327).

40

Chegworth. Gorse enclosure (OE *ceacge worð* → Chagewrth' 1201 → Chagworthe 1253 → Chegworth' 1339).

Cheke's Court (Tonge). The place is associated with the family of William Cheke (1270).

Chelsfield. Cēol's open land (OE *Cēoles feld* – Ciresfel, cillesfelle 1086 → Chilesfeld 1087 → Cilesfeld c.1100 → Chelesfeld 1185 → Chellisfelde 1226 → Chelsfeilde 1610). Cēol was also the owner of a wooded hill (OE *hyrst*) at the now lost place of Chelesherst in Rainham.

Cheney Wood (Rodmersham). Recorded as Chayney courte in 1549, it derives its name from the family of Robert Cheyne (1489). Cheney's Court, Chart Sutton, appears as Cheneys-Court in 1782, taking its name from that of the family of de Cheney of Patrixbourne who owned the house from the time of Edward I. Cheyne Court, Ivychurch, is named after Sir Thomas Cheney, who was granted the manor in 1553. Earlier, in 1537, Sir Thomas took possession of the Manor of Minster, and his name is perpetuated here in Cheyney Rock and Cheyney Marshes.

Cheriton. Church farmstead: farmstead with, or by, a church (OE *cirice tūn* → Ciriceton c.1100 → Ciriton' 1175 → Ceriton 1229 → Cheriton' 1240).

Cherry Tree Shaw. It appears in 1377 as Chersebemfeld, the name being derived from OE *cirisbēam feld:* 'open land marked by a cherry-tree'. The affix Shaw is from OE *scaga:* a copse.

Cherville House (Ickham). Open land of the churls, or peasants (OE *ceorla feld* → Cherlefeld 1270 → Cherlefelde 1338). In this name, -feld has become corrupted to -ville.

Chesley. Cæcca's clearing (OE *Cæccan lēah* → Chacheleye 1270 → Checheleye 1348 → Chesley-street *alias* Chicheley-street 1782).

Chessenden. Cēasta's woodland pasture (OE *Cēasting denn* → Chessingdenn', Chestenden' 1278 → Chesynden' 1292 → Chessenden' 1334).

Chested. Market place (OE *cēap stede* → Chepsted' 1240 → Chepstede 1313 → Chested 1489).

Chestfield Farm (Swalecliffe). Old castle (OF *chestel vieil* → Cestevile 1242 → Chesteuille 1332 → Chestevill 1346 → Chestefeld 1486). This is probably a manorial name, the 13th century family of Cestevile being natives of France.

Chestnut Street. Place where chestnut-trees grow (OF *chastaigniere* → Castayner 1214 → la Chastenere 1278 → Chesteynwode 1375). This remained a thickly wooded area until the late 15th century.

Chetney. Ceatta's island (OE *Ceattan ēg* → Chattenea 1192 → Cheteneye 1235). Chetney Marshes, in which the original island stood, is recorded as Chattene marsh in 1370.

Cheveney, Great and **Little.** Ceofa's island (OE *Ceofan ēg* → Cheuenay 1254 → Chiueneye 1261 → Chyvene 1308 → Chevene 1309). Great Cheveney, standing above the flat marsh-land of the Teise, is probably the original island. Cheveney and Cheveney Farm, lying only four miles away in Hunton, probably took their name from this early site.

Chevening (pronounced Cheevnin). Cifel's people (OE *Cifelingas* → Ciuilinga c.1100 → Chiveninges 1203 → Chiveninge 1247 → Chyvening 1271). Alternatively, it has been suggested that the place derived its name from the pronounced ridge beneath which it lies, and which may have been known to the British as 'Cefn' (← Welsh *cefn:* back, ridge). Those living at the foot of this ridge would have been known as the *Cefningas,* or ridge-dwellers.

Cheyne Court, Cheyney Rock and **Marshes.** See under CHENEY WOOD.

Chiddinghurst. There are no early forms for this place name, but since it is adjacent to CHIDDING-STONE, it seems highly probable that the two names are of the same origin and that Chiddinghurst was originally the 'wooded hill of Cidda's people' (OE *Ciddinga hyrst*).

Chiddingstone. Stone of Cidda's people (OE *Ciddinga stān* → Cidingstane c.1100 → Chidinggestan' 1218 → Chidingestone 1254 → Chyddingstone 1610). The stone was probably a boundary marker on this tribe's territory.

Chiddingstone Hoath. This name has the same derivation as CHID-DINGSTONE, being originally a stretch of heathland bordering the village. The affix 'Hoath' is from

OE *hǣð*: heath, heather-covered land.

Child's Bridge. Spring (OE *celde* – ME *chelde* – Chelde 1280 → Childe 1539 → Childebridge 1644). The place is close to a tributary of the Darent.

Childs Forstal. Spring (OE *celde* – ME *chelde* – Chelde c.1275 → Chealde 1348). The affix Forstal is a dialect word, used of land in front of farm buildings.

Chilham (pronounced Chillam). Cilla's settlement (OE *Cillan hām* → Cilleham 1086 → Chilham, Chilleham c.1140 → Chelham 1424 → Chylham 1610). The personal name is also found in connection with JULLIBERRIE.

Chillenden. Ceolla's valley (OE *Ceollan dene* → Ciollan dene c.833 → Cilledene 1086 → Cyllindænne, Cyllendene c.1100 → Chyllenden 1610). Ceolla also owned land at CHAL-LENDEN.

Chillmill. Spring mill: mill by a spring (OE *celde myln* → ME *chelde melle* → Childemelle 1327 → Chyldmelle 1332).

Chilmington Green. Cēolhelm's farmstead (OE *Cēolhelming tūn* → Chelminton' 1226 → Chelmynton' 1270 → Chelminton 1278).

Chilston Park. Child's farmstead (OE *cildes tūn* → Childeston' 1202 → Chilteston 1271 → Childeston 1289). This 'child' was probably a younger son (see CHILTON).

Chilton (near Alkham). Children's

farmstead (OE *cilda tūn* → Chilton' 1240 → Chiltone 1323). Chilton near St. Lawrence shares the same origin and is recorded as Chiltune c.1275, Chilton' in 1357. Chilton near Sittingbourne appears as Chilton' in 1240, Chiltone in 1334. The 'children' who owned these various farmsteads were the younger sons of a family, who inherited their property under the Kentish law of Gavelkind: the partible inheritance of land.

Chilverton Elms. Cēolwaru's farmstead (OE *Cēolware tūn* → Chelwarton' 1292 → Chelewartone 1332 → Chelwartone 1348). Cēolwaru was a Saxon woman.

Chimhams. 'Projecting rim settlement': settlement near a projecting rim (ME *chimbe ham* → Chimbeham 1203 → Chimbham 1254 → Chympeham 1278 → Chymham 1338). The 'projecting rim' refers to rising high ground here.

China Farm (Harbledown). It appears as Chaynes *alias* Cheynes, Cheineys in 1529, and as Cheney Court in 1790, taking its name from the family of Cheney to which the estate formerly belonged. 'China' is a corruption of Cheney.

Chingley. Shingle clearing (ME *cingel legh* → Chingele c.1200 → Chingeleghe 1253 → Chingley *alias* Shingley 1790).

Chipstead. Market place: place where a market is held (OE *cēap stede* → Chepsteda 1191 → Chepstede 1240 → Chipstede 1313).

Chislehurst. Gravel hill: wooded hill where the ground is gravelly (OE *cisel hyrst* → cysel hyrst 973 → Chiselhersta 1089 → Chiselhurste 1158).

Chislet. Cistern, aqueduct (OE *cistgelæt* → Cistelet 605 → Chistelet 1087 → Cistele c.1100 → Chislet 1610). It is possible that the aqueduct was connected with *Regulbium*, the Roman fort at Reculver, three miles from Chislet.

Chittenden. Citta's woodland pasture (OE *Citting denn* → Chityndenn' 1292 → Chytyngdenne 1314 → Chitindenn' 1346). The personal name is also found in CHITTY.

Chitty. Citta's island (OE *Cittan ēg* → Chiteye 1224). This would originally have been an island of firm ground in marshland: the district is still marshy.

Christian Court (Woodnesborough). It derives its name from the family of Jocelyn St. Cristian (1357), and is recorded as Christians Court in 1799.

Cinder Hill (Leigh). Hill where cinders are deposited (OE *sinder hyll* → Synderhelle 1239 → Sinderhell 1264). Cinderhill Wood, Brenchley, has the original meaning of 'cinder slope' (OE *sinder hielde*), being found as Cinderhild' in 1226. Both names show the places to have been in the vicinity of early iron works.

Cinque Ports (pronounced Sink Ports). Five ports (OF *cink porz* → de quinque portibus 1191 → the sink pors 1297 → the Cinque Ports c.1700). The original five ports were Hastings, Dover, Sandwich, Romney

43

and Hythe.

Clackett's Place. See under CLAY-GATE.

Clane Lane Marshes. This name, together with that of Great Clane Farm in the parish of Chalk, and Claylane Wood in the neighbouring parish of Cobham, is probably derived from OE *æt pære clæigan lane:* 'at the clayey lane'. Great Clane Farm appears as Clamlane in 1554.

Clappers Shaw. It is recorded as le Clapers in 1471, the name perhaps being a reference to a clapper bridge here. 'Shaw' is from OE *scaga:* a copse.

Clatfields. Glæppa's open land (OE *Glæppan feld* → glæppan felda 973 → Glepfeld', Glappefeld' 1254 → Clakefeld' 1292 → Clappefeld 1332).

Clavertye Wood (Elham). Clover enclosure (OE *clæfre tēag* → Clavertegh 1341 → Clav'tygh 1535).

Claxfield House and **Farm** (Lynsted). Clac's open land (OE *Claces feld* → Clakesfeld 1247 → Clasfeld, Claxfeld' 1332 → Claxfelde 1346). The personal name is of Old Norwegian origin.

Claygate. Gate leading on to clayey land (OE *clæg geat* → Cleygate 1270). Clackett's Place, Ryarsh, shares the same original meaning, being recorded as Cleygate in 1316, Claygate in 1348.

Claylane Wood. See under CLANE LANE MARSHES.

Claypits. Self-explanatory. The name appears as Claypet in 1509.

Clearhedges. 'Clear hedge': land cleared of hedges (ME *clere hegge* → Clerhegge 1380 → Cleren Heggem 1537).

Clement Street. The place derives its name from the family of Clement (1327), and is recorded as Clementeslond in 1374.

Cleve Hill and **Marshes** (Boughton-under-Blean). At the cliff (OE *æt pæm clife* → Clyue 1327). Cleve Court, Monkton, is from the same origin and appears as Cliue in 1240, Clyue (Clyve) in 1332.

Cliffe. Cliff, steep slope (OE *clif* → Clifwara gemære 778 → Clive 1086 → Clyffe 1610). The 8th century form means 'boundary of the cliff-dwellers'. West Cliffe has the same original meaning as Cliffe and is recorded as æt Clife 1042 → Westclive 1086 → W.Cliffe 1610. Cliff Farm, Minster, appears as South Cliff farm in 1584.

Cliffsend, Little. Self-explanatory (OE *clifes ende* → Cliuesend' 1240 → Clivesende 1280 → Clyuessende 1304 → Cliveshende 1318).

Cliftonville. This is a descriptive name given to the seaside resort which developed to the east of Margate during the mid-19th century.

Clinton Lane and **Wood** (Brasted). It takes its name from that of John de Clinton, Lord of the Manor of Broxham in Westerham towards the end of the 14th century.

Clip Gate Wood (Barham). Described as Clipgate in 1662, the name probably refers to a gate here which was closed by means of a clip or clasp of some kind.

Clowes Farm and **Wood** (Blean). Woodland enclosure (OE *clūs* → cluse 948 → Cluse 1240).

Coakham. Cobba's coombe, or valley (OE *Cobban cumb* → Cobbecumbe 1232 → Cobecumbe 1313). The present name is a contraction of these early forms. The personal name, Cobba, is also found in connection with COBHAM, COBHAMBURY and COPLAND'S WAYS.

Cobbes Place. See under LODGELAND.

Cobblers Bridge. Recorded as Cobeletesbrige in 1463, and as Cobbysbregge in 1465, the name is a manorial one, being originally associated with John and William Cobelot (1357). The place is on a stream flowing into the sea near Herne Bay.

Cobb's Wood (Ashford). It derives its name from the family of John Cobb of Ashford (1617). Cobb's Hall, Aldington, is recorded as Cophall in 1790, taking its name from the family of Cobbe or Cobbes who lived in the parish of Aldington from the 15th century onwards.

Cobham. Cobba's water meadow (OE *Cobban hamm* → cobba hammes mearce 939 → Cobbeham 1197 → Kobeham 1200 → Cobham 1226). The 939 form means 'boundary of the water meadow owned by Cobba'. The personal name is also found in COAKHAM, COBHAM-BURY and COPLAND'S WAYS.

Cobham Court, Bekesbourne, found as Borne Cobeham in 1385, takes its name from early 14th century owners who were natives of Cobham. Cobham Farm and Wood, Lenham, appears as Schelf Cobham or Shelvecobham in 1494, deriving its name from the family of William de Cobham, lord of the Manor of East Shelve in Lenham in 1320. Cobham Farm, Thornham, is named after the 13th century family of Cobbeham or Cobham who owned the manor here during the reign of King John.

Cobhambury. Stronghold of Cobba's people (OE *Cobbinga burh* → Cobbingeb'y 1232 → Cobbyngebure 1316 → Cobehambery 1329). Cobhambury Wood, Cobham, has the original meaning of 'Cobham borough': a borough, or manor, belonging to Cobham, and is recorded as Cobehambery in 1216, Cobhambiry in 1278.

Cobrahamsole Farm (Sheldwich). Sceobba's muddy pool (OE *Sceobban sol* → Sobesole 1270 → Schobesole 1332 → Copesham Sole, Copshole-farm, Copersole 1782).

Cockerhurst, Great. 'Quiver hill': wooded hill where wood is gathered for arrows (OE *cocer hyrst* → Cokerhirst 1254 → Kokerhurst 1314 → Cokerherst 1487). Alternatively, the place may have had some connection with the tribe settled at COCKERING.

Cockerils Wood (Preston). It derives its name from the family of William Cokerel (1327).

apply to Cobham Surrey!

Cockering Farm (Thanington). The quiver or sheath people (OE *cocer-ingas* → Cokeringe 1240 → Cock-ering' 1270). This was obviously a tribe of warriors noted for the arrows or spears which they carried in quivers (OE *cocer*).

Cockles Bridge. The place, lying on one of the many streams which drain the Denge Marsh, takes its name from that of Thomas Cokkel (1381).

Cockreed Lane. Cocca's cleared land (OE *Coccan rīed* → Cocride 1242 → Cockeryde 1283 → Cokerede 1313). Cocca also owned property at COX-ETT.

Cockshot. Cock-bird corner: corner of land frequented by cock-birds (OE *cocc scēat* → Cokschete 1348 → Cockshete 1507).

Coffin Shaw. It derives its name from the family of Hugh Coffin, or Cophin (1188). The affix 'Shaw' is from OE *scaga:* a copse.

Cold Blow. This was formerly the meeting-place of the Cornilo Hundred, the name of which had the original meaning of 'quern, or hand-mill, hill' (OE *cweorn hlǣw* → Corn-ilai 1086 → Cornelai 1159 → Quern-elawe 1226 → Querenlawe, Cornila 1240). Cold Blow may either be a corruption of Cornilo, or have received its name from its exposed position above LYDDEN – 'the sheltered valley'.

Coldbridge Wood and **Farm** (Boughton Malherbe). At the blackened bridge (OE *æt þǣm coligan brycge* → Calewebreg 1277 → Colewybregg'

1290 → Cologhbrugge, Colubregg 1352 → Colebregge 1362). Close by is Blackpit Wood, possibly a place where charcoal was once burnt: the blackened water of the stream on which Coldbridge stands must have caused discolouration of the stones, hence the original place name.

Cold Friday Street. It appears in 1799 as Cold Friday street and was an alternative name for the village of Woodnesborough Street. Friday Street is a common place name in southern England, denoting a small group of houses set apart from the main village: Friday was a day of ill-omen during the Middle Ages, and many Friday Streets once marked a road to a gallows.

Coldharbour. The place is recorded in 1346 as 'field called Caldham', and probably had the original meaning of 'cold water meadow' (OE *cald hamm*), the name later being altered to the common Coldharbour, which, like CALCOTT, was a wayside shelter for travellers in bad weather. Coldharbour Farm, North-bourne, appears as Cold Harbour in 1799 and marks the site of such a shelter.

Coldred (pronounced Coal-dred). Charcoal clearing: clearing where charcoal is burnt (OE *col hryding* → Colredinga gemercan 944 → Col-ret 1086 → Colrede c.1180 → Colred 1235). The 944 form means 'at the boundary of the charcoal clearing dwellers'.

Coldswood. Col's wood (OE *Coles wudu* → Coleswude 1240 → Coles-wode 1292 → Colleswode 1357). The personal name is also found in

46

connection with COLESHALL.

Cole Allen. Recorded in 1545 as Cold Alleyns, and in 1603 as Coales, this may originally have been a cold, exposed site on land belonging to a family named Alleyn or Allen.

Colebran Wood (Shadoxhurst). It derives its name from the family of Hamo Colebraund (1315).

Coleshall. Col's corner of land (OE *Coles halh* → Coleshalle 1327 → Colsall 1450 → Colshall 1690). Col was also the owner of a wood at COLDSWOOD.

Cole Wood (Cobham). Coal wood: wood where charcoal is burnt (OE *col wudu* → Colewood 1698).

Colgates. Recorded as Colgate in 1226, the name must be derived from OE *col geat*: charcoal gate, gate leading into woodland where charcoal is burnt.

Colkins. This is a manorial name, taken from the family of Sarra, John and Richard Colkyn (c.1350).

Collett's Field Cottage. The place appears in 1507 as Collett's Bridge, obviously deriving its name from that of some former owner.

Collier Street. It is associated with the family of William Colier (1348). This surname is also found in connection with Colliers Green; Collier's Hill, Mersham; Collier's Land Bridge, Penshurst; and Collyerhill Wood, Hastingleigh.

Colliers Green. See under COLLIER STREET.

Collington Wood (Tenterden). It is named after Nathaniel Collington, vicar of Tenterden from 1662 to 1682.

Collyerhill Wood. See under COLLIER STREET.

Combe Banks (pronounced Coom). Coombe, or valley (OE *cumb* → Cumbe 1327). Combebank Farm nearby in Sundridge shares the same original meaning, as do Combe Farm, Lympne; Combe Wood, Stowting; Coomb Farm, St. Mary's Hoo; Coombe near Woodnesborough; and Coombe Farm, Maidstone, Hawkinge and Poulton.

Combourne. Valley stream (OE *cumb burna* → Comburne 1327 → Combourne 1346).

Combwell. Valley spring (OE *cumb wielle* → to Cumwyllan c.950 → Cumbwell c.1160 → Cumbewell, Cumbwelle c.1194). It may have been from this spring that the stream in neighbouring COMBOURNE flowed.

Comp, Great and **Little.** Comp and Little Comp, near Leybourne, appear as Compe in 1461; and Great Comp near Wrotham is recorded as camp de Wrothā in 1240, Caumpes in 1251. The place names are derived from OE *camp*: field.

Coneyearth Wood (Godmersham). Cǣna's enclosure (OE *Cǣnan worð* → Keneworth' 1327). The present name is a corruption of the original, perhaps deliberately altered because of the number of rabbit warrens in the wood.

Conghurst, Old and **Little**. It is recorded as Conhurst 1254 → Cungherst 1313 → Congherst 1343. This is a difficult name to interpret. It certainly contains as a final element OE *hyrst*: wooded hill, and Conghurst stands on ground which slopes steeply towards the Kent Ditch. The first element might possibly be an Old English word *cong*, or *cung*, meaning a bend and referring to the several winding streams in the area.

Connetts. The place takes its name from the Eastchurch family of Colnette (1439).

Conningbrook (pronounced Cunninbrook). 'Royal marshy ground': marshy ground belonging to a royal estate (OE *cyne brōc* → Kunibroc 1226 → Cuninbrok', Conebrok', Conyngbroke c.1250 → Cunebrok' 1270). The place is close to KENNINGTON, which was originally a royal manor.

Conyer. Rabbit warren (OF *connière* → ME *conyngere* → Coneyire 1324). Conyer Wood, Hothfield, has the same original meaning and appears as le Conynger in 1326, Conyngere in 1347.

Cookham Farm (St. Paul's Cray). 'Cook settlement': settlement where cooking is done (OE *cōc hām* → Cokham 1241). Nearby was the now lost place of Kechyngrove, originally 'kitchen grove' (OE *cycen grāf*): perhaps this was at one time attached to Cookham, the grove supplying wood for the kitchen fires. Cookham Hill Farm, Rochester, has the original meaning of 'cock meadow: water meadow frequented by cock-birds' (OE *cocc hamm*)

and is recorded as Kocham in 1260, Cocham in 1338.

Cooling (pronounced Coolin). Cūla's people (OE *Cūlingas* → Culingas 808 → Colinges 1086 → Culinges 1203 → Colinge 1215 → Cowling 1610).

Coolinge (pronounced Coolinje). The corn people, or corn growers (OE *corningas* → Cornyng' 1327 → Cornynge 1348). The present name has been affected by COOLING.

Coombe. See under COMBE BANKS.

Coombegrove Farm (Hastingleigh). Recorded in 1535 as Combe Grove, the name refers to a grove growing in a coombe, or valley.

Cooper's Street. It appears in 1471 as Cowperstreet, and in 1484 as Couperstreet, the name being derived from the 14th century Ash family named Coupere. This surname is also found in connection with Cooper Farm, Pluckley; Coopers Corner, Sundridge; and Cooper's Wood, Wrotham.

Cooting Farm (Adisham). The cotdwellers, or cottagers (OE *cotingas* → Cottinges 1190 → Cotinge 1277 → Cotyng' 1327).

Copden Wood (Cranbrook). Coppa's farmstead (OE *Coppan tūn* → Copton c.1500). The personal name is also found in association with COPTGROVE and COPTON.

Copes. It takes its name from that of the family of Richard le Cope (1268).

Copland's Ways. Cobba's land (OE *Cobban land* → Cobelonde 1327 → Cobelond' 1347). The personal name is also found in COAKHAM, COBHAM and COBHAMBURY.

Copperhurst. 'Top wood': Wooded hill on a top or summit (OE *copp hyrst* → Cophurst 1254 → Cupherst 1346). Copperhurst is situated on high ground.

Coppings Gill. The name is derived from the family of John Copping (1522), the affix 'Gill' being from ME *gil*: a narrow valley. Copping's Farm, Leigh, appears as Copping Land in 1258, Coppings-Land in 1279, being associated with the forebears of John Coppyng (1327). Coppins Farm, Molash, takes its name from another John Copyn (1327).

Cop Street. It appears as Cobbistrete in 1366 and as Cobbestrete in 1487, the place originally being part of the property of William Cobbe (1348).

Coptgrove Barn. Coppa's grove (OE *Coppan grāf* → Coppegraue 1313 → Copgrave 1573). The personal name is also found associated with COPDEN and COPTON.

Copthall. Recorded in 1702 as Copthall, the name probably has the original meaning of 'capped hall': hall with a high roof (ME *copped hall*).

Copton. Coppa's stone (OE *Coppan stān* → Coppanstan 821 → Copton 1208). The stone would have been a boundary marker on Coppa's land here: he also had property at COPDEN and COPTGROVE.

Corbier Hall Wood (Thornham). It is named after the family of Robert Corbie of Boughton Malherbe, who owned the Manor of Thornham between 1378 and 1415.

Cornhill. Hill on which corn is grown (OE *corn hyll* → Cornhull' 1235 → Cornhill' 1240 → Cornhelle 1334).

Corn Hill (Rolvenden). Crane spring: spring frequented by cranes (OE *cran wielle* → Cranewell' 1254). The present name is a corruption of earlier forms.

Cossington. Cūsa's farmstead (OE *Cūsing tūn* → Cusintun c.950 → Cusintona c.1100 → Cusinton 1230 → Cossenton 1610). Cūsa owned another farmstead at COZENTON.

Cottingtoncourt. See under COTTINGTON HILL.

Cottington Hill (Minster). Cottagers' farmstead (OE *cotmanna tūn* → Cotmanton' 1278). During the 13th century a now lost Cottmannefeld is recorded close by: this would have been open land belonging to the cottagers (OE *cotmanna feld*). Cottingtoncourt Farm, Sholden, has the same origin as Cottington Hill, appearing as Cotmantone in 1304, Cotmanton in 1446. In both place names, the forms have been corrupted to Cottington.

Cotton Farm (Stone). At the cots, or cottages (OE *æt pǣm cotum* → Coten 1280 → Cotene 1316 → Cotton 1407).

Cotton Tree. Capped, or pollarded, tree (OE *coppede trēow* → Copintry 1405). A pollarded tree is one which has had its topmost branches pruned back.

Couchman's Wood (Cranbrook). It derives its name from the family of William Cowcheman (1500).

Coursehorne. 'Cross's horn': horn, or spit of land, associated with a cross (ME *crouches horne* → Croucheshorn' 1254 → Cursorn' 1278 → Courshorn' 1346).

Court-at-Street. The name appears in 1530 as Cortopstreet and may possibly refer to a street or way of some kind leading to or from a short stretch of enclosed marshland (ME *curt hop*).

Court-at-Wick. It is recorded in 1634 as Court at Week, 'Week' being derived from OE *wīc*: farm. 'Court' is probably a reference to a manorial possession.

Courtenwell. Short farmstead (ME *curt tone* → Corthone 1327 → Curtone 1348). The -well ending is a late addition to the name. The original farmstead appears to have been called 'short' in order to distinguish it from the nearby 'long' farmstead at LANGTON GREEN.

Courthope Wood (Shadoxhurst). The first element in this name is taken from the now lost place of Minchin Court, the wood formerly being part of that estate. The second element is probably derived from OE *hōp*: marsh enclosure. Minchin Court – the name is from OE *myncen*: nun – once belonged to St. James's Hospital in Thanington.

Courthopes Corner. Short marsh enclosure (ME *curt hop* → Kurthope 1226 → Courtehope 1334). There was another such place at Goudhurst, where a now lost Courthope is recorded in 1348.

Courtlands. Short farmstead's land (ME *curt tones land* → Curtoneslond 1349 → Courtlands 1738).

Court Wood (Cobham). It appears both in 1369 and in 1572 as North Court, in 1435 as North Courte Manor, and in 1572 again as northe Court Fylde, the place obviously being a possession of Cobham Manor.

Cousins Shaw. The name is taken from that of the family of Richard Cosyn (1301), 'Shaw' being derived from OE *scaga*: a copse.

Cowbeck Wood (Boxley). There are no forms earlier than the end of the 15th century, when the name appears as Cukebake.

Cowbeech. Recorded in 1690 as Cobeech Green, the name may possibly be derived from ME *cou beche*: 'cow beech', with reference to a particular beech tree here under which cows sheltered.

Cowden. Cow pasture (OE *cū denn* → Cudena c.1100 → Cudenne 1253 → Couden 1259 → Cowden 1610). Cowden near Hawkhurst has the same origin, being recorded as Coudenne in 1343. Cowden Farm, Brenchley, appears as Cudenna in 1279, Cowdenn' in 1334.

Cowharlands Shaw. The name appears to be associated with the family of William Crowland of West Wickham (1521).

Cowless Shaw. Cow lea, or meadow (OE *cū lǣs* → Cowles 1532).

Cowstead. Cuda's place (OE *Cudan stede* → Codestede 1190 → Cudesteda 1194). Cuda also owned property at CUDHAM and CULAND. Cowstead Farm, Minster, appears to have derived its name from a family who were natives of Cowstead proper, both places being in the same Hundred, and is recorded as Codestede 1226 → Cotestede 1313 → Codested' 1332.

Coxenhall Shaw. Cock-bird's corner of land: corner of land frequented by cock-birds (OE *cocces halh* → Cokeshall' 1278). The affix 'Shaw' is from OE *scaga*: a copse.

Coxett, Little. Cocca's seat, or dwelling (OE *Coccan (ge)set* → Cocsete 1247 → Coksete 1466). Coxett Wood here takes its name from the place. The personal name, Cocca, is also found in connection with COCKREED.

Cox Heath. See under COX STREET.

Coxhill. Cock's hill: hill frequented by cock-birds (OE *cocces hyll* → Cokeshull' 1327 → Cokkeshelle 1332 → Cokeshell' 1348).

Cox Street, Upper and **Lower.** It appears in 1278 both as Kokeystrete and as Kokeistrete, taking its name from that of a landowner to whom the original street, or way, belonged.

Cox Heath near Linton is recorded as Cokkyshoth in 1489, Coxhoth in 1585, being originally heathland belonging to the family of Gilbert le Cok' (1339). Cox Farm, Hougham, is associated with a 14th century family variously recorded as Cok', Kok' and Cook. Cox's Cottage, Sundridge, is similarly associated with a 14th century family found as Cok' or Cook'; and Cox's Farm, Snodland, takes its name from that of William le Cok' (1327).

Cozenton. Cūsa's farmstead (OE *Cūsing tūn* → Cusinton' 1235 → Cosynton 1450). Cūsa had another farmstead at COSSINGTON.

Crabble. Crab hole: hole in which crabs are found (OE *crabba hol* → Crabbehole 1227 → Crappolmyll 1537). The place is only two miles away from the coast, and lies on the River Dour: the name appears to be a reference to a creek or hollow of some kind in which crabs were caught.

Cranbrook. Crane marsh: marshy ground frequented by cranes (OE *cran brōc* → Cranebroca c.1100 → Cranebroc 1226 → Cranebrok 1270 → Cranbrooke 1610). Close to Cranbrook is a stream known as the Crane Brook. Cranbrook near Newington shares the same original meaning, appearing as Cranbrooke in 1782.

Cranford, The. Crane ford: ford frequented by cranes (OE *cran ford* → Craneford 1259 → Cranford 1308 → the Cranford 1778). This is a small tributary of the River Darent.

51

Cray, River. The name is derived from a British river-name which survived in the Middle Welsh word *crei*, meaning fresh, or clean. The river is recorded as Crægean in 814, Craie c.1200.

Cray, North. It derives its name from that of the CRAY river on which it lies, and appears as Craie 1086 → Northcræi c.1100 → Nortcraye 1226 → Northcray 1261 → North Craye 1610.

Crayford (pronounced Krayfud). Ford on the Cray river (OE *Crægan ford* → Crecgan ford 457 → Craiford 1202 → Crayford 1354).

Craylands. The place takes its name from that of the family of Walter Greylaund (1292).

Craythorne Firs. 'Crow thorn': thornbush frequented by crows (OE *crāwe þorn* → Crawethorn 1226 → Crauethorne 1313 → Craythorne 1799). The now lost place of Crauthorn in Hope All Saints had the same origin, being recorded as æt crawan þorne 984 → Crowthorne 1283 → Crauthorne 1347.

Creed Farm (Egerton). Weeds, or plants (OE *crēad* → Crede 1292). The name probably refers to 'a place where plants grow: a garden'.

Crippenden. Cryppa's woodland pasture (OE *Crypping denn* → Cryppenden' 1278).

Cripps. It derives its name from the 14th century family of Crips, found in the Eastchurch area.

Crisbrook, Upper. Cress marsh: marshy ground where cress grows (OE *cresse brōc* → Krisbrok' 1327 → Kyrsbroke 1334 → Crisbrok 1348). The place lies on a tributary of the Medway.

Crit Hall (Benenden). Crotta's hollow (OE *Crottan hol* → Crotehole 1292 → Crutehole 1402 → Crittall 1690). Crotta also owned a woodland pasture (OE *denn*) at the now lost place of Cruttenden in Headcorn, recorded as Crotinden' 1256 → Crotindenne 1270 → Cruttenden 1782.

Crittenden. Guðhere's woodland pasture (OE *Guðhering denn* → Westguterindenne 1227 → Guteringden' 1258 → Crotynden 1451). Why this place should have been known as 'west' during the early 13th century is not known.

Crixhall Farm (Staple). Cricket's corner of land: corner of land infested with crickets (ME *crikeles hale* → Crikesale 1278 → Krykeleshale 1292 → Crikleshale 1299 → Crekelesale 1389 → Cryksale 1484).

Crockenhill. 'Crock-house slope': slope on which stands a crockhouse, or pottery (OE *crocc ærn hielde* → Crokornheld 1388 → Crokerneheld 1390 → Crokkenhill 1471 → Croukhill, Crokenhill 1535).

Crockers Hatch Corner. See under CROCKHURST STREET.

Crockhurst Street. This place name appears to be derived from a British word *crūc*, hill, with the explanatory addition of OE *hyrst*: a wooded hill, and is recorded as Crokhurst in 1250. Crockers Hatch Corner, Speldhurst, probably shares the same origin, appearing as Crokherst in 1313. In 1525 the name appears in connection with a William Crocher, the hatch, or gate, presumably being on his land here.

Crockley Green. It is found recorded as The Crockhill in 1441, Crockey Green in 1559, and Crockers Green in 1607, and may originally have had some association with crocks or pots (OE *crocc*). Alternatively, like CROCKHURST STREET, the name may contain a British word *crūc*: hill. This last explanation seems the most likely one in view of the 1441 form.

Crocksfoot Hill. See under CROCK-SHARD FARM.

Crockshard Farm (Wingham). The place is recorded in 1254 as Croks-erde, deriving its name from OE *crocsceard*: potsherd, or piece of broken earthenware. In 1270 it appears as Crokestede – 'crock place' – denoting a spot where potsherds of an early date had been unearthed. A similar explanation may lie behind the name of Crocks-foot Hill, Willesborough, which is recorded as Crokkesford' in 1338. However, since there is no stream near the hill, which would produce the -ford ending, this may have been a mis-spelling, and the correct form have been Crokkesserd', derived from OE *crocsceard*: potsherd.

Crofton. Mound farmstead: farm-stead by a mound or hillock (OE *cropp tūn* → crop tun 973 → Croc-tvne 1086 → Croftona 1179 → Crofton 1271).

Cromer's Wood (Sittingbourne). It is associated with James and William Cromer of Sittingbourne (1598).

Cronk's Farm (Nettlestead). Hovels of the *Crangas*, or dwellers by a bend (OE *Cranga bȳras* → æt Cranga-byrum 801 → Crangabyras 811 → Crancheberi, Cronkesbery 1185 → Craunkebiry 1336). In 1336 the place is further described as 'aqua de Craunkebiry': water of Craun-kebiry – a stream flows past the farm, forming a right-angled bend, which would explain the name given to the original settlers here.

Crookhorn Wood (Snodland). Rad-,ulfus de Curbespine is recorded in the Domesday Book (1086) as ow-ner of the manor of neighbouring Birling. His family name, Curva Spina, or Curbespine, appears to have been anglicised to Crookhorn (probably another word for Crook-back), and is perpetuated in that of the wood.

Cross, Crouch. See under CROUCH HOUSE GREEN.

Crouch House Green. 'Cross house': house built near a cross (ME *crouche hus* → Crouchouse 1731 → Crouchhouse 1744). Crouch near Boughton-under-Blean has the sim-ple original meaning of 'cross' (OE *crūc*, ME *crouche*), and appears as Cruce in 1278, Crouche in 1332. Cross near Minster shares the same origin and is recorded as Cruce during the 13th century, The name refers to wayside, or 'preaching' crosses.

Crowdown Wood (Herne). Crow

pasture: woodland pasture frequented by crows (OE *crāwe denn* → Crowdenne 1485).

Crowhurst (near Lamberhurst). Crow land: shortened piece of land frequented by crows (OE *crāwe scyrte* → Croweserte 1240 → Croushert 1292 → Crowsherte 1334). The name seems to have been later confused with the more common Crowhurst.

Crowhurst (near Wrotham). Crow wood: wooded hill frequented by crows (OE *crāwe hyrst* → Crouhurst 1292).

Crowslands. Crow land: land where crows gather (OE *crāwe land* → Crowelande 1278 → Craulonde 1348).

Crump. The place derives its name from the family of Walter Crumpe (1325). Crump Farm, St. Nicholas at Wade, is similarly associated with the family of David Crompe (1503).

Crundale (pronounced Crundle). Chalk pit, quarry (OE *crundel* → Crundala c.1100 → Crundal' 1226 → Crundale 1242).

Cuckoldscombe. Cucol's coombe, or valley (OE *Cucoles cumb* → Cokelescombe 1211 → Coclescumbe 1253). Confusion with the word 'cuckold' has produced the present place name.

Cuckoo Shaw. It appears c.1500 as Cuckowescrofte Major, presumably being a large piece of enclosed land (croft) frequented by the cuckoo bird.

Cudham (pronounced Cuddam). Cuda's settlement (OE *Cudan hām* → Codeham 1086 → Codham 1269 → Cudeham 1278). The personal name is also found in connection with COWSTEAD and CULAND.

Culand, Great. Cuda's land (OE *Cudan land* → Codeland' 1254 → Codelonde 1338). The present name is a contraction of these forms. Cuda also had property at COWSTEAD and CUDHAM.

Culverden, Great. Dove pasture: woodland pasture frequented by doves (OE *culfre denn* → Culfredene 1254 → Culverdene 1278 → Culverdenn 1324).

Culverstone Green. 'Dove mire': miry or muddy pool frequented by doves (OE *culfre sol* → Culversole 1381). There are no later forms to show how this name developed to its present one.

Curlswood Park Farm (Nonington). Crūd's wood (OE *Crūdes wudu* → Crudeswod' 1254 → Croddeswode 1342 → Cruddyswood 1425).

Curteis Wood. See under CURTISDEN GREEN.

Curtisden Green. This was originally a pasture (ME *denne*) belonging to the family of John Curteys (1292). The same surname is found in connection with Curteis Wood, Stone-cum-Ebony, and Curteis Wood, Herne.

Cutnails. Cutta's corner of land (OE *Cuttan halh* → Cuttenhal' 1240 → Cuttenale 1327).

54

Cuxton. Cucola's stone (OE *Cucolan stān* → Cucolanstan 880 → Cuclestana, Cucclesstane c.975 → Coclestane 1086 → Cukelstan' 1240 → Cuckston 1610). The stone was probably a boundary marker on Cucola's land here.

D

Dachurst. Dæcca's wooded hill (OE *Dæccan hyrst* → Dachehirst 1295 → Dachurst 1372). The personal name is also found in connection with DAGNAM.

Dadman's. Recorded during the 16th century as Dodmannys, the name is a manorial one, derived from some early owner named Dodman.

Dagnam Farm (All Hallows). Dæcca's settlement (OE *Dæccan hām* → Dekeham 1240 → Dagenham 1278 → Dakenham 1313). Dæcca also owned a wooded hill at DACHURST.

Dalham. Dale settlement: settlement in a dale, or valley (OE *dæl hām* → Dælham c.980 → Delham 1246 → Dalham 1332).

Dam Bridge. It appears as Danne Bridge in 1790 and as Danbridge in 1801: the name is probably derived from ME *dene:* valley, since the place lies in the valley of a stream. Dambridge Farm here takes its name from that of the place.

Danaway. Valley way: way or path through a valley (OE *denu weg* → Denewei c.1230 → Deneway 1338 → Denaway Street 1598).

Dane Court. (Boughton-under-Blean). Valley (OE *denu* → Dane 1292). The same original meaning is shared by Dane Court and Dane Street, Chilham; Dane Court, Tilmanstone; Dane Court, St. Peters; Dane Farm, Upper Hardres; Dane House, Hartlip; and the now lost places of Dane in Boughton Aluph, and Dane Court, Gillingham.

Dane John (Canterbury). Dungeon (OF *donjon* → Le Dungon 1254 → Dongyon 1391 → Daungeon 1407 → Dongeon, Dungeon 1535 → Dane-John 1690). This is the name given to an early defensive mound, now a public garden, lying just within the city walls.

Dane Street. See under DANE COURT.

Daniel's Water. Recorded as Daniells water in 1634, it derives its name from the family of John Daniel (1346). Daniel's Wood, Bethersden, is similarly associated with Thomas Daniel (1417).

56

Danns Lane. It is associated with the family of Dan, recorded in the Mereworth area in 1500.

Dan's Hill (Chatham). The place possibly takes its name from that of the family of Arnold in the Dane (1313), whose name means 'dweller in the valley'.

Danson Farm (Bexley). Denesige's farmstead (OE *Denesiging tūn* → Densinton' 1301 → Danston' 1327).

Danton Farm (Cheriton). Dalesman's farmstead (OE *dælmanning tūn* → Dalmynton' 1327 → Dalmentone 1348). The present name is a contraction of these forms. Although 'dalesman' is a term now confined to the natives of northern England, in early times it was used generally to describe a valley-dweller.

Darent, River (pronounced Darren). The name, recorded as Diorente in 822, and as Dærent in 983, is derived from a British river-name, *Derventiō*, meaning 'river where oaks are plentiful'.

Darenth (pronounced Darren). The place derives its name from the DARENT river on which it stands, and is recorded as Darente, Dærintan 940 → Tarent 1086 → Derente 1185 → Darente 1205.

Dargate. 'Wild animal gate' (OE *dēor geat* → Deregate 1275 → Dergate 1458 → Dargate 1535). This name, probably a reference to a gate leading on to woodland, is shared by Dargets Wood, Chatham, which is found as Dergate in 1313.

Darland. Animal land: land frequented by wild animals (OE *dēor land* → Dirilaunde 1254 → Derlond, Dirlond 1450 → Darlande 1519). The name is shared by Darland Farm here.

Dartford (pronounced Darfud). This was originally the site of a ford (OE *ford*) crossing the River Darent, and is recorded as Tarentefort 1086 → Darenteford 1089 → Derentford 1196 → Derteford 1219 → Dartfoorde 1610.

David Street. It derives its name from the family of Richard and Godfrey Dauy, or Davy (1327).

Davington. Valley farmstead: farmstead lying in a valley (OE *denu tūn* → Denentune c.1100 → Deninton 1165 → Deniton 1200 → Davinton 1256 → Deniton, Davington 1279). The place lies in a valley below Davington Hill. The name appears to have developed from Deniton to Davington to distinguish this valley farmstead from those at the county's two DENTONs.

Dawbourne Wood (Tenterden). Dove stream: stream frequented by doves (ME *dufe burne* → Doueburne 1292 → Douebourne 1348).

Daw's Wood (Hackington). It is associated with the family of Thomas Dawe (1327).

Deal. Valley (OE *del* → Addelam 1086 → Dele 1154 → Dela 1159 → Dale 1275 → Deale 1610).

Deangate, Deans Furzes. See under DEAN STREET.

Deans Hill (Bredgar). Hill buildings: group of buildings on a hill (OE *dūn (ge)sella* → Dungesell' 1225 → Dongeshelle 1327 → Dongesell, Dungeshull 1332). The present name is a contraction of these forms.

Dean Street. It is recorded in 1324 as Denestrete, being a narrow road (ME *strete*) running through a valley (ME *dene*). 'Valley', together with the associated surname atte Denne or atte Dene – 'dweller in the valley' – also occurs in the names of Dean Court, Brenzett and Westwell; Dean Farm, Elmstead and Meopham; Deane Farm, Wingham; Deangate, Hoo St. Werburgh; Deans Furzes and Deans Wood, Chiddingstone.

Debden Court (Petham). Deep valley (OE *dēop denu* → Depedene 1403 → Depdane 1535).

Dedmar Hill (Meopham). Dudda's pool (OE *Duddan mere* → Duddem'e 1240 → Dodemer' 1270 → Dodemere 1381). The personal name is also found in connection with DODDINGTON, DOWNINGBURY, and the now lost place of Dodingdale in Canterbury.

Deerson Farm (Preston). Dægred's farmstead (OE *Dægredes tūn* → Deyreddiston' 1270 → Deyredeston 1290 → Derson 1498).

Deerton Street. Animal farmstead: farmstead where wild animals are caught (OE *dēor tūn* → Dertone 1334 → Deyrton' 1338).

Delaware. The place is associated with a local family variously recorded between 1199 and 1346 as de la Ware, La Ware, ate Ware and de la Warre – 'dweller by the wier' (OE *wer*).

Delce. Doles, divisions (OE *dālas* → Delce 1086 → Delse, Delce 1226). This seems originally to have been two estates, Great and Little Delce, since the name appears in 1147 as Delce majori & minori, in 1240 as Magna Delce, and in 1401 as Majori Delses & Minori Delses. The greater and smaller divisions of land finally joined to form one site some time during the 16th century.

Delf, The. Trench: something which is dug (OE *(ge)delf* → Waterdelfe 1382 → the Delf 1541 → the Delfe 1613). This is the name of an old canal at WORTH.

Delmonden Green. Dalesmen's woodland pasture (OE *dælmanna denn* → Delmunden 1206 → Delmyndenne 1347 → Delmynden 1507).

Denge (pronounced Denj). Valley district (OE *denu gē* → Denge 1292). The name is a reference to the valley of the Great Stour.

Denge Marsh. This was originally marshland belonging to DENGE, and is recorded as Dengemersc 774 → Dengemaris 1071 → Dengemersse 1253 → Denge Marshe 1610. The area is alternatively known as Dunge Marsh, giving its name to DUNGENESS.

Denly Hill (Hernhill). Woodland pasture clearing (OE *denn lēah* → Denelee 1214).

Denne Hill (Womenswold). Woodland pasture (OE *denn* → Denne 1226 → Denhill 1610). This origin is shared by the names of Denne Court, Woodnesborough, and Denne Manor Farm, Chilham.

Denne's Wood (Kenardington). It is associated with the family of Richard, Robert and Walter Denis (1327), natives of Kenardington.

Densole Farms (Swingfield). The farms are referred to in 1539 as Densall Minnis and Densall Bushes, the name probably being derived from OE *denn sol*: pasture pool, muddy pool in a woodland pasture.

Denstead Farm (Chartham). Valley place (OE *denu stede* → Denestede 1210 → Denstede 1346).

Denstroude. The place is recorded between 1216 and 1273 as Dwnsterue *alias* Dunesterue, Dunsterne and Dennstrue, and possibly has the original meaning of 'pasture of pestilence' (OE *denn steorfa*): Denstroude lies in a poorly wooded area, and the name may be a reference to unproductive, sour soil.

Dent-de-Lion (pronounced Dandylion). Recorded in 1610 as Dentdelion, the place is named after the family of William de Dandelyon (1382). Dent-de-lion, or 'lion's tooth', is, in fact, the origin of the flower-name.

Denton (East Kent). Valley farmstead (OE *denu tūn* → dene tun 799 → Danetone 1086 → Deniton' 1203 → Denintone 1253 → Denetone 1275 → Denton 1610).

Denton (West Kent). Valley farm-stead (OE *denu tūn* → Denetun, Danitona 964 → Danitone 1086 → Denetun 1321 → Denton 1610).

Deptford (pronounced Detfud). Deep ford (OE *dēop ford* → Depeford' 1293 → Deppeford' 1314 → Depford 1334 → Diepforde 1610). So named from the deep ford which crossed the Ravensbourne at this point before a bridge was built.

Dering Farm (Lydd) (pronounced Deerin). It takes its name from that of the family of Dering or Deryng, residents of Lydd during the 13th and 14th centuries. Dering Farm, Smarden, is associated with the place of Surrenden Dering in the neighbouring parish of Pluckley.

Derringstone. Dēoring's farmstead (OE *Dēoringes tūn* → Deringeston' 1262 → Deringgeston' 1321).

Detling (pronounced Dettlin). Dyttel's people (OE *Dyttelingas* → Detlinges 1086 → Dytlinge c.1100 → Dettlinge 1253 → Detling 1275).

Devenden. Dægfrið's woodland pasture (OE *Dægfriðing denn* → Deuerdenne 1253 → Deuyrindenn' 1346 → Deuerdenne 1365). The *u* in this name is the common medieval form for *v*. Dægfrið was also the owner of a stretch of water (OE *ēa*) at the now lost place of Deiferthesea, recorded in 833 not far from Rolvenden, which is close to Devenden.

Dibden. Deep valley (OE *dēop denu* → Depedene 1270 → Depeden' 1278).

Dibgate Wood (Saltwood). There are no forms for this name, but in a charter of 993 there is a reference to a *deop gatan* in this area, which is probably the origin of the name (← OE *dēop geat*: 'deep gate', or gate in a dip or hollow).

Dicker's Wood (Ruckinge). The place is associated with the family of Alan Dyker of Ruckinge (1327).

Dickley Wood (Lenham). Ditch clearing: clearing near, or containing a ditch (OE *dīc lēah* → boscus de Dykkele c.1250). Dickley Farm here has taken its name from that of the wood.

Digges Place, Upper and **Lower**. It is connected with the family of John Digges of Barham (1254).

Dignash. Together with Digge Farm which, like Dignash, is close to Westwell, the place was once the property of the family of Digge who owned land in Westwell from the time of Edward III. The -ash ending in this name no doubt refers to some prominent tree in the area.

Dingleden. Prince's woodland pasture (OE *pengeling denn* → Tenelyngden' 1226 → Thenglesdenn' 1383). Dialect pronunciation has altered the initial *th* to *d* in this place name. The original pasture must have been part of a Saxon royal estate. Dingleden Wood, Lyminge, is recorded as Dyngedown Wood in 1546, the name probably being derived from OE *dyncge dūn*: 'manured land hill', or hill with fertile soil.

Ditton. Ditch farmstead: farmstead surrounded by a ditch (OE *dīc tūn* → to dictune c.975 → Dictune c.1060 → Dictvne 1086 → Ditton' 1232 → Ditton 1610).

Divan Wood (Eastling). It derives its name from the family of John Dyve (1242), the final *n* of the name being produced by the medieval genitival form 'Dyven'.

Dobles. It is associated with the family of William Dobbel (1292).

Dockenden. Dokel's woodland pasture (OE *Dokeling denn* → Dokelinden' 1254 → Dokelyngdenn' 1340 → Doklyndenn' 1346).

Doddington. Dudda's farmstead (OE *Dudding tūn* → Duddingtun c.1100 → Dodintone 1210 → Dodington 1264). The personal name is also found in connection with DEDMAR HILL and DOWNINGBURY.

Dodhurst. Dodda's wooded hill (OE *Doddan hyrst* → Dodehurst 1262 → Dodeherst 1348).

Dornden. Thornbush pasture: woodland pasture marked by a thornbush (OE *porn denn* → Thorndenn' 1292). Dialect pronunciation has caused the initial *th* to be altered to *d*.

Dour, River. See under DOVER.

Dover. The waters (B *dubrā* → Dubris c.425 → Dofras 696 → on Doferum c.1000 → Douer 1610). The name refers to the River Dour here, which shares the same origin as Dover, and is first recorded in its present form in 1577. The area surrounding the river is described c.1040 as Doferware broc: marshy land (OE *brōc*) belonging to the *Doferware*, or people of Dover. The Dour did not begin to silt up until

Norman times and was once navigable well inland: Caesar sailed up it in 55 B.C. The original settlement of Dover was known to the Romans as *Dubris* and lay at the side of the river between two hills.

Dowde's Church. Dud's church (OE *Dudes cirice* → Dodes circe c.1100 → Dodescherche 1270 → Dodechirche 1312). Dud also seems to have been the owner of land in this area, recorded as Dudeslande c.975. He may also have given his name to Dowde's Wood, not far away in Snodland.

Dowels, The. This is a stretch of marshy land close to Appledore, and is recorded as The Dowles in 1558 and as The Douls, The Dowls in 1660. The name is probably derived from OE *dalas*: doles, or divisions, of land.

Dowle Street. It is associated with the family variously recorded as Doul, Dowele and Dowle from the 14th to the 16th century.

Down Barton. Barley farm (OE *beretun* → Berton' 1292 → Dounberton 1397). The affix Down refers to the place's downland site.

Downe. Hill (OE *dun* → Dune 1296 → Downe 1610). The same word is found in the names of Down Court, Doddington; Down Wood, Charing; The Downs, Tilmanstone; Downs House, Yalding; and West Down, Meopham.

Downingbury. Dudda's stronghold (OE *Dudding burh* → Dudingburie 1191 → Dondingbury 1279). Dudda's name is also found in

DEDMAR HILL and DODDINGTON.

Downs, The. See under DOWNE.

Drellingore. Dylla's bank or border (OE *Dylling ora* → Dillynger 1264 → Dyllyngore 1313).

Drove, The. Recorded as Droue in 1292, this was once a droveway along which cattle were driven, the name being derived from OE *draf*. Droveway House, Lyminge, is similarly recorded as Droue in 1348, and marks the site of an old droveway.

Dryhill. Self-explanatory (OE *dryge hyll* → Dreyhill 1464).

Dryland Farm (Molash). Self-explanatory (OE *dryge land* → Dreylaunde 1251 → Dreylonde 1347).

Duckhurst. A wooded hill (OE *hyrst*) belonging to an early landowner named Doke, the place is recorded as Dokeshurst in 1275, and as Duxherst in 1379. The same family name is found in connection with Duck Farm close by. Ducks Grove, Seal, is associated with John Ducke of Seal (1278); and Duck's Court, High Halstow, derives its name from the family of Duk' (1327).

Ducks Grove. See under DUCKHURST.

Dumbourne. Stream of the *Duningas*, or hill dwellers (OE *Duninga burne* → Danegebourne 1253 → Dunegeburn' 1272). There are no later forms to show how the present name evolved. The area is hilly, and a tribe living here may well have

61

used the stream as their watering-place.

Dumpton. Dudeman's farmstead (OE *Dudemaning tūn* → Dudemeiton' 1186 → Dodeminton' 1270 → Dodmanton' 1332 → Dodemayton' 1348). Dudeman also owned a farm (OE *wīc*) at the now lost place of Dudmanswike in Hope All Saints.

Dunbury. Dunna's stronghold (OE *Dunning burh* → Dunningbyr 1285 → Dounynb'y 1347). The personal name is also found in connection with DUNTON GREEN.

Dundle. Secret, or hidden, valley (OE *dierne dæl* → Derondalle 1563 → Derndale 1782).

Dungate. Hill gate: gate leading on to a hill (OE *dūn geat* → Dongate 1591).

Dungeness (pronounced Dunjeness). It takes its name from DENGE MARSH here, the affix -ness being derived from OE *næss*: headland or cape. The place appears as Dengenesse in 1335, Denge Nasse in 1610).

Dunkirk. Recorded in 1790 as Dunkirk *alias* the ville of the Hundred of Westgate, the place name has been adopted from Dunkerque in France: for a few years during the 17th century this was an English possession.

Dun Street (Boxley). It appears as Dunne Strete in 1535, the name being derived from OE *dūn*: hill. Dun Street, Westwell, has the same origin, being recorded as Donstrete in 1313. The 'streets' were original-ly narrow roads running up into the hills.

Dunstall Wood (Lenham). Hill site (OE *dūn steall* → Dunstall', Dounstall', Dunstalle 1348).

Dunton Green. Dunna's farmstead (OE *Dunning tūn* → Dunington' 1244 → Doninton 1264 → Duningston' 1292). Dunna also had a strong-hold at DUNBURY.

Durlock (near Ash). It appears as Durlock in 1616, and as both Durlock-Bridge and Durlocks Bridge in 1790, the name possibly being de-rived from OE *dēor loca:* animal enclosure. Durlock near Minster may share the same possible origin, being also found as Durlock in 1616.

Durndale. Secret, or hidden, valley (OE *dierne dæl* → Derendale c.1500). As with DUNDLE, the name originally referred to a remote place.

Duskins. Threshing valley: valley where threshing is done (OE *persing denu* → puscincg deono 824 → Thurkyng' 1270 → Thurskynge 1304 → Duskyn 1606).

Dymchurch (pronounced Dimchurch). Judge's church (OE *dēman cirice* → Deman circe c.1100 → Demechirch 1240 → Dymecherche 1270 → Deemchurche 1585). Al-ternatively, the original church may have been associated with Diuma, Bishop of Mercia during the 7th century, making the origin of this place name 'Diuma's church'.

Dyne's Wood (Bilsington). It is associated with the family of Robert

Dyn (1348). Dyne's Farm, Kemsing, takes its name from the family of Reginald Dyn (1278), and Dynes Farm, Bethersden, from the family of John Dyn (1514).

E

Each. (Place) of the oak (OE *ǣc* → Ece 1086 → Ecche, Heche c.1100 → Eche 1323).

Earde. Estate, land (OE *eard* → Erde c.1100 → Earde 1240).

Easole (pronounced Eesole). At the gods' deep pools (OE *æt ōesa wǣlum* → æt Œsewalum 824 → Eswalt 1086 → Eswalle 1253 → Easwole 1270 → Essole 1292). There are pools at Easole which were very likely regarded as holy pools in pre-Christian times. The place lies only four miles to the south-west of WOODNESBOROUGH, dedicated originally to Woden, chief of the Teutonic gods.

Eastborough. It is recorded in 1292 as Eastborgh', and since it lies to the east of COOLING, was probably known as 'the east manor, or borough'.

Eastchurch. Self-explanatory (OE *ēast cirice* → Eastcyrce c.1100 → Eastcherche 1208 → East Church 1610). The place lies on the eastern side of the ISLE OF SHEPPEY.

East Hall. See under EAST STREET.

Eastlands. Land lying to the east of the parish (OE *ēast land* → Estelond' 1278 → Estlonde 1279).

Eastleigh Court (Lyminge). East clearing (OE *ēast lēah* → Estlegh 1361 → Estleghe 1382).

Eastling. Ēsla's people (OE *Ēslingas* → Eslinges 1086 → Æslinge, Eastlinges c.1100 → Estlynge 1610). This tribe had a settlement at ISLINGHAM.

East Mountain Farm (Kennington). East men's farmstead (OE *ēast manna tūn* → Estmonton', Eastmuntun' c.1250 → Eastmanton' 1348). The farm lies to the east of KENNINGTON, giving the original settlers the name 'east men'.

Eastry (pronounced Ee-stree). Easterly district (OE *ēasterra gē* → in regione Eastrgena 788 → Eastorege 805 → Eastrige 1006 → Estrei, Estre 1086 → Eastry 1610). Once a region of Kent in Jutish times, the name is now preserved in the village of Eastry.

East Stour Farm (Chilham). East of the Stour (OE *ēast Stūr* → Estesture

1195 → Esture, Estesture 1278). The farm lies to the east of the River Stour, as does East Stour Farm, Ashford, which has the same original meaning and is recorded as Estesture in 1240, Esture in 1346.

East Street (Addington). The name refers to a street east of the parish, and appears as Eaststreete in 1657. East Street, Ash, shares the same origin, being recorded as East Street in 1491. The meaning of 'hall situated to the east of the parish' (OE *ēast heall*) is shared by the East Halls in Orpington and Murston; while East Hall, Boughton Monchelsea, was originally an 'east hedged enclosure' (OE *east haga*), appearing as Easthawe in 1462.

Eastwell. East spring (OE *east wielle* → Estwelle 1086 → Eastwelle 1267). Called 'east' to distinguish this spring from that at WESTWELL.

Eastwood. Wood to the east of the parish (OE *east wudu* → Eastwode 1285 → Eastwodd 1535).

Eaton Farm, Little (Lower Hardres). Island farmstead (OE *ēg tūn* → Eyton' 1327 → Eytone 1332). This was originally an island of firm ground in a marshy area.

Eatwell Shaw. The name appears to be a corruption of St. Edith's Well, which stands in the middle of the village of Kemsing.

Ebony. Ebba's river (OE *Ebban ēa* → Ebbanea 833 → Ebbene 1278 → Ebeney 1313). The 'river' probably refers to swamps in this marshy area.

Ebbsfleet. Creek or inlet of the *Hēopwell*, or stream where hips grow (OE *Hēopwelles flēot* → hyppeles fleot 1038 → Heppelesflet, Eppesflete c.1250→ Ebsfleet 1610).

Eccles. Meadow of the oak (OE *āēc lāēs* → Aclesse, of Æcclesse c.975 → Aiglessa 1086 → Ecclesse 1166 → Eccles 1208).

Eddington. Edda's farmstead (OE *Edding tūn* → Edington 1466 → Hedington 1506).

Eden, River. The name is a late back-formation from that of EDENBRIDGE.

Edenbridge. Ēadhelm's bridge (OE *Ēadhelmes brycg* → Eadelmesbrege c.1100→ Edelmebrigg 1214 → Edelnebrigg', Edelmesbrugg' 1226 → ponte Edelmi 1232 → Eden bridge 1610). The place lies on the River Eden.

Eden Farm (Minster). Yew pasture: woodland pasture marked by a yew-tree (OE *īw denn* → Idenne 1327 → Iden 1799).

Edenhurst. This was originally a hurst, or wooded hill, standing beside the River Eden.

Edward Shaw. The place is associated with the family of John and Jordan Edward (1338), 'Shaw' being derived from OE *scaga*: a copse.

Egerden (pronounced Ejer-dn). Ēadgar's woodland pasture (OE *Ēadgaring denn* → Egerindenn' 1278 → Egeringdenn' 1313 → Egeryndenn' 1348). The personal name is also found in connection with EGGERTON and EGGRINGE.

Egerton (pronounced Ejerton). Ecgheard's farmstead (OE *Ecghearding tūn* → Eardingtun c.1100 → Egardintone 1254 → Edgarinton' 1261 → Egerton 1610).

Eggerton Farm, Great (Godmersham). Eadgar's farmstead (OE *Eadgaring tūn* → Atgarenton' 1240 → Edgarinton' 1313 → Egarton 1690). Eadgar's name also occurs in EGERDEN and EGGRINGE.

Eggringe Wood (Godmersham) (pronouced Eggrinje). Eadgar's people (OE *Eadgaringas* → bosci de Adgeringe 1237). Eadgar himself had a farmstead close by at EGGERTON; his name is also found in EGERDEN.

Elbridge House (Littlebourne). Plank bridge (OE *pel brycg* → þæl brycge 948 → Telebrigg' 1226 → Thelebrigg' 1254 → Ellebregge 1347). The original bridge spanned the Nailbourne here.

Elham (pronounced Eelam). Eel meadow: water meadow where eels are trapped (OE *æl hamm* → Ælham c.1100 → Elhamme c.1195 → Ellham 1275 → Elham 1610). The same original meaning was shared by the now lost place of Elham at Crayford, recorded as Ellam in 1240, Elham in 1274.

Ellenden. Elm-trees' pasture: woodland pasture where elms grow (OE *elma denn* → Elmeden' 1278 → Elmenden' 1334 → Elynden 1415). Ellenden Farm, Dunkirk, has the original meaning of 'elder-tree pasture' (OE *ellen denn*), and appears as Elyndenne in 1346, Elynden in 1535.

Ellinge (pronounced Ellinje). Ægel's people (OE *Ægelingas* → Eylinge 1292 → Eyllinge 1338). The personal name is also found in connection with AYLESFORD and AYLESHAM.

Ellingham Farm (Kingsnorth). Ælfwynn's settlement (OE *Ælfwynne hām* → Eluineham 1272). Ælfwynn was a Saxon woman.

Ellington. Farmstead of Ealda's people (OE *Ealdinga tūn* → ealdincg tun 943 → Elinton c.1250). In a charter of 943 the place is referred to as Ealdingctuninga mearc: 'boundary of the farmstead of the *Ealdingas*'. The personal name, meaning 'old man, chieftain', is also found in ALDINGTON, YALDHAM and YALDING.

Elliots. It is associated with the family of Elyot, residents in the parish of Harty during the time of Elizabeth I. Elliott's Farm, Penshurst, takes its name from the family of Richard Elyot (1327).

Elliston Bottom. The place is recorded in 1572 as Ellynsole and may originally have had the meaning of 'muddy pool by an elder-tree' (OE *ellen sol*).

Elmers End. It derives its name from the Beckenham family variously recorded as Elmer, Aylmer and Eilmer between 1226 and 1332.

Elmhurst. Elm wooded hill (OE *elm hyrst* → Elmeherst 1327 → Elmherst 1348).

Elmley. Elm-tree clearing: clearing marked by an elm (OE *elm lēah* →

Elmele 1226 → Elmeley 1270).

Elmstead. Elm homestead: homestead by elm-trees (OE *elm hāmstede* → elmanstede, elmesstede 811 → Elmestede 1087 → Elmsted 1610). Elmstead near Bromley has the same original meaning, being recorded as Elmsted in 1320.

Elmstone. Ægelmǣr's farmstead (OE *Ægelmǣres tūn* → Ailmerestone 1203 → Elmereston' 1240 → Elmerston' 1254 → Elmestone 1610).

Elphees. It takes its name from that of the family of Elphee who appear in the Newenden register at the beginning of the 19th century.

Elphicks. See under ELVY.

Elsfield. Eli's open land (ME *Elis feld* → Elysfeld 1335).

Eltham (pronounced Eltam). Elta's settlement (OE *Eltan hām* → Elteham 1086 → Elltham 1210 → Eltham 1224).

Elverland. Ælfwaru's land (OE *Ælfware land* → Elverlond 1247 → Elveyrlond 1346). Ælfwaru, a Saxon woman, also had property at ELVERTON.

Elverton. Ælfwaru's farmstead (OE *Ælfware tūn* → Elwarton' 1254 → Aylwarton' 1288 → Eylwarton, Elwarton' 1293 → Eylewarton 1321). The same Saxon woman held land at ELVERLAND.

Elvington (near Eythorne). Ælfgyð's farmstead (OE *Ælfgȳðe tūn* → Ælvetone 1086 → Elfgethetun

1087 → Elvynton 1327 → Elvinton 1731). This Saxon woman may also have had a farmstead at Elvington near Hawkinge, which is recorded as Eluyntone (Elvyntone) in 1346.

Elvy The place, like Elvy Cottage, Westwell, probably derives its name from the family of Elfegh who are recorded in this area during the 14th century. The same name is found in connection with Elphicks, Horsmonden, where it appears as both Elphegh and Elfeg during the 14th century.

Enbrook Ægen's marshy land (OE *Ægenes brōc* → Einesbroc 1166 → Eynesbroc 1242 → Enybrok' 1304 → Eynebrok' 1311). The personal name also occurs in ANSDORE and EYNSFORD.

Engeham, Great and **Little** (pronounced Enjum). Eadda's settlement (OE *Eadding hām* → Eadinghame 1278 → Edyngeham 1313 → Engeham *alias* Edyngham 1471 → Engham Farm 1643). Eadda also had a farmstead at ADDINGTON.

English Wood (Hastingleigh). It is associated with the family of Emme, Robert and Thomas Englisshe (1348).

Ensden, Lower. See under ENSINGE.

Ensfield. Geon's open land (OE *Geones feld* → Jenesfelde c.1180 → Genesfeld 1206 → Yenesfeud, Yenefeld' 1283 → Yensfeld 1371).

Ensinge, Upper (pronounced Enzinje). Esne's people (OE *Esningas* → Ensingges 1226 → Ensinges 1240

→ Ensynge 1279 → Ensinge 1327).
Esne may have been an overseer
of some kind, since his name means
'servant': perhaps he was the leader
of a group of slaves or servants.
Upper Ensinge's neighbour, Lower
Ensden, shares the same name, and
was probably the woodland pasture
(OE *denn*) of these people.

Erith (pronounced Eerith). Gravelly
landing-place (OE *ēar hȳð* → Earhyð
695 → Earhið c.960 → Erhede
1086 → Erhethe 1278 → Eryth
1610).

Erriottswood. The place is recorded
as bosco de Heryet in 1232, and as
bosco vocato (woodland called)
Eriette in 1313, the name being
derived from OE *here-geatu*: army
trappings. This is the origin of the
feudal service of heriot: the return-
ing of weapons to a lord on the
death of a tenant. Erriottswood
appears to have been associated
with this service.

Etchden Farm (Bethersden). Gate's
pasture: woodland pasture entered
through a gate (OE *hæcces denn* →
Hecchisdenne 1194 → Ecchesdenne
1247 → Hacheden 1286).

Etchinghill (near Goudhurst).
Hollow of Totta's people (OE
Tottinga hol → Tottingehol' 1254
→ Totingehole c.1270 → Totinghole
mill 1333). Etchinghole close by
has exactly the same original meaning, though, as with Etchinghill,
there are no late forms to show
how the names evolved.

Etchinghill (near Lyminge). Tetta's
slope (OE *Tetting hielde* → Tettinge-
helde, Tettingheld' 1240 → Tetyng-

held' 1327). There are no later
forms to show when the initial *T*
was dropped from this place name.

Etchinghole. See under ETCHING-
HILL.

Etherington Hill (Speldhurst). Heath
ridge: ridge covered by heather
(OE *hǣð hrycg* → Hatheregg' 1278
→ Hatheregge 1301). Etherton Hall
and Etherton Lawn close by are a
contraction of this name.

Etherton Hall and **Lawn.** See under
ETHERINGTON HILL.

Ethnam. It is recorded in 1313 as
Echenham, and possibly has the
original meaning of 'oaken water
meadow' (OE *ācen hamm*): the
place is on low-lying ground close
to the River Rother.

Evegate (pronounced Eeve-gate).
Thieves' gate (OE *pēofa geat* → to
peofagadan 993 → Tevegate 1086
→ Theuegate 1246 → Thevegate
1346 → Theffegate 1452). The 993
charter also records a nearby place
as *æt peofacotan*: 'at the thieves'
cottage': probably the gate and
cottage were held by the same band
of thieves.

Everden Farm (Alkham). Eofor's
people (OE *Eoforingas* → Everings
1195 → Everinges 1211 → Evering
1270). The change in spelling
appears to have happened comparatively recently, since Everden is
recorded as Evering in 1610. The
personal name, Eofor, is also found
in connection with the now lost
places of Evering Acre in Pluckley,
and Eversley in Charing.

68

Everlands. Recorded in 1239 as Everlaund, this may originally have been land on which wild boar roamed (OE *eofor land).*

Evington (pronounced Eevington). Ibba's farmstead (OE *Ibbing tūn* → Ibbinctun 809 → Iuynton' c.1250 → Iuyngton' 1313 → Evynton 1481).

Ewell Minnis (pronounced Youill). Spring, source of a stream (OE *ǣwiell* → Ewell' 1226 → Ewelle 1253 → Ewell 1610). The affix 'Minnis' is derived from OE *gemǣnnes,* ME *menesse,* meaning 'land held in common'. Ewell Manor, West Farleigh, shares the same origin as Ewell Minnis, being recorded as Ewelle in 1198, Ewell in 1263.

Ewell, Temple. See TEMPLE EWELL.

Exhurst. Ash wooded hill (OE *æsc hyrst* → Exherste 1225 → Esherst 1255 → Eaxherst 1327 → Exherst 1450).

Exted. Oak-tree place (OE *āc stede* → Hacstede c.1100 → Acstede 1292 → Axstede 1347).

Eyhorne Hatch. See under EYHORNE.

Eyhorne (pronounced Ayorne). At the hawthorn-tree (OE *æt þǣm hægþorne* → æt heageþorne 831 → Haihorne 1086 → Haythorne, Aythorn', Hayhorne 1254 → Eyhorne 1610). This was the meeting-place of the Eyhorne Hundred. Eyhorne Hatch, Borden, appears to share a common origin, the affix 'Hatch' being derived from OE *hæcc:* hatch, gate.

Eynsford (pronounced Aynesfud). Ægen's ford (OE *Ægenes ford* → Ænesford c.960 → Elesford 1086 → Æinesford c.1100 → Ainesford' 1164 → Eynesford 1210). The original ford was a crossing on the Darent. Ægen's name is also found in connection with ANSDORE and ENBROOK.

Eythorne (pronounced Ay-thorn). Hēahgȳð's thornbush (OE *Hēah-gȳðe þorn* → æt Heagyðe þorne 805 → Egethorne 824 → Hagthorn' 1254 → Eythorn 1256). Hēahgȳð was a Saxon woman.

F

Faggs Wood (Warehorne). It is associated with the Fagg family, residents of neighbouring Orlestone since 1613, and of Warehorne since 1807.

Fairbourne. Fern stream: stream overhung with ferns (OE *fearn burna* → Fereburne 1086 → Fareburna 1164 → Farburne, Farnburn' 1242 → Est Farbourne, Farnebourn 1346). The name appears to have been given to the River Len at this point.

Fairbrook Farm (Boughton-under-Blean). Fair, or beautiful, marshy ground (OE *fæger brōc* → ffayrbrok' 1253 → Fairbrok 1318). Probably so called because of the abundance of waterplants growing at the edge of the stream here.

Fairby. The place derives its name from the family of John Feerby, residents of the parish of Hartley (1420).

Fairfield. Fair open land (OE *fæger feld* → Faierfeld c.1220 → Feyrefeld 1270 → Fairefeld' 1278 → Fayre feilde c.1550).

Fairlawn. It is recorded as Fayrelane in 1610, as Fair Lane in 1690, and as Fairlawn *alias* Fairlane in 1782, the place probably being near the site of a fair.

Fairseat. It appears as both Fairseat and Farsee Street in 1782, being so named because of the pleasant view from this point.

Fairtrough. Robert de Bel Arbre — 'dweller by the beautiful tree' — is recorded here in 1254, so the origin of this place name may well be derived from OE *fæger trēow:* 'beautiful tree'.

Falconhurst. See under HURST.

Falklands. It is named after Viscountess Falkland who acquired property here in Hadlow in 1768.

Fallon. Recorded as Stretchland *alias* Foreland in 1790, the original meaning of this name was probably 'land by a ford' (OE *ford land*): the place is on a stream and lies only half a mile from FORD-WATER.

Fanscoombe Wood (Wye). This was once known simply as 'fen' (OE *fenn*), coombe, or valley, being later added to the name, which is recorded as Fanne 1086 → Fennes 1242 → Faunescumbe 1307 → ffannescoumbe 1347.

Fant, Upper. Recorded as Fant in 1782, the place name possibly shares the same origin as Frant in Sussex which appears as Ferneth in 1230, Fant in 1630, being originally 'place overgrown with ferns' (OE *fearniðja).*

Farleigh, East (pronounced Farley). Fern clearing (OE *fearn lēah* → on Fearn lege 871 → Fearnleage 898 → Fernleah 1006 → Ferlaga 1086 → Farlege 1209 → Farlegh' 1226). Called 'east' to distinguish this place from West Farleigh, which shares the same origin and is recorded as Fernlege in 1042. The two names appear as Eastfarlegh and Westfarlegh in 1291, and as E. Farly and W. Farly in 1610.

Farleigh, West. See under FARLEIGH, EAST.

Farnborough. Fern mound: mound or tumulus overgrown with ferns (OE *fearn beorg* → fearnbiorg 862 → Farnberga, Farinberghe 1185 → Farnberg' 1226 → Farnborow 1610).

Farnell Wood (Rolvenden). Fern hill (OE *fearn hyll* → Farnehille 1440). Farnhill Sluice, Tenterden, shares the same origin, being also recorded as Farnehille in 1440.

Farnham. Fern meadow: water meadow where ferns grow (OE *fearn hamm* → ffarnham 1292 → ffarnhamme 1332 → ffarnhame 1346).

Farnhill Sluice. See under FARNELL WOOD.

Farningham. Settlement of the fern-dwellers (OE *fearninga hām* → Frinningaham 1042 → Foringeham 1086 → Færningeham c. 1100 → Ferningeham 1201). Farningham Farm, Cranbrook, may either share the same original meaning, or have taken its name from Farningham proper. There were other groups of 'fern-dwellers' – people living at a place where ferns grew thickly – at FARTHINGLOE and FRININGHAM.

Farthingloe, Great and Little. Hill of the fern-dwellers (OE *fearninga hlǣw* → Feringelai 1086 → ffarnynglo 1313 → Farthynglowe 1535).

Farthings. It is connected with John Farenthe (1309), a resident of Boxley parish.

Farthing Street. A fourth part, or quarter, of land (OE *fēorðung* → Ferthyng 1366). Farthing Wall, Cliffe, shares the same original meaning, being recorded as Le Verthing in 1370.

Faversham (pronounced Favver-sham). Wright's, or smith's, settlement (OE *fæferes hām* → Fefresham 812 → Faversham 1086 → Faveresham 1154 → Feversham 1610). The old name for the stream which flows through Faversham was the Fishborne: 'fish stream' (OE *fisc burna*), recorded as Fisseburne in 1226 and as ffyssheburn' in 1254.

Fawke Common. Together with Fawke Farm here, the place derives its name from the family of Richard le ffalke (1327).

Fawkham (pronounced Faykum). Settlement of the Falcons (OE *Fealcna hām* → Fealcna ham 964 → Fealcnaham, Fealcna hames c.980 → Falkeham 1210 → Faukham 1245 → Falkeham 1610). 'The Falcons' was a tribal name, possibly given because the tribe used these birds in hunting.

Felborough Wood (Chilham). It takes its name from that of the Hundred of Felborough, which had the original meaning of 'fallow mound' (OE *fealu beorg*) and is recorded as Ferliberg 1086 → Feleberga c.1100 → Felebergh 1284. Felborough Wood may have been the meeting-place of the Hundred.

Felderland. Land of the *Feldware*, or open land people (OE *Feldwara land* → Feldwareland' 1226 → ffeldwerlonde 1352 → Feldworland 1376). The *Feldware* were a tribe who made their home on open or treeless land.

Fenn Street. Fen (OE *fenn* → Venne 1298 → Fenne, Fenstrete 1305 → Fenstrete 1316). Obviously a road of some kind had been built across fenland here by the beginning of the 14th century.

Field Green. Hay (OE *fileðe* → ffilethe 1324 → Filtth 1327). Field Farm, Egerton, shares the same origin — possibly a reference to a place where hay was stored — and is found recorded as ffilethe and ffylethe at the beginning of the 14th century.

Fig Street. It derives its name from the family of Alan ffyk' of Sevenoaks (c. 1300).

Filborough. Fallow mound (OE *fealu beorg* → ffelebergh' 1292 → Fylbarow 1489 → Filborow, Fylborowe 1566).

Filchborough. Recorded as Filchborow in 1782, the origin of this name may have been 'Filica's mound, or tumulus' (OE *Filican beorg*).

Filmer Wood (Wichling). Foul or dirty pool (OE *fūl mere* → ffulm'e 1258 → Filmer 1498).

Filston Hall (Shoreham). Viel's farmstead (ME *Vieles tone* → Vieleston' 1203 → Vielestone 1212 → Vielston alias Filston 1782). The personal name is of French origin.

Finchcocks. Recorded as such in 1782, the place derives its name from the family of Finchecock, who owned the manor from the mid-13th century.

Finchurst. 'Heap's wood': wooded hill where heaps of wood are gathered (OE *fīnes hyrst* → East Fynesherst 1328 → ffynsherst 1348 → Est Vynesherst 1355). Why the place should be called 'east' is not known.

Finglesham (pronounced Finglesam). Prince's settlement (OE *pengeles hām* → penglesham 832 → Flengvessam 1086 → Fenglesham 1206 → Finglesham 1226). This must once have been part of a Saxon royal estate: a rich Anglo-Saxon cemetery was uncovered here in the early 1950s.

Finnis Wood (Womenswold). It is probably to be associated with the family of de ffyneaws (1347).

Fishall Hall, Great (Hadlow). This place, together with adjacent Little Fish Hall, acquired its name through association with the medieval family of ffissher or Fyssher, and is referred to as Fishers Hall in 1690.

Fisher's Wood (Hunton). It takes its name from that of the family of John ffysshere (1352). The name is also found in connection with Fisher's Farm, Staplehurst, and Fisherstreet Farm, Badlesmere.

Fishpoolhill Wood (Littlebourne). Fish pool (OE *fisc pōl* → Fispole c.1250 → Fysshpole 1416 → Fysshe-pole 1538).

Fleet. Creek or inlet (OE *flēot* → Fleote 798 → Fletes 1086 → Flete 1212). Fleete Farm, Garlinge, has the same original meaning, appearing as Flete c.1250.

Flegis Court (Hawkinge). This is the alternative name for the Manor of Hawkinge and is recorded as Fleggescourt in 1346, deriving its name from the 13th century family of Fleg, or fflege, natives of Flegg in Norfolk who settled here.

Flemings. It is described in 1512 as the maner of Flemyng in Woodnesborough, taking its name from that of the 14th century family of fflemyng, or Flemyng.

Fletcher's Green. The place is associated with the family of Thomas ffleccher (1354). This occupational surname is also found in connection with Fletcher's Farm, Pembury.

Flightshot. Shortened piece of land (OE *flicce scyrte* → Flisserte 1270 → Flissherte 1338 → Flyssherte 1461).

Flishinghurst. Plussa's wooded hill (OE *Plussing hyrst* → Plussinghirst 804 → Plussinghurst 1278 → Pulsingherst 1313). There are no later forms to show when initial *P* changed to *F*: this may have been due to a misreading when the name was being copied down. Plussa was also the owner of a woodland pasture (OE *denn*) at the now lost place of Plusshenden in Headcorn, which appears as Plussyngdene in 1327, Plusshenden in 1538.

Fobles Wood (Capel). It appears in 1407 as Fobles farm, no doubt deriving its name from that of some former landowner.

Folkestone (pronounced Fokestun). Folca's stone (OE *Folcan stān* → Folcanstan 696 → Folcestan 927 → Stan 993 → Folcstane 1052 → Fulchestan 1086 → Folkston 1610). Folkestone was the meeting-place of its Hundred, the stone acting as a landmark at which people met.

Folks Wood (Lympne). It is associated with the family of John ffolke (1357).

Foord. See under FORD.

Foots Cray. Recorded as Crai 1086 → Fotescræi c.1100 → Fotescraye 1210 → Footescray 1610, the place, which is on the River Cray, takes its affix from the name of Godiune, or Godwine, fot, who held the manor here during the time of Edward the Confessor.

Force Green. It derives its name from the family of Martin le Forst (1254).

Ford. Self-explanatory (OE *ford* → Forde 1278 → Ford 1309). The place lies on the North Stream. Ford Place, Penshurst, is found as Forde in 1450 and as Fordplace-

farm in 1738. The village of Foord, near the coast at Folkestone, appears as fforde in 1357.

Fordcombe. Recorded as ffyrecoumbe in 1313, the origin of this name may possibly be 'fir valley: valley where fir-trees grow' (OE *fyre cumb*). The change in name must be due to the village's proximity to the Medway.

Fordwater. Self-explanatory (OE *ford wæter*). The place is close to a tributary of the East Stour.

Fordwich (pronounced Forditch). Ford farm: farm close to a ford (OE *ford wīc* → Forduuic 747 → Fordwic 1042 → Fordwik c.1100 → Fordwich 1610).

Foreland, North. Foreland, cape (OE *foran land* → Forland 1326 → the Forland of Tenet (Thanet) 1432 → North-Foreland 1690). Called 'north' to distinguish this promontory from the South Foreland near Dover.

Foresham. It derives its name from the family of Stephen de Forshame, a native of Forsham, who is recorded in Sutton Valence parish in 1351.

Forest Hill (Lewisham). Self-explanatory. It is recorded as la fforest de Leuesham in 1292 and as Forest-place in 1619.

Forsham. Frosty water meadow (OE *forst hamm* → fforsthamme 1261 → Forshamme 1290 → fforsham 1327).

Forstal (pronounced Fostle). Recorded in 1348 as fforstalle, this is a dialect word used of land in front of farm buildings and is derived from OE *foran steall*: 'before the place'.

Fosten Green. Frosty woodland pasture (OE *forst denn* → Forsden' 1254 → ffosdene 1327 → fforsdenn' 1347).

Foulmead. Bird meadow: mead or meadow frequented by birds (OE *fugol mæd* → Fugelmed c.1250 → Fulmede 1313 → ffoulmed 1334).

Four Elms. The name is a late one, given to the recently developed village north of Edenbridge.

Four Throws. Four trees (OE *fēower trēow* → Fourtrowes 1790).

Fowley Island. Bird island: island frequented by birds (OE *fugol ēg* → Fughele c.1250 → Fowley 1610). The island lies off Teynham Level, in the Swale estuary.

Foxen. Fox farmstead: farmstead troubled by foxes (OE *fox tūn* → Foxton 1202 → ffoxstone 1348).

Fox Grove. Grove frequented by foxes (OE *fox grāf* → Foxgrave 1275 → Foxgrove 1355).

Foxholt. Fox hollow: hollow frequented by foxes (OE *fox hol* → Foxole 1278 → Foxhole 1535).

Fox's Cross. It derives its name from the family of John le Fox (1278).

Frangbury. Fronca's stronghold (OE *Froncan burh* → Fraungeber 1327 → Fronckebery 1338 → Frankebury 1348).

Franks. Recorded in 1610 as Franks, the place is associated with a Yorkshire family named Frank who owned property here during the time of Henry III.

Fredville. Cold place (OF *freide ville* → Freydevill 1266 → Fredvyle 1401). So called because of its exposed position.

Freeland Wood (Ruckinge). Free land (OE *frēo land* → Friland 1256 → Freland' 1327).

Freezingham. Settlement of the *Fresingas*, or people of Frisian descent (OE *Fresinga hām* → Fresinghā 1236 → Fresingham 1313). This tribe, whose ancestors from the European mainland probably invaded the district along the waterways here, were also associated with nearby FRENCH HAY and FRENCHHURST.

French Hay. Hedged enclosure of the *Fresingas*, or people of Frisian descent (OE *Fresinga hæg* → Frisingehegh' 1254 → Frisingeheye 1256 → Frenchyngeheye 1292 → Frenchyngheye 1313).

Frenchhurst. Wooded hill of the *Fresingas*, or people of Frisian descent (OE *Fresinga hyrst* → Fresynghurst 1270 → Farrencheherst 1487 → Frinchinhurst, Frenchurst c.1550).

French Street. It is associated with the family of John le ffrenche (1332). French House, Lympne, derives its name from the family of John and Thomas le ffrensche (1348).

Friars, The. Recorded in 1690 as Friers, the place is named after a priory founded here in 1240 for friars of the Carmelite Order.

Frid Wood, Fridhill Wood. See under FRITH.

Friday Hill (Erith). It appears in 1544 as Fridayes-hole, and may have been a hollow (ME *hole*) which for some reason was regarded as evil or cursed, since Friday was looked upon as a day of ill-omen during the Middle Ages.

Frienden (pronounced Frenden). Helfriðs woodland pasture (OE *Helfriðing denn* → Helfreðingdenn 814 → Frendenne 1239 → ffreindene 1278 → Frynden, Hylfrenden 1297).

Friezley (pronounced Freezley). Friðu's clearing (OE *Friðes lēah* → Friðesleah 804 → Fretheslee c.1250). The personal name also occurs in connection with FRITTENDEN.

Frindsbury (pronounced Frinsbury). Friend's stronghold: strong-

hold held by a friend, or ally (OE *frēondes burh* → Freondesberi 764 Freondesberia c.975 → Frandesberie 1086 → Fryndesbury 1610).

Friningham. Settlement of the *Fearningas*, or fern-dwellers (OE *Fearninga hām* → Ferningeham 1086 → Freningham 1206 → Frimingeham c.1270). Other 'fern-dwellers' were settled at FARNINGHAM and FARTHINGLOE.

Frinsted. Fenced-in place, enclosure (OE *freoðenstede* → Fredenestede 1086 → Frethenested' 1235 → Frenestede 1243 → Frensted 1610).

Frith. Woodland (OE *fyrhðe* → Frith' 1254). The same word is found in the names of Frith Farm at Bilsington, Guston and Hawkhurst; Frith Hall, East Farleigh; Frith Wood, East Farleigh and Hawkhurst; Frid Farm, Bethersden; Frid Wood, Borden; Frid's Wood, Boughton Malherbe; and Fridhill Wood, Sheldwich.

Frith, North. North woodland (OE *norð fyrhðe* → Northfryth 1285 → Northfrithe 1541 → Frith North 1690). Called 'north' to distinguish this place from a now lost South Frith in the Tonbridge area, recorded as South fryth in 1610.

Frittenden (pronounced Frittendn). Friðu's woodland pasture (OE *Friðing denn* → Friððingden 804 → Frithindenne 1243 → Fritindenne c.1275 → Frytenden 1610). Friðu owned a woodland clearing at

FRIEZLEY. 1346.

Frogham. Frogs' water meadow (OE *froggena hamm* → Frogenham 1270 → Frogeham 1346 → Frogham 1610).

Frogholt. It appears in 1790 as Frogwell, a name probably derived from OE *frogga wielle:* 'frog spring'.

Frognal (near Teynham). Frogs' corner of land: corner of land where frogs are found (OE *froggena halh* → Froggenhale 1279 → Frogenale 1332). Frognal near Chislehurst was originally known as Frogpool, a name derived from OE *frogga pōl.*

Frogs Hill (Newenden). Frog wood: wooded hill where frogs are found (OE *frogga hyrst* → Frogherst 1338).

Frog's Hole. Frogs' hollow (OE *froggena hol* → ffroggenhole 1262). Frognall Farm, Wickhambreux, shares the same original meaning, being recorded as North-, South-frogenhole in 1360.

Fryarne Park. This seems originally to have been part of the estate of a monastery, being recorded as Monkenlands in 1535 and as Monken Lands in 1644. The name Fryarne is probably derived from ME *frerene:* 'belonging to the friars'. Fryarne Park is believed to be identical with the now lost place of Halyrode, which had the original meaning of 'holy rood, or cross' (OE *hālig rōd*), and is found as Halirodes in 1208, Halyrode in

Fuller Street. Described as Fuller Street farm in 1651, the place may either have been the site of an old fulling mill, or have taken the name of a family named Fuller. Fuller Farm, Smarden, is associated with the family of Thomas Fuller de Smarden (1450); Fuller's House, Staplehurst, with Radulfus ffuller (1340); and Fullers Shaw, Maidstone, with 'John Reede the ffullere in Maydestane' (1381), who was obviously connected with the Maidstone fulling mills.

Fullers Shaw. See under FULLER STREET.

Fulston Manor (Sittingbourne). Fugul's farmstead (OE *Fugules tūn* → Fugeleston 1197 → Fulgeston' 1198 → Fuelestun' 1225). Fugul also owned a woodland clearing (OE *lēah*) at the now lost place of Fausley in Hothfield, recorded as ffoglesle 1292 → Foghelesle 1313 → Fowsleys 1663 → Fausley alias Fousley 1790.

Fulwich Lane (pronounced Fullich). Bird's farm: farm where birds or fowl are kept (OE *fugoles wīc* → Foleswyk' 1270 → Foleswich' 1327 → Fulleswych c.1375 → Fullege 1778).

Funton. Fountain, spring (OF *fontaine* → ffontine 1347 → Fonteine maner' 1410 → Funton 1598).

77

G

Gablehook. Recorded as Gable or Caple Hooke's sometime during the 17th century, the name is either a manorial one, or, possibly, refers to a hook or spur of land associated with a chapel (ME *capel*).

Gabriels. The place appears as Gabriels in 1625 and as Gabriell's in 1744, taking its name from that of a landowning family in the Edenbridge area.

Gadshill (Higham Upshire) (pronounced Gads-hill). God's hill (OE *godes hyll* → on Godes hylle 973). There is another Gadshill near Gillingham, the names referring to pre-Christian places of worship.

Gafford's Bridge. Goat's ford: ford over which goats are herded (OE *gātes ford* → Gatesford' 1313 → Garteforde 1344 → Gatford 1588). The place lies close to a tributary of the Beult.

Galley Hill (Swanscombe). The name is possibly derived from that of Robert Galyan in Swanescampe (1292).

Gammon's Land. It is associated with the family of Geman (1348).

Gardener's Wood (Throwley). The place derives its name from the Throwley family of John and Roger le Gardiner (1270).

Garlinge (pronounced Garlinje). Green bank, or rising ground (OE *grēne hlinc* → Groenling c.824 → Grenling' 1254 → Gerlinge, Grelinge c.1275 → Garlyng 1474). Garlinge Green has the same original meaning, appearing as Grellynch' in 1327.

Garretts. Recorded as such in the time of Elizabeth I, the name may be derived from the Eastchurch family of Gerard (1369).

Garrington. Gārwynn's farmstead (OE *Gārwynne tūn* → Warwintone 1086 → Garwynnetun c.1100 → Garwintun 1194 → Garwynton' 1247). Gārwynn was a Saxon woman.

Gass Lane. It is associated with the family of John, Richard and William Gosse (1348).

Gasson's Wood (Chiddingstone). The place derives its name from the Hever family of William Gasson (1648).

Gatteridge Farm (Denton). Goat wood: wooded hill where goats graze (OE *gāt hyrst* → Gatherste 1304 → Gateherst 1444 → Gatehurst Fm 1655). The farm is referred to during the 15th century as le Sowth, le North Gateherst, showing it to have been once two separate holdings. The change from -hurst to -ridge is a late one.

Gattons (North Cray). Goat farmstead (OE *gāt tūn* → Gatton' 1301). Gattons at Cliffe possibly shares a common origin, being recorded as Gatton's in 1718. Alternatively, this may be a manorial name.

Gaysham (pronounced Gaysam). Gæg's settlement (OE *Gæges hām* → Gaysham 1312 → Gayesham 1446 → Gaysum 1778).

Gibbins Brook. This small tributary stream of the East Stour was once part of the lands of a tribe known as the *Gimmingas*, or Gimma's people, whose name was preserved in the now lost borough of Gimminge in this area. The stream is referred to as Gibbins-brook in the borough of Gimminge in 1790, its name being a corruption of the original tribal name.

Gibbon's Wood (Rolvenden). It takes its name from the family of Robert Gybbon of Rolvenden (1509).

Giddinge (pronounced Giddinje). Gydda's people (OE *Gyddingas* → Geddingge 687 → Geddingc 799 → Getinge 1086 → Geddynge 1292).

Gilden Hill (Sutton-at-Hone). Golden hill (OE *gylden hyll* → Gyldenhill 1406 → Gilden-Hill 1778). Probably so called because of the profusion of yellow flowers growing here.

Gilling Drove. Recorded as Gildenge c.1250, this was once a droveway for cattle, earlier associated with the tribe of the *Gildingas* who were settled at ILEDEN.

Gillingham (pronounced Jillingham). Settlement of Gylla's people (OE *Gyllinga hām* → Gyllinge ham c.975 → Gelingeham 1086 → Gillingeham 1206 → Gillingham 1226).

Gillman's Brimstone. This name, for which there are no records, appears to be associated with John Brim, a resident in the Chelsfield area in 1301. 'Brimstone' is probably derived from ME *Brimes tone*: Brim's farmstead. The first part of the name is manorial.

Gillridge. Golden ridge: ridge covered with golden flowers (OE *gylden hyrcg* → Gilderigge 1353 → Gildregge c.1450).

Gill's Green. It takes its name from that of the family of Matillda Gille (1327). Gill's Farm, Darenth, is connected with William Gelle of Darenth (1368), and is recorded as Gillis in 1522.

Gilridge. Bright, or gleaming, ridge (OE *glæd hrycg'* → Gladerugg', Gladeruge 1202 → Gledrig' 1226). The name – which has obviously been influenced by GILLRIDGE, four miles away – is probably descriptive of a sunny ridge of ground.

Gilwyns. The place is associated with the family of John and Richard Gylewin (1278).

Glassenbury. Stronghold of the *Glæstingas*, or resplendent ones (OE *Glæstinga burh* → Glestingeberi 1301 → Glastingb'i 1327 → Glassenbury 1484 → Glastyngbury 1502). The tribe may have been nicknamed 'resplendent, or brilliant' because of their shining weapons.

Glovers Bridge. The place, situated close to the River Beult, derives its name from the families of Henry Glouere (1327) and John and Richard Glover (1450). Gloversbridge Farm here is named after the place.

Goat Lees. Goat clearing: clearing where goats graze or are penned (OE *gāt lēah* → Gatele 1247 → Gotele 1313). The name appears to have developed to Gotely and later divided to produce its present form.

Goddard's Green (near Benenden). It is associated with the family of Matilda Godard, recorded as living in the Rolvenden Hundred in 1348. The family also gave its name to Goddard's Green near Cranbrook. Goddard Farm, Bonnington, derives its name from the family of Goddard who owned the Manor of Bonnington during the 18th century.

Godden Green. Recorded in 1516 as Godden, the place takes its name from that of John Godwyne (1327). Goddens at Wrotham is similarly associated with the family of Thomas Godden (1528). The now lost place of Godden in Tenterden had the original meaning of 'goat's woodland pasture' (OE *gātes denn*), and appears as Gattesden' 1240 → Gatesdenn 1278 → Gatisden *alias* Godden 1453.

Goddington (near Chelsfield). Recorded as Godinton' 1240 → Godingeston, Godingstone 1271 → Godinton 1330, the place derives its name from the family of Goddington or Godinton, natives of GODINTON, who held the manor here during the 13th century.

Goddington (near Harrietsham). Godda's farmstead (OE *Godding tūn* → Godyntone 1318). Godda had another farmstead at GODINTON.

Godinton. Godda's farmstead (OE *Godding tūn* → Godinton' 1240 → Godyngton 1434).

Godmersham (pronounced Godmershum). Godmǣr's settlement (OE *Godmǣres hām* → Godmǣres ham 824 → Gomersham 1086 → Godmarsham 1610).

Godwell. It is recorded as such in 1313, and may possibly have had the original meaning of Godda's spring (OE *Goddan wielle*). This personal name is found in GODDINGTON and GODINTON.

Gogway. This name, recorded in 1473 as Gogwey, contains the dialect word 'gog', meaning a bog or quagmire. The original track or way (OE *weg*) must have been a very muddy one.

Gold Hill (Shoreham). Self-explanatory (OE *gold hyll* → Goldhelle 1332). The same meaning, descriptive either of a sunny hill, or one on which yellow flowers grew, is shared by Goldhill House, Hadlow, which is found as Goldhull in 1338.

Goldingbank Wood. See under GOLD STREET.

Goldings Wood (Luddesdown). It is described in 1537 as 'woodland called Goldwynes', the name being a manorial one.

Goldstone. Goldstān's farmstead (OE *Goldstānes tūn* → Goldstaneston 1202 → Goldstanestone 1294). The present name is a contraction of these forms.

Gold Street. This street, or narrow road, belonged to an early owner named Goldyng, and is recorded as Goldyngestreete 1460 → Golding strete 1572 → Gouldstreete 1630. Goldingbank Wood, Brabourne, derives its name from the family of William Goldyng (1348).

Goldwell (Great Chart). Marigold spring: spring where marsh marigolds grow (OE *golde wielle* → Goldewelle 1313 → Goldwell 1347). This is probably also the origin of the Goldwells at Aldington and Biddenden.

Golford Green. Recorded in 1700 as Goldford Green, the name is probably derived from OE *golde ford*: 'marsh marigold ford', a description of waterside plants growing by the stream here.

Goodcheap Farm (Hinxhill). Good market (OE *gōd cēap* → Godchep 1270). Perhaps the name refers to an early 'cut-price' place.

Goodley Stock. Marigold clearing (OE *golde leah* → Goldelegh 1278). The affix 'Stock' is probably derived from OE *stocc*: a stock, or tree stump.

Goodnestone (near Eastry) (pronounced Gunston). Gōdwine's farmstead (OE *Gōdwines tūn* → Godwineston 1196 → Guodwinestone 1279 → Goodwinston 1610). Goodnestone, near Faversham, shares the same origin, being recorded as Godwineston in 1208. Both farmsteads, or manors, probably belonged to Earl Godwine of Wessex, also Earl of

81

Kent, who was the father of Harold II, last king of Saxon England. Earl Godwine is traditionally believed to have given his name to the Goodwin Sands, an island which was drowned by the sea in 1097. The Sands, a dangerous bank lying off the coast around the Deal area, are recorded as Godewynsonde 1371 → the Goodwyn 1513 → the Goodwins 1790.

Goodwin Sands. See under GOODNESTONE.

Gore (near Eastry). Wedge-shaped piece of land (OE *gāra* → Gare 1283 → Gore 1302). The same original meaning is shared by Gore, near Upchurch; Gore Court, Otham and Tunstall; Gore Farm, Darenth; Gore Green, Higham Upshire; Gore Street, Monkton; Nether Gore Wood, Adisham; Goretop Lane, Worth; and Upper and Little Gore End Farm, Birchington.

Gore Green, Gore Street. See under GORE.

Gorham Wood (Bicknor). 'Gore settlement': settlement by a gore, or wedge-shaped piece of land (OE *gāra hām* → Garham 1185).

Gorrell Bridge. Dirt spring: spring with discoloured water (OE *gor wielle* → Gorewelle 1278 → Gorewell' 1356). Alternatively, the stream here may have been used as an open sewer, since *gor* means 'dung, dirt; filth'.

Gorsley Wood (Bishopsbourne). Recorded in 1541 as Gosley, the origin of this name may either have been 'gorse clearing' (OE *gorst lēah*), or 'goose clearing: clearing where geese feed' (OE *gōs lēah*).

Gosmere Farm. See under GUSHMERE.

Goss Hall (Ash). Goose corner: corner of land where geese are kept (OE *gōs halh* → Gosehal' 1202 → Gosehale 1254).

Gosshill. Gorse-covered hill (OE *gorsten dūn* → Gorsindon 1195 → Gostendon c.1385). The present name is a contraction of these forms, with -don changing to -hill.

Goudhurst (pronounced Gowdhurst). Battle hill: wooded hill on which a battle has been fought (OE *gūð hyrst* → Gmthhyrste c.1100 → Guthurst, Guhtherste c.1200 → Gudherste 1232 → Guthhurste 1278 → Goutherst 1316 → Goodherst 1610). The name commemorates a battle or combat fought on this high ground in Saxon times.

Grafty Green. Grass enclosure (OE *gærs tēag* → Grasteghe c.1250 → Grastye, Garstye, Grauftegh' 1270).

Grain, Isle of. Gravelly, or sandy, shore (OE *grēon* → Grean c.1100 → Grien 1205 → Gren 1232 → Greyn, Grane 1535 → Ile of Greane 1610). The Isle of Grain was once a true island, separated from the Kentish mainland by the Thames and Medway.

Grainy Farm. See under GRAVE-NEY.

Grandacre Farm (Waltham). Great cultivated piece of land (OF *grand* + ME *æcer* → Grandek' 1226). Grandacre also appears as Gartaker' in 1334 and as Gartakere in 1347 (← OE *grēat æcer*: great piece of cultivated land).

Grange. Green farm: farm surrounded by fields (OE *grēne wīc* → Grenic c.1100 → Grenche 1226 → Grenech 1348 → Grawnge 1535). Perhaps the name was altered to 'Grange' in the 16th century to avoid confusion with GREENWICH, which has the same original meaning.

Graveney (pronounced Grayney). At the graven river (OE *æt þǣm grāfen ēa* → æt Grafonǣa 811 → Gravenea 832 → Grafenea 946 → Gravanea 1006 → Graueney 1610). This was the name originally given to the stream at Graveney, running through a broad ditch which gave it its name: a river flowing through a trench, or 'graven' ditch. It is recorded as Grafon eah in 814. A native of Graveney, Stephen de Graveney, gave his name to Grainy Farm, Hartlip, when he held the manor there during the reign of Edward I.

Gravesend. At the grove's end (OE *æt þǣm grāfes ende* → Gravesham 1086 → Grauessend 1157 → Gravesend' 1232). The park to the east of Gravesend may be the original grove at the 'end', or edge of which the settlement developed.

Grays, Little. Together with Grays Farm here, the place derives its name from the family of William le Grey (1284).

Great Bursted Farm (Bishopsbourne). Stronghold place (OE *burh stede* → Beristede 1216 → Burstede 1270 → Borstede 1284).

Great Lines. This is a hill near Chatham, taking its name from the 18th century earthworks on it which formed part of the land defences of the town during the Napoleonic Wars.

Greatness. At the gravelly stubble field (OE *æt þǣm grēoten ersce* → Gretaniarse Greatnearse 821 → Gretenersce c.1100 → Greteness 1206)

Greatstone-on-Sea. This name, together with that of neighbouring Littlestone-on-Sea, is modern, the two coastal resorts being comparatively recent developments.

Greenacre Farm (Elham). Spectre's piece of cultivated land (OE *grīmes æcer* → Grimeshaker 1275 → Grimesekere 1304 → Grims Acres 1790). Obviously this piece of land was believed to be haunted by a spectre or ghost of some kind.

Greenborough Marshes. Green mound, or barrow (OE *grēne beorg* → (marsh of) Grenebergh 1375). The name must refer to a grassy hillock in this flat, low-lying area.

83

Green Farm (Shorne). Recorded as Grene manor in 1338, the farm marks the site of the now lost place of Merston, which had the original meaning of 'marsh farmstead' (OE *mersc tūn*), being recorded as Meriston' in 1242, Merston in 1265.

Green Hill (Lenham). Self-explanatory (OE *grēne hyll* → Grenehelle 1313). The same origin is shared by Green Hill, Otham, and Greenhill Farm, Herne. Greenhill House, Egerton, is on the site of a 'green slope' (OE *grēne hielde*), recorded as Grenehelde in 1237, Grenehilde in 1254.

Greenhithe. Green landing-place: landing place at a grassy spot (OE *grēne hȳð* → Grenethe 1264 → Grenehethe 1339 → Grenehithe 1343 → Greenhyth 1610).

Greenland Shaw. Green, or grass-covered land (OE *grēne land* → Greeneland 1648). The affix 'Shaw' is from OE *scaga*: a copse.

Greenstreet. See under GREEN STREET GREEN.

Green Street Green (near Darenth). Green road: Roman road overgrown with grass (OE *grēne strǣt* → Grenestrete 1240). Green Street Green, near Farnborough, shares the same origin (Grenstrete in 1292), as does Greenstreet near Teynham (Grenestrete in 1278). OE *strǣt* is derived from the Latin *via strata*: metalled, or paved way.

Greenway Court (Hollingbourne). Green way: way, or track, overgrown with grass (OE *grēne weg* → Greneweie 1240 → Grenewaye 1408 → Grenway court 1610). The same original meaning occurs in the name of Greenway Cottages, Lower Hardres, which appears as Greneweye in 1242.

Greenwich (pronounced Grinnidge). Green farm: farm surrounded by green fields (OE *grēne wīc* → Grenewic 964 → Greenwic 1044 → Grenviz 1086 → East, West Grenewych 1291 → Greenwych 1610).

Greet. Gravel: gravelly or gritty land (OE *grēot* → Grete 1240).

Gregg's Wood. See under GRIGG.

Grigg. The place is associated with the family of John, Henry and William Grigge of Headcorn (1450). Gregg's Wood, Tonbridge, is similarly connected with the family of Robert Grigge (1347).

Grimshill Wood (Blean). Slope of Grimm's people (OE *Grimminga hielde* → Gremyngehelde 1313 → Gryminghelde 1332 → Grimgill 1790).

Groombridge. Servants' bridge (ME *gromena brigge* → Gromenebregge 1318 → Grombrugg 1355 → Grumbrygge c.1480 → Groomebridge 1601). What connection there was between servants and a bridge at Groombridge – which straddles the Kent/Sussex border – is not known;

but there is a local tradition that the place name owes its origin to a Saxon named Gromen who built a moated stronghold where Groombridge Place now stands.

Grove. Self-explanatory (OE *gräf* → Graue 1254 → Grove 1341). The same origin is shared by The Grove, Sutton-at-Hone; Grove Court, Chislet; Grove End, Tunstall; Grove Farm, Newington; Grove Farm and House, Sellindge; Grove Hill, Wickhambreux; Grove Manor Farm, Woodnesborough; and Groves, Staple.

Grove Ferry. 'Passage hill': hill with a passage, or way, across it (OE *fær hyll* → Ferehelle c.1250 → Grove Ferry 1600). The affix 'Grove' seems to have come from Grove Court nearby. Groveferry Hill here retains the original form 'Ferryhill'.

Grovehurst (Horsmonden). Grove wooded hill (OE *gräf hyrst* → Grofhurste 1240 → Grofhurst 1309). The same original meaning occurs in the names of Grovehurst, Pembury (Grofherst in 1332); and Great Grovehurst, Milton (Grofhurst in 1324, Groveherst in 1610).

Grubs Croft. 'Grubbed-up valley': valley where the soil has been broken up (ME *grobben dene* → Grobbindane 1322 → Grubbyndane 1327). There are no later records of this name to show how it developed to its present form, but it is possible that a croft, a small piece of arable land, here belonged to a family

who took their name from this place, so that at some time it was known as Grubbin's Croft.

Guildsted (pronounced Gillsted). Offering place (OE *gield stede* → Hildestede 1198 → Ildestede 1236 Ylstede 1457 → Yelsted 1690). This seems to have been a place where pagan offerings or sacrifices were made, *gield* having the various meaning of 'tribute, worship, offering', etc.

Guilton (pronounced Gilltun). Golden farmstead (OE *gylden tūn* → Geldenton 1218 → Gildenetune 1278 → Gildentoune 1337). The adjective may have been descriptive of the colour of the stone from which the buildings were built, or of the foliage, flowers or crops in the vicinity of the farm.

Gumping Common. Gunna's pound, or enclosure (OE *Gunnan pund* → Gunnepende 1479 → Gunnepend 1482).

Gusborne. Goose stream: stream used by geese (OE *gōs burna* → Goseburn' 1292 → Gossebourne 1332 → Gosebourne 1359).

Gushmere. Recorded as Gusselm'e 1240 → Gosselm'e 1332 → Gussemere 1348, the origin of this name appears to be 'goose muddy pool pool': pool by a muddy pool where geese drink (OE *gōs sol mere*). Gosmere Farm, one and a half miles from Gushmere, shares the same origin.

85

Gussels, Little. Goose muddy pool: muddy pool frequented by geese (OE *gōs sol* → Gosehale, Gosesole 1292 → Gosole 1347).

Guston. Gūðsige's farmstead (OE *Gūðsiges tūn* → Gocistone 1086 → Gusistune, Guthistun 1087 → Guthsieston 1229 → Gussiston' 1254 → Guston 1610). Guston Farm, Ash, takes its name from that of a native of Guston who settled in this area, and is recorded as Gustone in 1338.

Gutteridge Gate. Godric's wood (OE *Godrices wudu* → Godricheswude 1268 → Goodrich Wood 1555 → Godrick alias Gutteridge field 1728).

H

Hackington. Hacca's farmstead (OE *Haccing tūn* → Latintone 1086 → Hakinton' 1186 → Hakington', 1226).

Hacklinge (pronounced Hacklinje). Hollow-dwellers (OE *halclingas* → Halklinge 1240 → Halkling 1302 → Hacklinge field 1675). OE *halc* had the meaning of 'small hollow in a slope': perhaps this tribe was so named because it made its home in the vicinity of Hacklinge Holes and Hacklinge Hill.

Haddling Wood (Northbourne). Hæddel's people (OE *Hæddelingas* → Hedelinge 1240 → Edelynge 1313 → Hedlyng 1535).

Hadlow. 'Head hill' (OE *hēafod hlǣw* → Haslow 1086 → Hadlo 1214 → Haudlo 1280 → Hadloe 1610). The hill here was probably described as 'head', or chief, because it was more prominent than others in the area.

Haffenden. Herefriδ's woodland pasture (OE *Herefriðing denn* → Efreδingdenn 863 → Herferthyng' 1244). The present name is a corruption of these forms. Haffenden Farm, St. Mary in the Marsh, derives its name from John Haffenden of Tenterden, who owned an estate in the parish towards the end of the 18th century.

Hail Beech Wood (Ospringe). Recorded in 1380 both as Caldhelbeche and as Ealdhelbeche, the origin of this name may either be 'cold hill beech-tree' (OE *cald hyll bēce*), or 'old hill beech-tree' (OE *eald hyll bēce*).

Haine (pronounced Hayne). Hedged enclosure (OE *(ge) hæg* → Hæg 697 → Hayne 1434).

Halden Place. See under HIGH HALDEN.

Hale (near Chiddingstone). Corner of land (OE *halh* → Hale 1278). The same word, together with the surname atte Hale — 'dweller by the corner of land' — also occurs in the names of Hale near Gillingham; Hale Farm, Lamberhurst; Hale Oak, Chiddingstone; Hale Place and Street, East Peckham; Hale Wood and Hale Field Wood, Penshurst; Hale's Place, Tenterden; Hall Farm, Seal; Hall Wood, Stansted; and Hayle

87

Place, Loose. Hales Place at Hackington is named after Sir Edward Hales, who lived there during the 18th century.

Hale, Upper and **Nether.** Manor house, hall (OE *heall* → Halle 1292 → le Nedyr Hall 1456). This is also the origin of the names of Hall Farm, Hothfield; Hall Place, Barming, Bexley, Harbledown and Leigh; and Hall's Place, Otterden.

Haley Shaw. Holloway, or way through a hollow (OE *hol weg* → Holewey 1278). The affix 'Shaw' is from OE *scaga*: a copse.

Half Yoke. Yoke, or measure of land (OE *geoc* → Yoke 1325 → Halfyoke 1419 → Half Yoke *alias* Halfway Oke 1782).

Halke House (Sheldwich). Small hollow (OE *halc* → Halk' 1278 → Halke 1327).

Hall, Little. It appears in 1431 as Haghe, and is described in 1790 as 'Haghe *alias* Hawe, now commonly called Hawle'. The origin of this name is OE *haga*: enclosure.

Hallborough. Recorded in 1650 as Halebury, the name appears to be derived from OE *heall burh*: 'hall stronghold', referring to a well-fortified manor house.

Halling (pronounced Hawling). Hall-dwellers (OE *heallingas* → Healling wara mearc 880 → Hallinges 1086 → Hallynge 1189 → Halling 1202). The 880 forms means 'boundary of the hall-dwelling people': probably the hall was a building shared by several families. Another group of 'hall-dwellers' owned a wooded hill at the now lost place of Hallinghurst in Smarden, which appears as Hallingehurst in 1254 (← OE *heallinga hyrst*).

Hall Place. See under HALE, UPPER and NETHER.

Halstead. Place of shelter for cattle (OE *(ge) healdstede* → Haltesteda c.1100 → Halsted 1201 → Aldestede 1212 → Halstede, Haltsted 1291).

Halstow, Lower. See under HIGH HALSTOW.

Halton Court (Alkham). Hall farmstead: manor (ME *halle tone* → Halton 1408).

Ham. Water meadow (OE *hamm* → Hama 1086 → Hammes c.1100 → Hamme 1253 → Ham 1610). This word, together with the surname atte Hamme – 'dweller by the water meadow' – is also found in connection with Ham Bridge and Ham Brooks Wood at Ham; Ham Farm, Barham; Ham Green, Upchurch and Wittersham; Ham Hill, Birling; Ham Street, Orlestone; and Ham Marshes, Graveney.

Hamden. Water meadow pasture: woodland pasture on low-lying ground (OE *hamm denn* → Hamdenne 1313 → Hamden' 1359). In 1278 the place is recorded as Hamedenebrig', showing that there was a bridge spanning the River Beult here at that time.

Ham Green, Ham Street. See under HAM.

Hamlet Hole. It derives its name

88

from the family of Nicholas Hamelot of Hadlow (1292), the 'Hole' being a hollow or dip in the land here.

Hammill. Water meadow forest: forest bordering on to a water meadow (OE *hamm weald* → Hamolde 1086 → Hamwolde 1174 → Hamwold, Hamwol 1226 → Hammewolde 1240). The present name is a contraction.

Hammond's Corner. The place is associated with the family of William Hamon of Lydd (1270). Hammond's Farm, Goudhurst, is connected with Mary Hammon of Goudhurst (1642).

Hampstead Mill. Homestead (OE *hāmstede* → Hamsted' 1240 → Hamstede 1332 → Hampstede 1338).

Hampton (near Brabourne). Home farm (OE *hām tūn* → Hamptone 1235 → Hampton 1307). Hampton, near Herne, shares the same original meaning and is found as Hampton' in 1226. Hamptons, West Peckham, is recorded as Hampton in 1480.

Handen. At the high woodland pasture (OE *æt þǣm hēan denne* → Hendenne 1334 → Heandenn' 1346 → Handenn' 1347).

Hand Wood (Thanington). This appears to be a corruption of the name Honywood: the family of Honywood were at one time owners of nearby COCKERING FARM.

Hanslett's Forstall. Recorded as Hengsellewode in 1313 and as Hansells or Hansletts-forstal in 1782, the origin of this name is possibly

'stallion hill: hill where a stallion grazes' (OE *hengest hyll*), which would produce the Hengselle form of 1313. The affix 'Forstall' is a dialect word used of land in front of farm buildings.

Harbledown. Herebeald's hill (OE *Herebealding dūn* → Herebolddune 1175 → Herebaldon 1196 → Herbeldon 1229 → Harbledoune 1610).

Harbourland. Hereburh's land (OE *Hereburge land* → Hereburglond 1313 → Havurland 1540). Hereburh was a Saxon woman.

Harbourne House (High Halden). Hȳra's stream (OE *Hȳring burne* → Hyringburne 968 → Hereburn' 1278 → Herbourne 1407). The stream is a tributary of the Highknock Channel. Hȳra also owned a woodland pasture at HERONDEN.

Hardacre Farm (Preston). Self-explanatory (OE *heard æcer* → Hardeaker 1538). The name may be compared with that of MELLIKER, where the soil was soft and easily turned.

Hardres, Upper and **Lower** (pronounced Hards). Hard, stony ground (OE *harad* → in haredum 786 → haredā 809 → Hardes 1086 → Hardres 1191 → Heghhardres, Nitherhardres 1242 → Upper hardres, Nether hardres 1610).

Harefield Farm (Selling). Battlefield (OE *herefeld* → Harefeld 1251 → Herefelde 1313). Harville Farm, Wye, probably shares the same origin, being recorded as Northharifield in 1271. Nothing is known of the early battles which the name commemorates.

Hare's Brooks. Hare marsh: marshy ground frequented by hares (OE *hara brōc* → Harebroke 1485).

Harewell. Hare spring: spring frequented by hares (OE *hara wielle* → Harewelle 1253 → Harwell 1690).

Harlakenden. Herelāc's woodland pasture (OE *Herelācing denn* → Harlakinden' 1240 → Herlakenden' 1254 → Harlakendenne 1316).

Harman's Corner. It derives its name from the family of William Hereman (1235).

Harmansole Farm (Lower Hardres). Heremod's hollow (OE *Heremodes hol* → Heremodeshole 1278 → Hermodesole 1334).

Harpole. Filthy pool (OE *horh pōl* → Horpole 1189 → Horepole 1270).

Harrietsham (pronounced Harrisham). Heregeard's water meadow (OE *Heregeardes hamm* → Herigeardes hamm 964 → Hergeardesham 1043 → Hariardesham 1086 → Herietesham 1215 → Haretsham 1610).

Harringe Court (Sellindge) (pronounced Harrinje). Here's people (OE *Heringas* → Herring 1250 → Herrynge 1304). Alternatively, this may have been the settlement of a tribe known as 'the fighting men' (*heringas*), from the Old English word *here:* army, troop.

Hartanger. Hart slope: wooded slope frequented by harts or stags (OE *heorot hangra* → Hertange 1086 → Herthangre 1242).

Hartley. Hart clearing: clearing frequented by harts or stags (OE *heorot lēah* → Erclei 1086 → Hertlegh' 1226 → Hertleye 1275 → Hartley 1610). Hartley at Cranbrook has the same original meaning, being recorded as heoratleag 843 → Hertle c.1200 → Hertleya 1253.

Hartlip. 'Hart leap': leaping-place for harts or stags (OE *heorot hlīep* → Heordlyp c.1100 → Hertleppe 1207 → Hartlep 1219 → Hartlyppe 1610). The name may refer to a spot where deer mated. Hartlip Hill here is recorded as Hertlepeshelle in 1316: 'hart leap's hill'.

Hartridge. Wooded ridge (OE *harað hrycg* → Hatherugg' 1292 → Hartheregge 1327 → Herterege 1505). The name is still descriptive of the area.

Hartsdown. Hart's hill: hill frequented by harts or stags (OE *heorotes dūn* → Hertesdowne 1451).

Hartsheath. Recorded during the 15th century as Hersherde *alias* Herscherte *alias* Harshett, the second element in this name appears to be derived from OE *scyrte*: shortened piece of land. The forms are too late for the first element to be explained with any certainty.

Hartsland. This was originally land belonging to John Hert, a husbandman, or cottager, in Penshurst in 1450. In 1778 the place is recorded as Newhouse *alias* Harts, confusion having arisen between Hart's Land here, and NEWHOUSE nearby.

Harty, Isle of. Hart or stag island (OE *heorot ēg* → Hertei 1086 →

Heortege c.1100 → Herteye 1242 → Harty 1610). The Isle of Harty lies at the south-eastern end of the Isle of Sheppey, separated from it by the Capel Fleet.

Harvel. Hart land: open land frequented by harts or stags (OE *heorot feld* → heorot felda 939). There are no further records of this name, but it no doubt developed to Hertfelde (late 13th century), the present name being produced by dialect pronunciation of 'Hartfield'.

Harville Farm. See under HAREFIELD FARM.

Harwarton. Recorded as Harwarton manor in 1539, the place was earlier associated with Thomas Hereward of Speldhurst who is found here in 1292. The place name, which appears as Herewordtone in 1327, is derived from ME *Hereward tone*: farmstead belonging to the Hereward family.

Hastingleigh (pronounced Hastenlye). Clearing of Hæsta's people (OE *Hæstinga lēah* → Hæstinga lege 993 → Hastingelie 1086 → Hastingleye 1225 → Hastingleygh 1610). This appears to have been an eastern extension of the territory of the *Hæstingas*, a Saxon tribe whose main settlement was at Hastings in Sussex.

Hatch Hill (Luddesdown). Recorded in 1537 as Hechehill, this was originally a hill with a hatch, or gate, leading on to it, the name being derived from OE *hæcc hyll*. The word 'hatch', together with the surname atte Heche – 'dweller by the hatch' – is also found in connection with Hatch Farm, Ware-

horne; Hatch Spring, Hoath; Mersham Hatch, near Mersham; and the now lost place of Hatch in Chislet.

Hault Farm (Petham). Recorded as Haute in 1278 and as Hauts Place in 1790, the place derives its name from the family of Ivo de Haut (c.1180).

Haven Street. The former name for this place was Haydon Street, which had the original meaning of 'heather-covered hill' (OE *hǣð dūn*) and appears as Hathdune c.975 → Hadone 1086 → Heydon' 1270. The modern form of Haven seems to have been in use from the early 17th century onwards.

Haviker Street. Found in the 13th century as Hauekere and Heuakere, this name may originally have meant 'head land': strip of arable land lying at the head, or top, of a field (OE *hēafod æcer*).

Hawden. Hæfa's woodland pasture (OE *Hæfan denn* → Hauedenne 1301 → Haweden' 1422).

Hawe. Hedged enclosure (OE *haga* → Hagh' 1278 → Haugh 1483 → Haw 1690). Hawe Farm, Sturry, shares a common origin, and is found as Haghe in 1332.

Hawkenbury (near Headcorn). Stronghold of the bog-dwellers (OE *focginga burh* → focgingabyra 814→ Fokingbery 1275 → Hokyngbery 1331). The place is on low-lying ground close to the River Beult and one of its tributary streams: the dwellers here were known as 'the bog-dwellers' because of the boggy or marshy area (OE *focge*) in which they lived.

Hawkenbury (near Tunbridge Wells). Stronghold of Hōc's people (OE *Hōcinga burh* → Hokyngbury 1258). Hōc himself owned a woodland pasture at HOCKENDEN.

Hawkhurst. Hawk wood: wooded hill frequented by hawks (OE *heafoc hyrst* → Hauekehurst 1254 → Haukhurst 1278 → Hawkherst 1610).

Hawkinge (pronounced Hawkinje). Heafoc's people (OE *Heafocingas* → Hauekinge 1204 → Hawekingg' 1218 → Hawking 1610).

Hawkridge. Hook ridge: ridge with a hook or spur (OE *hōc hrycg* → Hokeregge 1256).

Hawk's Nest. The name appears to be a comparatively late one, first recorded in 1782 as Hawksnest.

Hawkwell, Little. Hawk spring: spring frequented by hawks (OE *heafoc wielle* → Hawkewell 1279 → Haukewell, Hawkwell 1381). Hawkwell Place here derives its name from the original site.

Hawley. At the holy clearing (OE *æt pæm hāligan lēage* → Hagelei 1086 → Halgelei c.1100 → Haleghele 1253 → Halghele, Halwele 1303 → Halghwelee 1355).

Hawthorn Corner. See under AGNEY.

Hay Farm (Eastry). Hedged enclosure (OE *(ge)hæg* → Haye 1242 → Heye 1327). Hayland Farm, Smarden, shares the same origin, being recorded as Haye in 1254.

Hayden Wood (Lamberhurst). High woodland pasture (OE *hēah denn* → Heah dæn 838 → Hedenn 1275 → Headenne 1327).

Hayes. Brushwood, underwood (OE *hæs* → Hesa 1177 → Hese 1254 → Heys 1610). Hayes Wood, Pembury, shares a common origin, appearing as Hese in 838, Hese in 1260.

Hayland Farm. See under HAY FARM.

Hayle Place. See under HALE.

Hayman's Hill (Horsmonden). Described as Hammons Hill in 1782, it derives its name from the 14th century family of Hamon or Haymond.

Haysden. Brushwood pasture: woodland pasture overgrown with brushwood (OE *hæs denn* → Hesdenn' 1232 → Hasden 1324 → Hesdene 1407). Haysden and Upper Haysden are distinguished from each other by the forms Easthesedenne 1332, Westhesdenne 1381.

Haytham Green. Recorded as Etham in 1258, the name probably shares the same origin as nearby IGHTHAM.

Hayton Manor (Stanford). Enclosure farmstead: farmstead with a hedged enclosure (OE *(ge) hæg tūn* → Hægtune 1035 → Hayton c.1140 → Heyton' 1254).

Hayward's Hill (Throwley). It is associated with John le Heyward (1292). This family name is also found in connection with Hayward Farm, Stanford; Hayward House,

Fairfield; and Haywood, near Tonge.

Haywood. See under HAYWARD'S HILL.

Hazelden. Hazel pasture: woodland pasture where hazels grow (OE *hæsel denn* → Hasilden' 1256 → Heseldenne 1327 → Heselden 1403). Hazeldene Cottage, Edenbridge, shares the same origin, being described in 1536 as 'garden in Edenbreg called Haseldens'.

Hazel Hall. See under HAZEL STREET.

Hazeling Wood (Ickham). (Place) associated with a hazel-tree or bush (OE *hæseling* → Haselyng 1535 → Hasteling wood 1635).

Hazelpits. Hazel copse (OE *hæslett* → Heselette 1332). There are no later forms to show how the present name evolved.

Hazel Street. Hazel bush (OE *hæsel* → Hesele 1334 → Hasele 1347). Hazel Hall and Wood, West Peckham, are on the site of a hazel thicket (OE *hæsel holt*), the name appearing as Hæsl holte 964 → Aisiholte 1086 → Haselholte 1343.

Hazelwood. Self-explanatory (OE *hæsel wudu* → Heselwode 1332 → Hasylwode 1450). Hazlewood and Hazlewood Farm, Wilmington, derive their name from the family of John Hasylwood of Wilmington (1528).

Hazlewood. See under HAZEL-WOOD.

Head Barn Wood (Strood). Recor-

ded in 1698 as Head Barne wood, the name may originally have implied a wood lying above, or beyond, a barn.

Headcorn. Hydeca's fallen trees, or debris (OE *Hydecan hruna* → Hedekaruna c.1100 → Hedecrune 1240 → Hedecrone 1248 → Hedcorne 1610).

Heane Barn and Wood (pronounced Hayne). Family, household (OE *hīwun* → Hen 1086 → Hean 1253). The meeting-place of the Heane Hundred was probably in this area.

Hearnden Green. Corner pasture (OE *hyrne denn* → Herindenn' 1313 → Herynden' 1338).

Heasledown Farm (Waldershare). It appears in 1799 as Heasleden Down, the name probably having the original meaning of 'hazel pasture' (OE *hæsel denn*).

Heathen Street. The name is derived from OE *hǣð feld*: 'heather-covered open land', and is recorded in 1599 as Heathy feild. The present form appears to be a corruption.

Heaverham. Boar meadow: water meadow frequented by wild boar (OE *eofor hamm* → Euerham, Everham 1313).

Hectorage Farm (Tonbridge). This was originally a 'heather-covered hill' (OE *hǣð hyrst*), the name appearing as Le Hethehirst in 1292. Three years later, in 1295, it is recorded as Hetherede – 'heather rid' – the present name being a corruption of this form.

Hedgingford Wood (Hawkhurst). Enclosure of Hæcga's people (OE *Hæcginga worð* → Heggingeworth' 1310). Change of -worth to -ford is quite common.

Heel Lane. Slope (OE *hielde* → Helde 1327). Heel Farm, Stalisfield, also appears as Helde in 1327; and the original meaning is shared by Hell Wood, Woodchurch: Helde in 1261.

Hell Wood. See under HEEL LANE.

Helsted. Hill place (OE *hyll stede* → Elstede 1336 → Helstedes lane 1436 → Helstedefelde c.1500). This last form refers to land surrounding the growing village.

Heminge (pronounced Heminje). Hemma's people (OE *Hemmingas* → Hemminge 1272 → Hemmyng' 1370).

Hempstead. Hemp place: place where hemp is grown (OE *henep stede* → Hempstede 1327). Hemsted, near Lyminge, shares a common origin, being recorded as Empestede 1240 → Hemstede 1275 → Hempstede 1278.

Hemsted (near Cranbrook). Homestead (OE *hāmstede* → Hæmstede 993 → Hamstede 1254 → Hæmstede 1391).

Hemsted (near Lyminge). See under HEMPSTEAD.

Henden. At the high woodland pasture (OE *æt þæm hēan denne* → Handenne 1332 → Heandenn 1355 → Henden 1407). The now lost place of Henden in Woodchurch also had this meaning, being recorded as Hiendeñe in 1327, Hendenne in 1346.

Henfoote Farm (Herne). Cock ford: ford frequented by cock-birds (OE *hana ford* → Haneford' 1270 → Henforde 1489).

Henghurst. At the high wood (OE *æt þæm hēan hyrste* → Henhurst 1240 → Hyanh'st 1334 → Henhurst 1619).

Hengrove. Grove frequented by hen-birds (OE *henn grāf* → Hengraue c.1250 → Hengrave 1308).

Henhurst (near Cobham). Hen wood: wooded hill frequented by hen-birds (OE *henn hyrst* → of hennhystæ c.975 → Hanehest 1086 → Henneherst 1219 → Henherst 1244). Henhurst Wood, Yalding, shares the same original meaning, being found as Henherst in 1226, Henhurste in 1243.

Henhurst (near Staplehurst). Narrow wooded hill (OE *enge hyrst* → Engherst 1270 → Hengherst 1327 → Henherst 1488).

Henley. Hen clearing: clearing frequented by hen-birds (OE *henn lēah* → Henle 1227). Henley Street, Luddesdown, has the same origin, appearing as Henle in 1323, Henley in 1572. The now lost place of Henley in Eltham is found as Hanlee 1243 → Haunle 1257 → Henley 1270, the name being derived from OE *æt þæm hēan lēage*: 'at the high clearing'.

Henley Street. See under HENLEY.

Hensill. At the high buildings (OE
æt þǣm hēan gesellum → Hennes-
hill' 1254 → Heansell' 1338 →
Henselle 1348).

Henwood. At the high wood (OE
æt þǣm hēan wude → Henwude
1272 → Heanewode 1313 → Hen-
wode 1338). The name is probably
a reference to high ground just south
of Henwood. Henwood Green, Pembury, has the original meaning of
'hen wood: wooded hill frequented
by hen-birds' (OE *henn hyrst*), and
appears as Henherst in 1314.

Henwood Green. See under HEN-
WOOD.

Heppington House (Nackington).
Hebba's farmstead (OE *Hebbing
tūn* → Hebbinton' 1181 → Hebyn-
ton 1346 → Hepyngton 1407).
Hebba's tribal settlement was at the
now lost place of Hebbinge in
Boughton Aluph.

Hepsbrook Wood (Pembury). There
are no early forms for this name,
but it seems almost certainly to be
associated with the now lost place
of Hepsbroke, six miles away in
Penshurst, which had the original
meaning of 'marshy ground within
a hook (formed by streams)' (OE
hæpse brōc), and is recorded as
Hapsebroc 1191 → Hapesbrok' 1254
→ Heppesbroke 1538.

Hereson (pronounced Heersun).
Hēahrēd's farmstead (OE *Hēahrēdes
tūn* → Heyredeston c.1225 → Her-
stone 1799).

Hermitage. Described in 1361 as
the 'land of the hermit of Long-
esole', the original name of this

place was Longsole – 'long muddy
pool' (OE *lang sol*) – recorded as
Langheshole in 1246 and as Longe-
sole in 1351. The present name
must be a reference to the chapel
of St. Laurence, mentioned here
in the mid-14th century.

Hernden (Chart Sutton). See under
HERNDEN, Sandhurst.

Hernden (Eastry). Hearda's woodland pasture (OE *Hearding denn* →
Hardingden' 1254 → Hardinden
1283 → Harynden 1431).

Hernden (Sandhurst). Corner pasture: woodland pasture in a corner
(OE *hyrne denn* → Hernindene 1170
→ Herindenn c.1210 → Herenden'
1254). Hernden near Chart Sutton
probably shares the same original
meaning, being recorded as Harnden
in 1649.

Herne. Corner (OE *hyrne* → æt
Hyrnan c.1100 → Hirne 1264 →
Herne 1298). Herne Bay and Herne
Common both take their name
from that of the original settlement,
which seems to have developed in a
corner, or angle, of land.

Hernhill. At the grey hill (OE *æt
þǣm hāran hylle* → Haranhylle
c.1100 → Harenhull 1247 → Harn-
hulle 1250 → Hearnhill 1610). Hern
Hill, Ruckinge, has the same origin,
appearing as Harnhell' in 1278,
Harnhelle in 1334.

Heronden. Hȳra's woodland pasture
(OE *Hȳring denn* → Hyringdenne
833 → Heryndenne 1327 → Herindenn' 1334). The personal name
is also found in connection with
HARBOURNE.

Hersden. Hersa's people (OE *Hersingas* → Hersing' 1270 → Hersynge 1338 → Hersinge 1574 → Hersing *alias* Haseden 1790). This tribe possibly owned a stretch of marshland at the now lost place of Hersing Marsh in Iwade, which is recorded as such in 1216 (← OE *Hersinga mersc*).

Hever (pronounced Heever). At the high bank (OE *æt þǣm hēan ȳfre* → Heanyfre 814 → Heure c.1200 → Hevere c.1240). Hever Court Farm, Ifield, takes its name from the Hever family of Radolphus de Havor (1284). Hever Place, Kingsdown, which appears as Hevere in 1379, is similarly associated with a family originating from Hever, Jacob de Hevre being recorded in the Kingsdown area in 1242. Heverswood, Halstead, derives its name from yet another native of Hever, Thomas de Heure (1327).

Heverswood. See under HEVER.

Hewitts (Chelsfield). Cutting: place where a clearing has been made in woodland (OE *hīewet* → Hewette 1268). Hewitts, Willesborough, shares a common origin, being recorded as Heuwette in 1307, Hewete in 1338.

Hexden. Hæcci's woodland pasture (OE *Hæccing denn* → Hechindenn 1251 → Heccyngden' 1292 → Hechyngdenn' 1313). Hexden Channel nearby shares the abbreviated form of this name.

Hextable (pronounced Hex-tubble). High staple: staple, or post, standing high up (OE *hēah stapol* → Hagestapel 1203 → Heghstaple 1327 →

Exstapul 1471 → Hackstaple 1778). The post was probably used as a landmark on the high ground here.

Hickmans Green. The place derives its name from the family of Hickman, being described in 1708 as 'Hickmans, land and tenements in Boughton'. Hickman's, Speldhurst, is associated with Richard Hikeman (1327).

Hicks Forstall. Recorded as atte fforstalle (at the forstal) in 1313, it takes its name from that of the 14th century family of Hicke, Hycke, or Hik, 'forstal' being a dialect word used of land in front of farm buildings.

Higham, Great and **Little** (pronounced Hyam). High settlement (OE *hēah hām* → Hecham 1204 → Hegham 1254 → Heygham 1270). The same original meaning is shared by Higham near Hadlow; Higham near Patrixbourne; Higham Farm, Littlebourne; Higham Hill, Monks Horton; and Highams, Goudhurst.

Higham Upshire (pronounced Hyam Up-shire). It has the same origin as HIGHAM and is found recorded as Heahhaam c765 → Hehham 774 → Hecham 1086 → Hygham 1511. The affix 'Upshire', meaning 'up, or higher, district' (OE *upp scīr*), appears as Upschire in 1240, Upshere in 1435.

Highborough Hill (Eastry). Though there are no records of this name, it is probably derived from OE *hēah burh*: 'high stronghold'.

High Brooms. The place, together with Broom Hill close by, is situated on high ground and appears as Brom-gebrug' 1270 → Bromelaregg 1318 → Brombridg 1560. The first element in this name is certainly OE *brōm:* broom; the second element may either be 'ridge' (OE *hrycg*) or 'bridge' (OE *brycg*).

Highfield Cottage. High open land (OE *hēah feld* → Heyfelde 1422).

Highgate. The name is self-explanatory, being recorded in 1507 as Highgate Crosse and in 1551 as Highgate.

High Halden (pronounced Hawlden). Heaðuweald's woodland pasture (OE *Heaðuwealding denn* → Hadinwold-ungdenne c.1100 → Hadewold-ineden' 1184 → Hathwoldenne 1253 → High Halden 1610). Halden Place, Rolvenden, shares the same original meaning, appearing as Hadwoldenn', Hathewolden' 1278 → Hathewald-enne 1292 → Haldene 1327 → Halden' 1347.

High Halstow. Holy place (OE *hālig stōw* → Halgesto c.1100 → Halgh-estowe 1270 → Halwestowe 1289 → High halsto 1610). Called 'High' to distinguish this place from Lower Halstow, which shares the same origin and is recorded as Halgastaw c.1100 → Halegestowe 1199 → Halgesto 1226 → Halstoe 1610.

Highlands (Mereworth). Self-explanatory (OE *hēah land* → Heyelond' 1270 → Heghelonde 1332). The same meaning is shared by Highlands, Sutton-at-Hone, and Highlands, Woodchurch.

High Reed. High cleared land (OE *hēah rīed* → Heghrede 1381).

High Snoad Wood (Challock). Recorded in 1535 as Highsnoth, the original meaning of this name seems to have been 'high piece of detached woodland' (OE *hēah snād*).

Highstead. High place (OE *hēah stede* → Hestede c.1250 → Hegh-sted 1314 → Hyghsted 1535). Highsted Forstal, Sittingbourne, shares the same meaning, and is recorded as Hecsted 1197 → Heghsted' 1254 → Heystede 1313.

Highsted Forstal. See under HIGH-STEAD.

High Tilt. Tilth, crop, harvest (OE *tilðe* → Tilthe 1236 → Tilðe 1278 → Tylthe 1292). Tilt's Farm, Boughton Monchelsea, has the same origin, appearing as Tilthe in 1278.

Hildenborough. Hill pasture (OE *hyll denn* → Hylden' 1240 → Hil-denne 1291 → Hildenborough 1389). This last form means 'borough, or manor, of Hilden'.

Hilders. It is described in 1399 as 'Helderes tenement in Chidding-stone', the original tenement, or house, taking the name of some former owner.

Hillborough. Holy mound or tum-ulus (OE *hālig beorg* → Halibergh', Haleberge 1270 → Halbergh 1359 → Helborough 1500 → Helburg *alias* Hillborough 1790). The name may be a reference to an ancient barrow dedicated to a heathen god.

Hills Court (Ash). Hills (OE *hyllas* → Hulles 1200 → Helles 1278).

Hinksden. Stallion pasture: wood-

land pasture where a stallion is kept
(OE *hengest denn* → Hengesdenn'
1334 → Hengsden, Henxden 1338
→ Hengstdenn' 1347).

Hinxhill. Hengest's hill (OE *Henge-
stes hyll* → Hengestesselle 864 →
Hangsel c.1140 → Hengesell', Henx-
hulle 1254 → Hengselle 1275 →
Henxhelle 1291).

Hoad Wood (Swingfield). Heath,
heather-covered land (OE *hǣð* →
Hothe 1327). Hoades Court, Sturry,
recorded as Hoad-Court in 1690,
shares the same original meaning;
as does Hode Farm, Patrixbourne,
which appears as La Hothe in 1276.

Hoaden. Heath hill: hill on heathland (OE *hǣð dūn* → Haddon' 1240
→ Hodoun 1282 → Hodone 1348).

Hoath (pronounced Hothe). Heath,
heather-covered land (OE *hǣð* →
Hothe 1278 → Hoath 1610). Hoath
Farm, Canterbury, has the same
origin and is recorded as Hothe in
1317; Hoath Wood, Ospringe, is
Hethe in 1380; and Hothe Court,
Blean, is Hothe in 1347.

Hoathly. Heath clearing: clearing
on heathland (OE *hǣð lēah* →
Hodlegh' 1240 → Hodeley 1278
→ Hothelygh 1551 → Hothligh
1618).

Hobbs Wood (Staplehurst). It derives
its name from the family of Richard
Hobbe (1327).

Hobday's Wood. The name is derived from that of the family of
Hobday who owned the manor at
nearby ANVIL GREEN for many
years.

Hoblingwell Wood (St. Paul's Cray).
The place is recorded in 1424 as
Powkelane *alias* Hobdodlane, both
names incorporating those of
demons: 'powk' is from OE *pūca*,
a goblin, while 'hobdod' appears to
be an early form of hobgoblin.
Thus the original lane here was believed to be haunted by mischievous
demons.

Hockenden. Hōc's woodland pasture (OE *Hōcing denn* → Hokindenne
1240 → Hokyngdenn' 1278 → Hok-
yndenn 1305). The personal name
is also found in connection with
HAWKENBURY.

Hockley. 'Hook clearing': clearing
near a hook, or spur of land (OE
hōc lēah → Hockele 1322).

Hodiford. Hoda's enclosure (OE
Hoding worð → Hoddeworth 1250
→ Hodingwrth' 1254 → Hodiford
1640 → Hoddiford 1664). Change
from -worth to -ford is not unusual
in place names.

Hodsoll Street. Hod's hollow (OE
Hodes hol → Hodeshole 1198 →
Hodesole 1271 → Hodsale 1442 →
Hudsoll 1512).

Hoggs Bridge. It derives its name
from the family of Thomas Hogge
of Headcorn (1383), the bridge
spanning a tributary of the Beult.

Hogshaw Wood (Milsted). Hog
copse: copse where hogs grub about
(OE *hogg scaga* → Hoggeschawe
1357 → Hogshawes 1493).

Holbeam. Hollow beam, or tree
(OE *hol bēam* → Holbeme 1240 →
Holbeam 1327). The same origin

is shared by Holborn Dane Shaw close by, recorded as Holbean-farm *alias* Holborne in 1778.

Holborn Dane Shaw. See under HOLBEAM.

Holborough. Hollow mound: mound in a dip or hollow (OE *hol beorg* → æt Holan beorge 838 → Holebergh' 1240 → Holeberghe 1292).

Holbrook. Hollow marsh: marshy ground in a depression or dip (OE *healor broc* → Hallerebrok' 1292 → Hallebroke 1332 → Halbrokland 1546). The place is on low-lying ground close to a stream.

Holden. Hollow pasture: woodland pasture in a hollow (OE *hol denn* → Holedene 1254 → Holedenne 1334).

Hole Park. Hollow, dip in the ground (OE *hol* → Hole 1278). Hole Cottage, Cowden, shares the same origin, being recorded as The Hole in 1603.

Hollanden, Great. Holly pasture: woodland pasture marked by a holly tree (OE *holegn denn* → Hollingdene 1270 → Holinden 1275 → Holyndenne 1353).

Hollands Hill (East Langdon). Hollow lane: lane running through a hollow (OE *hol lane* → Hollan' 1235 → Hollane 1292).

Hollicondane (pronounced Hollycondayne). It appears in 1799 as Hallicandane, but lack of any earlier forms makes definition of the place name impossible.

Hollingbourne. Stream of the *Hol-ingas*, or hollow-dwellers (OE *Holinga burne* → Holingeburna, Holinganburnan c.975 → Holingeborne 1086 → Holingeburne c.1100 → Holingbourne 1253 → Hollingborne 1610). The name refers to a tribe living close to the River Len.

Holloway Carvett. Holloway, way through a hollow (OE *hol weg* → Holewey 1348 → Holweye 1357). The affix 'Carvett' is probably derived from the name of a landowner in this area. There was another holloway at the now lost place of Holoway Court in Snodland, which appears as Holeweye c.1300, Holoway Court in 1782.

Holman's Wood (Sandhurst). It derives its name from the 16th century family of Holman who lived in neighbouring Newenden.

Holm Mill. Mill near a hollow (OE *hol myln* → Holemiln' 1254 → Holemelle 1327 → Holmelle 1332). Home Lake here shares the same original meaning.

Holmstone. Holly stone: stone close to a holly tree (ME *holm stone* → The Holmestone c.1460).

Holmwood. Holly wood (ME *holm wude* → Holmwode 1351).

Holt Street. Thicket (OE *holt* → Holstrete 1547 → Old Street *alias* Holt-street 1790). 'Holt', together with the surname atte Holte – 'dweller by the thicket' – also occurs in the names of Holt Farms, Elmstead; Holt Hill, Ditton; Holt's Farm, Sutton-at-Hone and Penshurst; and Holts Shaw, Meopham.

Holwood. Hollow wood: wood in or near a hollow (OE *hol wudu* → Holewoode Hill 1601).

Holywell. Holy spring (OE *hālig wielle* → Hailiwelle c.1250 → Halywelle 1343). Holywell Park, Ash, was originally the property of the prioress of the Benedictine nunnery of Halywell in London, from which the Park derives its name, being recorded as Haliwelle in 1327, Halywell in 1778.

Homefield Shaw. Settlement land: open land near a settlement (OE *hām feld* → Homfeld' 1352). Homefield Spring, Cudham, shares the same origin, appearing as West Homfeld in 1322.

Home Lake. See under HOLM MILL.

Homersham Farm (Smarden). Hūnmǣr's water meadow (OE *Hūnmǣres hamm* → Omeresham 1254 → Omereshamme 1270 → Homereshamme 1334 → Homersham 1450). The water meadow would have bordered on the Sherway stream here.

Home Street. Holly tree (OE *holegn* → ME *holm* → Holme 1332). Home Farm, Smeeth, has the same meaning, being found as Holme in 1313.

Honeychild. Honey spring (OE *hunig celde* → Hunichilda 1135 → Hunechilde 1189 → Honichild 1227). The name is probably a reference to the sweetness of the spring water.

Honeyden. Recorded in 1745 as Honeyden *alias* Hunisden, the place name is probably derived from OE *hunig den*: 'honey pasture', a woodland pasture where hives were kept.

Honey Farm. See under HONEY WOOD.

Honey Wood (Hackington). Honey wood: wood where bees nest (OE *hunig wudu* → Honywode 1328). Honeywood Plantation, Postling, shares the same origin and is recorded as Huniwude in 1240, Honywode in 1357. These were obviously woods where honey was collected from the nests of wild bees. Honey Farm, Pluckley, appears to be named after the stream which flows by it: it appears as Oneghe in 1292, the name being a reference to the sweet-tasting water of the stream.

Hoo (pronounced Who). Spur of land (OE *hōh* → Ho c.1250 → Hoo 1327). This is a promontory of land jutting out into the sea between the estuaries of the Thames to the north and the Medway to the south.

Hoo All Hallows. See under ALL HALLOWS.

Hoo St. Werburgh (pronounced Who St. Werborough). Spur of land (OE *hōh* → Hou 1086 → Sancta Wereburh de Hoo c.1100 → Hoo Scē Wereburge 1245). To distinguish it from HOO, the place has taken the name of its church, dedicated to St. Werburgh, a princess of Mercia who died c.700.

Hook, Great and **Little.** Hook, projection of land (OE *hōc* → Hoke 1254). This word, together with the family name atte Hoke — 'dweller by the hook' — is also found in connection with Hook Farm, Bromley; Hook Green, Wilmington, Southfleet and Meopham; and Hook Wood, Chatham.

Hook Green. See under HOOK.

Hope All Saints. Piece of enclosed marshland (OE *hōp* → Hope 1240 → Hope omīum Scor' 1254 → Alterhalghenehope 1270). This last form contains the Middle English words for 'all saints', from the church here which is dedicated to All Saints. *Hōp*, together with the surname atte Hope — 'dweller by the marsh enclosure' — also occurs in the names of Hope Cottage, High Halden; Hope Farm, Hawkinge; Hope House, Sandhurst; and Hoplands, Westbere.

Hoplands. See under HOPE ALL SAINTS.

Hopper Shaw. It derives its name from the family of William Hopper of Bethersden (1588). Hoppers, St. Mary's Hoo, is associated with the family of William Huberd' (1316). Hopper's Bank, Hever, derives its name from the 14th century family of Hoppere.

Hopper's Bank. See under HOPPER SHAW.

Horden. 'Horn pasture': woodland pasture on a horn of land (OE *horn denn* → Hordenn' 1278 → Horden' 1334 → Horndenne 1347). The place is situated close to a hill which must be the original 'horn' in the name.

Horish Wood (Boxley). Filthy ground washed by water (OE *horh (ge)wæsc* → Horewessh 1313 →

Horweshe 1535). The name is probably a reference to an open sewer.

Horlands. Filthy wood: wooded hill where the ground is dirty or filthy (OE *horh hyrst* → Horherst 1267 Horehurst 1445). There are no later forms to show when -hurst was altered to -lands.

Hornbrook, Great and **Little**. 'Horn marsh': marshy ground by a horn of land (OE *horn brōc* → Horinbrok c 1230 → Hornbroke 1327). The place is on a projection above lowlying ground.

Horne's Place. See under HORNS GREEN.

Horns Green. Horn, projection of land (OE *horn* → Horne 1292). Horne's Place, Appledore, has the same origin, appearing as Horne in 1276.

Horn Street. Corner of land (OE *hyrne* → Herne 1348). Probably so called because the place lies in a corner of Cheriton parish.

Horse Croft Hole. Described c.1500 as Horcrofte, the origin of this name appears to be 'filthy croft' (OE *horh croft*), referring to muddy ground here.

Horsham. Horse meadow: water meadow where horses graze (OE *hors hamm* → Horsham 1382 → Horsham Croft 1598).

Horsmonden (pronounced Hawzmun-dn). This was originally 'horse stream pasture': woodland pasture through which flows a stream where horses drink (OE *hors burne denn*),

101

the name being recorded as Horsbundenne c.1100, Horsburdenne in 1147. At the beginning of the 13th century the place became known as the 'horsemen's woodland pasture' (← OE *horsmanna denn*), the name appearing as Horsmindenn' 1232 → Horsmundenne, Horsmendene 1254 → Horsmondenn 1265. Presumably the horsemen, or horsekeepers, built a settlement by the small stream flowing here.

Horsted. Horse place: place where horses are kept (OE *hors stede* → Horstede c.675 → Horsted' 1240). Traditionally, the place takes its name from Horsa, the Jutish leader, since it is believed that he was buried here after his death at the Battle of Aylesford.

Horton. Filthy farmstead: farmstead where the ground is filthy or muddy (OE *horh tūn* → Horatun 874 → Hortone 1086 → Horton 1610).

Horton Kirby. The place name has the same origin as HORTON, the affix 'Kirby' coming from the name of Gilbertus de Kirkeby, lord of the Manór of Horton from 1253, whose family are believed to have originated from Kirkby in Lancashire. Horton Kirby is recorded as Hortune 1086 → Hortoñ 1198 → Horton Kirkeby 1379 → Horton Kerby 1610.

Hothe Court. See under HOATH.

Hothfield. Heather-covered open land (OE *hǣð feld* → Hathfelde c.1100 → Hedfield 1210 → Hathfeld 1270 → Hothfield 1610).

Hougham (pronounced Huffam).

Huhha's settlement (OE *Huhhan hām* → Hucham, Huham 1086 → Huhcham c.1100 → Hugham 1178 → Hougham 1271). The personal name is also found in connection with HOWFIELD.

Houndshurst. Hound's wood: wooded hill frequented by hounds or dogs (OE *hundes hyrst* → Hundeshirst 1251 → Hundesherst 1278 → Houndesherst 1480).

Housendane Wood (Charing). Hūsa's woodland pasture (OE *Hūsing denn* → Hussingdenn 836 → Houssyndenne 1327 → Housyndenn' 1348). Hūsa was also the owner of a stretch of water at HUSON.

How Bridge. Spur of land (OE *hōh* → Ho c.1245 → Hoo 1343 → Howe 1711). The bridge spans a tributary stream near Deal.

Howbury Lane. Little spur of land (OE *lytel hōh* → Hov 1086 → Littelho, Litleho 1226 → Littel Ho 1242 → Hobury 1379). 'Bury' is a late addition, meaning 'manor, borough'.

Howfield Farm (Chartham). Huhha's open land (OE *Huhhan feld* → Hughefeld c.1205 → Huggefeld 1284 → Hugefelde 1313). Huhha's settlement was at HOUGHAM. Howfield Place, Stone, is on the site of woodland called le Hoo in 1292, the name being derived from OE *hōh*: spur of land, with -field added at a later date.

How Green. It appears as Hokegrene in 1440, the name probably being derived from OE *hōc*: hook, hook-shaped land.

Howlets (Edenbridge). The name is probably to be associated with the family of John de Holegh' of Edenbridge (1304). Howletts, Luddenham, derives its name from the family of Robert Owlett (1522). Howlett's Farm, Chilham, is connected with William Hughelot (1327). Huggit's Farm, Stone-cum-Ebony, is similarly connected with Thomas and William Hughelot (1327).

Howt Green. Thicket (OE *holt* → Holt 1278 → Holte 1334).

Hubbard's Hill (Sevenoaks Weald). Side of a hill (OE *hugborde* → Hubord' 1200 → Hobord 1275 → Hobbordheth 1514). This last form refers to heathland in the vicinity.

Hucking. Hoca's people (OE *Hōcingas* → Hocking 1225 → Huckinges 1270 → Huking c.1290 → Huckyng 1610).

Huggin's Wood.(Hoo St. Werburgh). It derives its name from the family of John Huggin (1634).

Huggit's Farm. See under HOWLETS.

Hulberry. Hielte's stronghold (OE *Hieltes burh* → Holtysbury 1348 → Heltesbury 1371 → Hiltesbury 1475). The present name is a contraction of these forms.

Hulse Wood (Wilmington). The place is probably named after Richard Hulse, a landowner in the Dartford area during the latter part of the 18th century.

Hunstead Wood (Chartham). Hound place: place where hounds or dogs are kept (OE *hund stede* → Hounsted 1535).

Huntbourne. Hunta's stream (OE *Huntan burne* → Huntebourne 1347). The personal name is also found in connection with HUNTINGFIELD and HUNTON.

Hunters Forstal. It appears as Hunter Street in 1474 and as Hunter-street in 1479, the name probably being a manorial one. 'Forstal' is a dialect word used of land in front of farm buildings.

Huntingfield. Open land of Hunta's people (OE *Huntinga feld* → Huntyngefeld' 1278 → Huntingfeud 1285 → Huntyngfeld' 1327). Hunta owned a stream at HUNTBOURNE and a farmstead at HUNTON.

Hunton. Hunta's farmstead (OE *Hunting tūn* → Huntintune c.1100 → Huntingtun' 1226 → Hunton 1610). The ford here is described as Huntyngtonesford in 1313.

Hunt Street. It is associated with the family of Richard Hunt of West Farleigh (1632).

Hurst. Formerly known as Falconhurst, this was originally a wooded hill (OE *hyrst*) on land belonging to the 13th century family of Robert Falconarius, falconers to the King. The place is recorded as Herst in 1212, Fauconherst in 1278. OE *hyrst* is also the origin of the names of Hurst near Bexley; Hurst Farm, Chilham and Otterden; Hurst Wood, Charing and West Peckham; and Hursthill Farm, Hothfield.

Hurst, Long. See LONG HURST.

Hurstfield Farm (Marden). Herebeorht's open land (OE *Herebeorhtes feld* → Herdefeld' 1232 → Hereberdesfeld', Herdesfeld' 1292 → Herberisfelde 1347 → Herebertesfeld 1367 → Herysfelde 1538). Herebeorht owned a farmstead at the now lost place of Harbilton in Harrietsham.

Hursthill Farm. See under HURST.

Huson Farm (Tenterden). Hūsa's river (OE *Hūsan ēa* → Husneah 863 → Howseney 1538). The 'river' is a stream which flows close by. Hūsa also owned a woodland pasture at HOUSENDANE WOOD.

Hyde's Forest (Chevening). It derives its name from the family of Hyde who lived in neighbouring Sundridge during the 17th and 18th centuries.

Hythe. Landing-place (OE *hȳð* → on Hyðe 1052 → Hede 1086 → Heða 1176 → Heth 1228). West Hythe here is recorded as Westhithe in 1305.

I

Ibornden (pronounced Eye-born-dn) Yew stream pasture: woodland pasture bordering a stream by which yews grow (OE *īw burna denn* → Iburden' 1254 → Ibornedenn' 1292 → Iburnden 1427). The place is close to a stream.

Ickham (pronounced Ickum). Yoke settlement: settlement near a yoke of land (OE *geoc hām* → Iocc ham 785 → Geocham c.875 → Gecham 1086 → Iecham c.1100 → Icham 1233). A 'yoke' was a measurement of land equalling a quarter of a *sulung*, or between 50 and 60 acres.

Icknor. Recorded as Ictenore in 1300, the final element in this name is derived from OE *ōra:* bank or border. The first element is probably a personal name.

Ide Hill. Eadgyð's hill (OE *Ēadgȳðe hyll* → Edythehelle c.1250 → Ide hill 1610). Eadgyð was a Saxon woman.

Idenborough. The place is probably associated with the family of Henry and William Edyn (1327), 'borough' being a medieval manor.

Iden Green (pronounced Eye-den). Yew pasture: woodland pasture marked by a yew-tree (OE *īw denn* → Idunne 1194 → Ydenne c.1200 → Idenne 1293 → Iden 1473). Iden Manor, Staplehurst, shares the same original meaning, being recorded as Idenn' in 1258, Idenne in 1348.

Idleigh Court (Ash). Geda's clearing (OE *Gedan lēah* → Didele 1086 → Yedeleye 1226 → Yedeleghe 1338 → Idelegh' 1355).

Iffin Farm (Thanington). The youthful dwellers (OE *geoguðingas* → Yethyngge 1315 → Ithynge 1338 → Gytthyng, Ythgthyng 1349 → Yffyng 1465). OE *geoguð* had a meaning of youth, young people; junior warriors.

Ifield (pronounced Eye-field). Yew land: open land where yew-trees grow (OE *īw feld* → Yfeld 1174 → Ifeld 1235 → Ifield 1610).

Ightham (pronounced Eye-tum). Ehta's settlement (OE *Ēhtan hām* → Ehteham c.1100 → Eitham 1232 → Hightham 1254 → Heghtham, Eyteham 1278). Ightham Mote has the same origin as Ightham, with the addition of ME *mote:* a moat, or defensive ditch. Mote Farm nearby takes its name from the place.

Ileden. Gilda's people (OE *Gildingas* → Gilding 873 → Gildinge 1038 → Ildinges 1168 → Gilding, Illinges 1200 → Ildynge 1334 → Ileden 1610). Gilda's name is also found in connection with GILLING.

Impkins. Æmic's pool (OE *Æmicing mere* → Emecing mere 940). There are no forms later than this 10th century one to show how the present name evolved.

Inges Shaw. It takes its name from that of Isolda Ynge (1327), 'Shaw' being derived from OE *scaga:* a copse.

Ingleden. Igilwulf's woodland pasture (OE *Igilwulfing denn* → Igoluyndenne 1250 → Yguluyndeñe 1334 → Igolynden' 1434 → Igollynden 1545). The present place name is a contraction of these forms.

Ingress Abbey (Swanscombe). Formerly belonging to the Priory of Dartford, the abbey is recorded as Ingress in 1538. The name has the same meaning as Modern English ingress: entrance, and denotes a place where novices were trained.

Island Road. The place is described in 1502 as Fresshe Eyland, Salt Eyland, 'fresh' and 'salt' referring to the water surrounding the original island close to Chislet.

Isles Bridge. The place is recorded as Ilysbregge 1381 → Illysbridge 1437 → Ilesbregge 1509, and it has been suggested that the name may be connected with an *elesexincg* found in a charter written some time before 914. This word, from OE *eleseaxing,* means, literally, 'associated with an alien Saxon', *i.e.* not an Anglo-Saxon. Perhaps a late Saxon invader from the Continent held land near the stream here over which a bridge was later built.

Islingham Farm (Denton). Settlement of Esla's people (OE *Eslinga hām* → Æslingaham 764 → Eselingham 1107 → Hesslingeham 1210 → Eslyngham 1325). This tribe are also found at EASTLING.

Ittinge Farm (Elmstead) (pronounced Ittinje). Eade's people (OE *Eadingas* → Edinges 1240 → Edinge 1278 → Edynge 1346). Eade himself had a settlement at ADISHAM.

Ivychurch. Ivy-covered church (OE *īfig cirice* → Iuecirce c.1100 → Ivichurch, Ivechirch 1242 → Ivy Church 1610).

Ivy Hatch. Heavy hatch or gate (OE *hefig hæcc* → Heuyhatche 1325 → Ivy Hatch 1700 → Heavy Hatch 1714).

Iwade (pronounced Eye-wade). 'Yew wading place': ford, or wading place, where yews grow (OE *īw gewæd* → Ywada 1177 → Iwade 1235). Iwade lies on a stream which flows into the West Swale River.

J

Jack's Court (Lydd). Recorded as Jakys Court c.1460, and as Jakescourt in 1503, the place derives its name from the family of William Jakes (1348).

Jacob's Lane. It is associated with the family of Stephen Jacobe of Hoo St. Werburgh (1480).

Jarvis Downs Wood (Ospringe). The place is possibly connected with the family of John Gerueys (1327). Jarvis Farm, Woodchurch, takes its name from that of John Jervise of Woodchurch (1542).

Jeskins Court (Cobham). The name is derived from the family of John Josekyn of Cobham (1327).

Jesson Farm (St. Mary in the Marsh). Geffrey's farmstead (ME *Geffreyes tone* → Geffreyeston' 1254 → Jeston 1560 → Jeson 1565 → Gefferston Bridge, Lane 1790).

Jone Wood (Harrietsham). It is associated with the family of Thomas Jon of Harrietsham (1481).

Jordan's Wood (Paddlesworth). It takes its name from that of John

Jordan (1348). Joyden's Wood, Dartford, is connected with the family of William Jordayne of Dartford (1556).

Joyce Green. The place derives its name from the family of Richard Joce (1334).

Joyden's Wood. See under JORDAN'S WOOD.

Judd's Hill (Ospringe). Recorded as Judd House in 1690, the place is named after the builder of this house in 1652, Daniel Judde.

Judge Wood (Bidborough). Associated with the family of Galfridus Jud (1327), the wood is described as Juddes in 1445.

Jullieberrie Down. There are no forms to indicate the origin of this name, but it seems possible that the meaning was 'Cilla's mound, or tumulus' (OE *Cillan beorg*), since Cilla's settlement was close by at CHILHAM. Traditionally, the Down and Jullieberrie's Grave, a Neolithic long barrow half a mile south-east of Chilham, were named after one of Julius Cæsar's tribunes, Laberius,

107

who is supposed to have been buried in the barrow after a battle here between the Britons and Romans. The words *Jul. Laber.*, a Latin abbreviation of *Julii Laberius:* 'Julius's Laberius', are thus believed to have been the origin of Jullieberrie.

Jumping Downs. There are no forms of this place name, but in a charter of 799 there is mention of a *Humbing lond* in this area, derived from OE *humbing land:* humping, hillocky land. This is probably the original meaning of the name Jumping Downs.

K

Kearsney (pronounced Kurzney). Place where cress grows (OF *cressonniere* → Kersunere 1242 → Kersonere 1285 → La Kerseneye 1323). Kearsney Abbey lies beside the river at TEMPLE EWELL.

Kelsey Manor (Beckenham). The name appears to be a manorial one, taken from that of the owners of this manor during the 13th century.

Kelsham. Cylli's water meadow (OE *Cylles hamm* → Keleshamme 1244 → Kelesham 1343). The personal name may also be connected with KILLING WOOD.

Kemberland Wood (Sturry). Cynebeorht's land (OE *Cynebeorhtes land* → Kenebertelande c.1230 → Kenbersteslond 1334 → Kenebertelonde 1348). The present name is a contraction of these forms.

Kemnal Manor (Chislehurst). Cyma's hollow (OE *Cyman hol* → Kemeshol', Kemehal' 1240 → Kemenhole 1301 → Kymenhole 1387 → Kenmale 1480).

Kempe's Corner. It derives its name from the family of John Kempe (1334). Kemp's Hill, Lydd, is similarly associated with William Kempe of Lydd (1379). Kemphall Farm, Westbere, is connected with Walter and William Kempe (c.1250), the 'hall' perhaps being the original farm building.

Kemphall Farm. See under KEMPE'S CORNER.

Kemsing (pronounced Kemzin). (Place) associated with Cymesa (OE *Cymesing* → Cymesinc 822 → æt Cymesing 958 → Cimisinga c.1100 → Chemesing 1156 → Kemesing' 1224 → Kensing 1610).

Kemsley Street. Cyme's clearing (OE *Cymes leah* → Kemesle 1198 → Kemeslegh' 1254 → Kemeslee 1347). Kemsley, near Milton Regis, perhaps shares the same original meaning, but this cannot be certain since the name is first recorded in 1410, as Kempsele.

Kenardington. Cyneheard's farmstead (OE *Cynehearding tūn* → Kenardintone 1211 → Kynardinton 1242 → Kenardington 1610).

Kench Hill (Tenterden). Recorded in 1538 as Kentyshild, the origin of this name is either a slope (OE *hielde*) associated with the Middle English family name of Kent; or it is, literally, 'Kent's slope', since the place is not far from the county boundary with Sussex.

Kenfield Hall (Petham). King's open land (OE *cyninga feld* → Kenegefeld 1223 → Kenefeld 1286). The land was once part of a Saxon royal estate.

Kennaways. Recorded as Kenewys in 1347 and as Kenwayes in 1631, the place derives its name from the 13th century Ospringe family of Kenewy.

Kennelling Farm (Stalisfield). (Place) associated with Cyneweald (OE *Cynewealding* → Cyneuuold-incge 824 → Kenewolding 1270).

Kennington. Royal manor (OE *cyne tūn* → Chintun 1072 → Chenetone 1086 → Kenintuna 1157 → Kenington' 1254 → Kenington 1610).

Kensham Green. Hovel-dwellers' settlement (OE *casinga hām* → Casing-eham c.1180 → Cassinghā 1236 → Casingeham 1279). The present name is a contraction of these forms.

Kent. The county name is derived from the British word *cantus:* rim, or border, a word which was later applied to the whole of this south-eastern area to mean 'border land, coastal district'. Cæsar described it as Cantium in 51 BC, and it is later found as Cantia c.730, Cent in 835. The early inhabitants of the county were known as the *Cantwara*, or Kent people, whose capital was at CANTERBURY.

Kentlands. Recorded as Kent in 1348, the place was originally land belonging to the widespread medieval family of de Kent.

Kent Street. It is associated with the family of John de Kent (1334). Kent House, Beckenham, takes its name from Margaret de Kent of Beckenham (1286).

Kent Water, The. Described as Kent Water in 1610, this is a stream which forms part of the county boundary between Kent and Sussex. It has given its name to Kentwater Farm and Kentwater Mill, lying beside it. Kent Brook is another boundary stream separating the two counties.

Kenward. It derives its name from the family of Kenward who owned land in Yalding from the time of Henry VIII.

Keppel. Chapel (OF *capele* → Capele 1270 → Chapele 1278 → Capel 1327).

Keston (pronounced Kesstn). Cyssi's stone (OE *Cysses stān* → Cystaninga mearc 862 → Cysse stanes gemæro 973 → Chestan 1086 → Kestan 1205). The stone was used to mark the limit of Cyssi's land here, since the charter forms of 862 and 973 refer to 'Cyssi's stone's boundary' (OE *mearc, gemǣre:* boundary, border).

Kettle Corner. Described in 1374 as Ketylysstret, this was originally a street, or narrow road, belonging to a family named Ketyl. Kettle Farm nearby has also taken this family name. Kettleshill Farm, Seal, derives its name from that of the family of Robert Ketel (1313); and Kittles Corner, Stansted, contains the same surname.

Kettleshill Farm. See under KETTLE CORNER.

Kevington. Recorded in 1610 as Keuington, and in 1690 as Kevington, the original name of this place may have been OE *cȳfing tūn*: tub's farmstead', the word tub being used in a topographical sense with reference to the mound on which Kevington stands.

Keycol. See under KEY STREET.

Key Street. Quay or wharf (ME *keye*) on Watling Street: the place is recorded as Kaystrete in 1254, Keystrete in 1313. Keycol, which also lies on WATLING STREET, is described in 1598 as Kee Coll Croft, 'Kee Coll' meaning the 'hill near the quay' and being a reference to Keycol Hill here. The old Kentish dialect word 'key' found in these place names refers to wharves which were once sited on the small streams to the north of Keycol and Key Street.

Kidbrook. Kite marsh: marshy ground frequented by kites (OE *cȳta brōc* → Chitebroc c.1100 → Ketebroc 1202 → Ketebrock' 1278).

Killick's Bank. It is associated with the 14th century family of Kedelak or Kedelac.

Killing Wood.(Hawkinge). The place appears as Kellingesdene in 1263 and as Killingdane in 1323, the name perhaps having the original meaning of 'valley of Cylli's people' (OE *Cyllinga dene*). The personal name, Cylli, is found in connection with KELSHAM.

Kilndown. Kiln hill: a hill on which there is a kiln (OE *cylene dūn* → Kelnedoune 1391).

King Farm (Woodchurch). The farm appears to be associated with the now lost place of Kennetune in Woodchurch. This is recorded as Kynton' 1327 → Kyntone 1346 → Kennetune c.1415, and had the original meaning of 'royal manor' (OE *cyne tūn*).

Kingsborough. King's mound or barrow (OE *cyninges beorg* → Kyngesbergh' 1334 → Kyngesborroughe 1546). A burial mound here appears to have been associated with an early king.

Kingsden Farm (Egerton). King's woodland pasture (OE *cyninges denn* → Kingesden' 1237). This would once have been part of a royal estate.

Kingsdown, West. King's hill (OE *cyninges dūn* → Kingesdun 1170 → Kingesdon 1217 → Kingesdowne 1610). Probably called 'west' to distinguish the Down here from that at EASTDOWN nearby. The same meaning of 'king's hill', or hill on a royal estate, is found in Kingsdown near Deal, which appears as Kyngesdoune in 1318; and in Kingsdown on the Isle of Sheppey, which is Cyninges dune in 850, Kingesdune in 1182.

Kingsfield. The place is recorded as Kingesland in 1209, Kyngesmersh in 1299, and as Kyngesfeld in 1324. This was obviously once part of a royal estate containing marshland (OE *mersc*) and open land (OE *feld*).

Kingsford Street. King's open land: land belonging to a royal estate (OE *cyninges feld* → Kyngesfeld 1278 → Kyngesforde 1348). The name ending may have changed from -field to -ford because of the place's proximity to the East Stour.

Kingsgate. So called because it was at a 'gate', or cliff-gap here that Charles II came ashore on 30th June 1683. The place was originally known as King's Gate.

Kingsland. 'King's folk land': royal land held by freemen (OE *cyninges folc land* → cyninges folcland 858 → Kyngeslond 1327).

Kingsnoad. King's detached land: detached land belonging to a royal estate (OE *cyninges snād* → Kyngesnode 1256). Kingsnorth Wood here shares the same original meaning, but the name has developed in a different form and is recorded as Kyngessnothe c.1230, Kyngsnoth in 1535. Kingsnorth, south of Ashford, also has the same meaning as Kingsnoad, appearing as Kingesnade 1226 → Kyngesnode, Kingessnode 1254 → Kynsnoth 1610.

Kingsnorth. See under KINGS-NOAD.

Kingston. King's manor (OE *cyninges tūn* → Cincgestune 1016 → Kingeston' 1172 → Kingston 1610).

King's Wood (Broomfield). Recorded as Cyninges firhðe in a charter of 850, and described as 'woods called le Kingeswode and le Frithe' in 1468, this was originally a 'king's woodland' (OE *cyninges fyrhðe*). King's Wood, Wye, the name of which is self-explanatory, appears as Kingeswode in 1155 (← OE *cyninges wudu*).

Kippen, Kippington. See under KIPPINGS CROSS.

Kippings Cross. The place derives its name from the family of William and Thomas Kypping of Brenchley (1510). Kippen, near Frinsted, is similarly associated with the family of Elya Kypping' (1332); and Kippington, near Sevenoaks, with the family of William Kyppe of Sevenoaks (1313) – the place was originally a farmstead (ME *tone*) belonging to them and is recorded as Kyppingtone in 1408.

Kits Bridge. Kite bridge: bridge frequented by kites (OE *cȳta brycg* → Kettebregge 1250 → Kytbregge c.1425). Kits Bridge lies close to the Royal Military Canal.

Kit's Coty House. Recorded as Kyts cothouse in 1610, the name is derived from B *ked coed*: 'tomb wood', or tomb in a wood. This famous Megalithic burial chamber was once covered by a long barrow, described in the 18th century as being 200 feet in length. Since then the soil has been eroded, exposing the three upright stones and huge capstone.

112

Kittington Farm (Nonington). Cottage homefarm: homefarm where there are cottages (OE *cȳte hāmtūn* → Kethampton' 1226 → Kethamtone 1304 → Ketyntone 1334 → Ketynton 1450).

Kittles Corner. See under KETTLE CORNER.

Knell Farm (Ash). Elm-trees (OE *elmas* → Ulmis 1210 → Elmes 1240 → Nelmys 1454).

Knight's Place (Cobham). Recorded as Knyghtes Place in 1487, and as Knight's Place Fm in 1698, the place is so called from the fact that it was once the property of the Knights Templars. Knights Place, Pembury, takes its name from the family of Knyght who lived in Pembury during the 14th and 15th centuries.

Knock Farm (Stoke-cum-Ebony). Hillock (OE *cnocc* → Cnocke 1194 Knokke 1253).

Knockhall. At the oak thicket (OE *æt þǣm āc holte* → ME *atten oc holt* → Nockholte 1332 → Nockhole 1442). The present form of this place name has resulted from the final *n* of *atten* – 'at the' – being attached to the following word.

Knockholt (pronounced Nockhole-t). At the oak thicket (OE *æt þǣm āc holte* → Ocholt 1197 → Okholte 1270 → Nocholt 1353 → Nokholt wood 1397). Ralph Scot possessed the Manor of Knockholt during the reign of Henry III and gave his name to the place for a time: it appears as Scottes Ocolt in 1322 and as Scottesokholte in 1324.

Knockmill. Hillock (OE *cnocc* → La Knocke 1313). At some time a mill was working here, giving the place name its present form.

Knole (pronounced Nole). Knoll, hillock (OE *cnoll* → Cnolle 1327 → Knolle 1381).

Knowel Hill. See under KNOWLE, THE.

Knowle, The. Knoll, hillock (OE *cnoll* → Cnolle 1226 → Knolle 1327). This word, together with the family name atte Cnolle – 'dweller by the knoll' – also occurs in Knowle Farm, Sturry; Knowle Hill, Ulcombe; Knowle Wood, Barham; Knowles Bank, Tonbridge; and Knowel Hill, Herne.

Knowlton (pronounced Nole-ton). Knoll farmstead: farmstead near, or on, a knoll (OE *cnoll tūn* → Chenoltone 1086 → Cnoltune c.1100 → Cnolton 1226 → Knoltone 1253 → Knowlton 1610).

Knox Bridge. Hillock (OE *cnocc* → Knok' 1278 → Knocke 1346). The family name of atte Knocke – 'dweller by the hillock' – recorded here in the 14th century, accounts for the form 'Knockes bridge', which has produced the present place name. Knox Bridge is on a tributary of the Beult.

L

Lackenden Wood (Ickham). Luca's valley or dale (OE *Lucing dæl* → Lukindale c.1210 → Luckedale 1267 → Lokendale 1431 → Lokyndenne 1441). Luca also owned a farmstead at the now lost place of Luketone, recorded in 1355 near Goudhurst.

Lacton Green. Kitchen garden (OE *lēactūn* → Leketun 1266 → Leketone 1307 → Lecton 1528). Lacton Hall here derives its name from the place. Leacon Farm, Westwell, shares the same original meaning, being recorded as Lecton' in 1254. Leighton Manor, Cowden, is found as Lecton' in 1260, Leighton in 1591.

Laddingford. This was originally the site of a ford (OE *ford*) crossing the River Teise, which seems to have been known in early times as the Lodena, or Lodna, a name derived from a British river-name *Lutnā*: 'the muddy one'. Laddingford was once therefore the 'ford across Lodena', and is recorded as Lodeneford 1201 → Lodene fford 1289 → Lodneford 1346 → Lodingford 1782.

Ladd's Cottages, Ladds Court Lade's Ashes. See under LADWOOD.

Lade Wood (Lenham). The name is derived from OE *lād*: way or path, probably referring to a sheep track: it is described in the 13th century as Sheplade.

Ladwood. Recorded as Ladwude in 1240 and as Ladewode in 1332, this was once woodland owned by the family of Lad or Ladde who were resident in the Acrise area during the 13th and 14th centuries. The same surname is also found in connection with Ladd's Cottages, Dartford; Ladds Court, Chart Sutton; Lade's Ashes, Boughton-under-Blean; and Lad's Farm, Snodland.

Ladydown Farm (Preston). Lady's hill: hill on land owned by a lady (OE *hlǣfdige dūn* → Leuedy Doune 1335 → Ladydoune 1356).

Lake Farm (Sutton Valence). Watercourse (OE *lacu* → Lake 1327). The name must refer to a tributary of the Beult nearby.

Lamberden. Recorded in 1278 as Laum'den, the origin of this place name may possibly be 'loamy woodland pasture' (OE *lām denn*). Lamberden Wood, Bethersden, may also share this original meaning but there are no forms for the name. Close to Lamberden is Lomas, which appears to be associated with the family of Lomas, found in the Newenden parish register in 1661: the origin of the family name was atte Lomere – 'dweller by the pool in loamy ground (OE *lām mere*) – of which Lomas is the genitival form.

Lamberhurst. Lambs' wooded hill: wooded hill where lambs feed (OE *lambra hyrst* → Lamburherste c.1100 → Lamberhurst 1226). In 1270 the place is referred to as Lamburneherst, a form which contains OE *burna*: stream – the stream at Lamberhurst is recorded as le Burne in 1428. Lamberhurst Cottages, Shoreham, share the same original meaning, the name appearing as Lamberherst in 1332.

Lambert's Land. Found as Lamberteslond' in 1313 and as Lamberts land in 1535, this was originally land belonging to a man described as 'Adam Lambert le fflemmeng' in in 1259.

Lamb's Cross. The place derives its name from the family of William Lambe of Chart Sutton (1470) and is recorded as Lambes in 1670.

Lamorbey (pronounced Lammerbie). Originally associated with the family of Thomas Lamendby (1513), the place is recorded as Lamienby in 1778.

Lancup Well. This is a lake to the north of PENSHURST Place, the name appearing as Lannepewelle in 1465 and as Lancup-well in 1778. The second element is derived from OE *wielle*: spring; the forms are too late for the first element to be explained with any certainty.

Langdon, East and West. At the long hill (OE *æt pǣm langan dūne* → Langandune 861 → Langedone 1201 → Estlangedoun, Westlangedone 1291→E.Langdon, W.Langdon 1610). Langdon Abbey near Dover shares the same original meaning, as does Langdon Court, Faversham, recorded as Langedon' in 1240, Langedoune in 1332. Langdown House, Eythorne, preserves the name of a now lost South Langdon.

Langdown House. See under LANGDON.

Langhampark Lodge (Bishopsbourne). Long water meadow (OE *lang hamm* → Langeham 1313 → Langhamme 1334).

Langley. At the long clearing (OE *æt pǣm langan lēage* → Longanleag 814 → Langvelei 1086 → Langeleg' 1226 → Langele 1242 → Langley 1610). Langley Court, Beckenham, stands on the site of another 'long clearing', the place being recorded as langan leage 862 → Langele 1278 → Langelee 1292.

Langton Green. There are no records of the name, but it may possibly be derived from OE *lang tūn*: long farmstead. Nearby there was a 'short farmstead' at COURTENWELL.

Larkfield. Open land where larks nest (OE *lāwerce feld* → Lavrochesfel 1086 → Lauercefeld c.1100 → Lauerkefeld 1175 → Lau'kefeld 1240 → Larkfield 1610).

Lashenden. Læcca's woodland pasture (OE *Læccing denn* → Lachindenn' 1240 → Lechinden' 1270 → Lecchynden' 1338).

Lavington Farm (Wye). Lāfa's woodland pasture (OE *Lāfing denn* → Lauyndenn', Lavyndenne c.1225).

Layham's Farm (West Wickham). Fallow water meadow (OE *lǣge hamm* → Leyham 1289).

Layne. See under ROLVENDEN LAYNE.

Leacon Farm. See under LACTON GREEN.

Leaveland. Lēofa's land (OE *Lēofan land* → Levelant 1086 → Liofeland, Liveland c.1100 → Leveland c.1180). Lēofa owned a farmstead at LUTON.

Lee. Clearing (OE *lēah* → Lee 1086 → Leahei c.1100 → Lee, Legh' 1278). The same original meaning is found in the names of Lee Green, Cliffe; Lee Priory and Farm, Ickham; and Lea Farm, Lenham.

Leeds. The place takes its name from the stream here, which in early times was known as the *Hlȳde*: the loud, or noisy one. The original settlement was called *Hlȳdes* – 'belonging to the noisy one' – and is recorded as Esledes 1086 → Hlyda, Hledes c.1100 → Ledes 1194 → Lhedes 1235 → Leeds 1610).

Lees Court (Sheldwich). Lea, meadow (OE *lǣs* → Lese 1327 → Lees Court 1690).

Leesden. This place name is composed of two Old English words, *lǣs*: meadow, and *denn*: woodland pasture, and is recorded as Leseden' in 1338. Probably the reference is to pasture lying above meadowland.

Leesons. Leowsa's valley (OE *Leow-san dene* → Leowsan dene 987 → Lyston 1346).

Leg Lane. It derives its name from the family of John Leg' of Birling (1368). The same surname is found in connection with Legg Farm, Kenardington; Legg's Lane, Speldhurst; and Leggs Wood, Frittenden.

Leigh (pronounced Lye). Clearing (OE *lēah* → Lega c.1100 → Leghe 1239). The same meaning is shared by Leigh Green, Tenterden, and North Leigh, Elmstead, which is rather oddly recorded as Sutleghe (South Leigh) in 1242.

Leighton Manor. See under LACTON GREEN.

Len, River. The name is a back-formation from LENHAM. An early name for the river appears to have been derived from OE *wōh pring*: 'crooked press', referring to the Len's winding, compressed course. This name is the origin of OTTRIDGE.

Lenacre (pronounced Lennaker). Flax land: cultivated piece of land on which flax is grown (OE *līn æcer* → Linacher 1200 → Lynacre 1242 → Linacre 1254). Len-

116

acre Hall, Boughton Aluph, has a common origin, appearing as Lynacr' in 1327, Linacre-hall in 1790.

Lenham (pronounced Lennam). Lēana's settlement (OE *Lēanan hām* → Leanaham 858 → Lænham 961 → Lenham 1087).

Lessness Heath. Meadow headland: headland with a lea or meadow on it (OE *lǣs nǣss* → Lesneis 1086 → Lesnes 1197). This was the meeting-place of the Lesnes Hundred.

Lested Cottage. Clearing place: place where there is a clearing (OE *lēah stede* → Leystede 1258 → Lestede 1327).

Lett's Green. It is associated with the family of Galfridus Lete (1332).

Lewisham (pronounced Lewishum). Lēof's settlement (OE *Lēofes hām* → Lievesham 918 → Leofsnhæma 987 → Levesham 1086 → Leuesham 1211 → Lewsham 1610). The personal name is also found in connection with LEWIS HEATH.

Lewis Heath. Lēof's heathland (OE *Lēofes hǣð* → Lewesheth' 1240 → Leueshothe 1327 → Leuweshothe 1348). Lēof's settlement was at LEWISHAM.

Lewsome Farm (Lenham). Lēofric's farmstead (OE *Lēofrices tūn* → Lieurechestune 1176 → Liefrichestun' c.1225 → Leuereston' 1261 → Leu'estone 1332).

Lewson Street. Lady's stone (OE *hlǣfdige stān* → Leuedeyston' 1292 → Lewdistonstreet 1475 → Lewsham 1690). The stone probably marked the boundary of land belonging to a Saxon woman here.

Leybourne. Lilla's stream (OE *Lillan burne* → Lillanburnan c.975 → Lelebvrne 1086 → Leeburn' 1194 → Leiburne 1226 → Layborn 1610). Lilla was the owner of a church at LILLECHURCH.

Leysdown. Clearing's hill: hill associated with a clearing (OE *lēages dūn* → Legesdun c.1100 → Leesdon' 1175 → Leysdon 1247).

Libbetwell. It is recorded as Lubickwell in 1598 and as Lubeck-well in 1782. The second element in this place name is derived from OE *wielle*: spring, but the forms are too late for the first element to be interpreted.

Lidsing (pronounced Lidsin). The loud, or noisy people (OE *hlīodesingas* → Lidisinga c.1100 → Lidesinges 1251 → Lidesinge 1296 → Lydsing 1610). This is a tribal nickname.

Lillechurch. Lilla's church (OE *Lillan cirice* → Lilecirce c.1100 → Lillecherche 1186 → Lillechurche 1226). Lilla was also the owner of a stream, at LEYBOURNE.

Lillesden (pronounced Lillesdn). Lil's woodland pasture (OE *Liles denn* → Lellesdenn' 1240 → Lellesdenne 1327 → Lellisden', Lilisden' 1338). Lil's farmstead was at LINTON.

Lilley Farm (Capel). Lime-tree clearing: clearing marked by a lime (OE *lind lēah* → Lindlehe 1240 → Linleghe 1327 → Lyndlegh' 1348).

117

Lily Hoo in Yalding derives its name from the Yalding family of John de Lilleye (1364), whose forbears originated from Lilley. The affix 'Hoo' is from OE *hōh*: spur of land.

Lily Hoo. See under LILLEY FARM.

Limekiln Wood (Otterden). The name is self-explanatory, being recorded as Lymekyll-wood in 1724.

Limepits Cross. Loam pit: pit or hollow where the ground is loamy (OE *lām pytt* → Lombpette⁻1334 → Lompette 1369).

Lindridge (Lamberhurst). Lime-tree ridge (OE *lind hrycg* → Linderegge 1232 → Lindrigge 1254). Lindridge near Staplehurst shares the same origin, being recorded as Linderigg' in 1226, Lindrege in 1278.

Linkhill. The name appears as Lincheden' in 1254 and is derived from OE *hlinc denn*: 'rise pasture', or woodland pasture on rising ground.

Linton. Lil's farmstead (OE *Liling tūn* → Lilintuna c.1100 → Lillington' 1226 → Lintone 1327 → Lynton, Lylyngton 1535). Lil owned a woodland pasture at LILLESDEN.

Lipwell. 'Leap spring': spring where animals leap, or copulate (OE *hlīep wielle* → Leapwelle 1291).

Littlebourne. Little stream (OE *lytel burna* → Littelborne 696 → Liteburne 1086 → Litleburne 1197 → Littleborne 1610). This is probably an early name for the Little Stour, on which the place lies.

Little Boutshole Shaw. It derives its name from the family of le Bolte (1270) and was originally known as Bolte's hole, or hollow. The affix 'Shaw' is from OE *scaga*: a copse.

Littlebrook Farm (Stone). At the little marshy land (OE *æt þæm lytlan brōce* → Lytlanbroce 995 → Litlebroc 1203 → Littlebroc 1210).

Little Buckland. See under BUCKLAND.

Little London (Lydden). Recorded as Londun in 1270, it may have been given the name of the country's largest city as a joke to emphasise the place's insignificance: there are many Little Londons to be found in England. However, the origin of this name may equally well have been 'long hill' (OE *lang dūn*) or 'long valley' (OE *lang denu*). Little London, Waltham, certainly has this latter meaning and is recorded as Langedene 1254 → Langedane 1316 → Longedane 1332.

Littlepett. See under PETT.

Littlestone-on-Sea. See under GREATSTONE-ON-SEA.

Liverton Street. Lēoflǣd's farmstead (OE *Lēoflǣde tūn* → Liffletune 1220 → Liffleton', Leffletun c.1230 → Lifletun' 1239). Lēoflǣd was a Saxon woman.

Loddenden. Ludel's woodland pasture (OE *Ludeling denn* → Lodelyngdenn' 1292 → Ludelyndenn' 1313 → Lodelinden' 1348). Ludel's farmstead was at LODDINGTON.

Loddington Farm (Linton). Ludel's

farmstead (OE *Ludeling tūn* → Lode-lyngtone 1332 → Lodlynton' 1338 → Lodyngton 1407). Ludel owned a woodland pasture at LODDEN-DEN.

Lodgeland. It is recorded in 1790 as Cobbes-place *alias* the Lodge-land, and was originally known as Cobbes Place, a name derived from the family of John Cobbe of New-church (1313).

Lodgelees Farm (Denton). Descr-ibed in 1658 as Lodge Lease-House, the name probably refers to a lodge built on a meadow (OE *lǣs*).

Lomas. See under LAMBERDEN.

Lomer Farm (Meopham). It is as-sociated with Richard le Lom'e of Meopham (1258) and his descen-dant, Nicholas Lomer of Meopham (1349).

Longage Farm (Lyminge). Long hedge (OE *lang hecg* → Longehegge 1322).

Longbeech Wood (Westwell). Long beech-tree (OE *lang bēce* → Lange-beck 1226 → Langebech' 1261 → Longbeche 1535 → Longbeach 1690).

Longbridge Bridge. This was the meeting-place of the Longbridge Hundred which is recorded as Lange-brige 1086 → Langebrug' 1226 → Langebregge 1253 (← OE *lang brycg*: long bridge).

Longbrooks. Long marshy ground (OE *lang brōc* → Longebrok' 1313 → Longebroke 1332).

Longfield. Long open land (OE *lang feld* → Langafelda 964 → Langa-fel 1086 → Langefelde 1253 → Longfeild 1610).

Longford. Self-explanatory (OE *lang ford* → Longford 1425). The place is close to the River Darent.

Longhoes Wood (Cuxton). Long spur of land (OE *lang hōh* → Longhoo 1392).

Long Hurst. Recorded as Longhurst in 1780, the name is derived from OE *lang hyrst*: long wooded hill. Lonkhurst's Farm here takes its name from the family of Lonk-hurst who lived in the area in the early 19th century.

Longlands, Lower (Tilmanstone). This is a wood which is described in 1513 as le longfryth: the long wood-land (OE *lang fryhðe*).

Longport Farm (Newington). Long town (OE *lang port* → Langeport 1292). Port is probably used here in its alternative Middle English sense of 'market place'.

Longreach. Long strip of land (OE *lang rǣc* → Longereche c.1250).

Longridge. At the long ridge (OE *æt þǣm langan hrycge* → langan hrycg 788 → Langerigg' 1254).

Longrope Wood (Orlestone). This name contains OE *rāp*: rope or cord, a word which was used with refer-ence to a measurement of land. There are no records for the name, but a field called Mydelrape is found in this area in 1292. Roper Lane, Hoo St. Werburgh, has the original meaning of 'rope land': land measuring a rope's length, and is recorded as Roplande in 1278, Ropelonde in 1334 (← OE *rāp land*).

Long's Corner. The place derives its name from the family of Richard Long of Bethersden (1607).

Longsole. See under HERMITAGE.

Lonkhurst's Farm. See under LONGHURST.

Loose (pronounced Looz). Pigsty (OE *hlōse* → Hlose c.1100 → Lose 1204 → Loose 1610). The village appears to be on the site of an early pig farm.

Lords. It is associated with the family of Lorde who owned the manor here until the reign of Richard II, and who probably originated from · nearby LORENDEN. Lord's Wood, Stone, is named after William Lord (c.1400), a local landowner.

Lorenden. Woodland pasture of Lord's people (OE *Lordinga denn* → Lurdinga dene 993 → Lurdingeden' 1227 → Lourdynggedene). The present name is a contraction of these forms. This tribe also owned another woodland pasture, at the now lost place of Lorringden in Challock.

Lossenham. Hlossa's settlement (OE *Hlossan hām* → Hlossanham 724 → Lossenham 1205).

Loudon Wood (Ashford). Recorded as Lowden in 1617 and as Louden in 1693, this was probably a low

denn, or woodland pasture: the name also appears as louden field in 1619.

Lovehurst Manor (Staplehurst). 'Remnant wood': what is left of a wooded hill (OE *lāf hyrst* → Lofherst c.1210 → Lofhurst 1219 → Lofeherst 1535). The name probably refers to a wood on the outskirts of the forest which once covered this area.

Lovelace. It is recorded as Lovelace Place in 1561, deriving its name from the family of John Lovelace (1367).

Love Street. The name appears as Lovys street in 1508 and as Love street in 1526, the place taking its name from that of John Loue, or Love (1327). The same surname is found in connection with Lovestreet Farm, Reculver.

Lowden. Lufa's valley (OE *Lufan dene* → Louedane 1380 → Lovedane, Louedane 1399 → Lowden *alias* Lovedane 1620). The personal name is also found in connection with LUCKETT FARM.

Loyterton. Hlōðhere's farmstead (OE *Hlōðhering tūn* → Luteryngton' 1324 → Lutryngton' 1327 → Loteryngton' 1356).

Luckett Farm (Preston). Lufa's cot or cottage (OE *Lufan cot* → Luuekote, Luuecote c.1225). Lufa's valley was at LOWDEN. Luckett's Farm, Blean, appears to be named after a Mrs. Leggett of Blean who left a yearly charity gift to the parish in 1820.

Luckhurst. There are no records for this name, but it is possibly derived from OE *Lucan hyrst*: Luca's wooded hill, which would have developed to a medieval Lukehurst form.

Luddenham (pronounced Luddnum). Luda's settlement (OE *Ludan hām* → Dodeham 1086 → Ludeham 1211 → Lodenham 1242 → Ludenham 1610). The personal name is also found in connection with LUDWELLS.

Luddesdown. Hlūd's hill (OE *Hlūdes dūn* → Hludesduna, Hludes dune c.975 → Ledesdune 1086 → Hludesdune c.1100 → Ludesdon 1186 → Luddesdowne 1610). Hlūd was also the owner of a mound or barrow (OE *beorg*) nearby, since a *Hludes beorh* is recorded in the area in a charter of 939.

Ludgate. Swing-gate (OE *hlidgeat* → Lydegate 1338).

Ludwells. Luda's hill (OE *Ludan hlǣw* → Lodelawe 1313). The present name has developed from this 14th century form. Luda's settlement was at LUDDENHAM.

Lullingstone. Lulling's farmstead (OE *Lullinges tūn* → Lolingestone 1086 → Lullingestuna c.1100 → Lullingeston 1208). As early as Domesday (1086) Lullingstone was divided into two separate estates, both having the same origin but being distinguished by different name endings – the one in 'ton', the other in 'stone': they are recorded as Lullyngeston' and Lullyngestan' in 1278, and as Lullyngeston' and Lullyngestane in 1380.

Lunsford. Lull's enclosure (OE *Lulles worð* → Lullesworthe 1278). Change from -worth to -ford in place names is quite common.

Lusted. Enclosure, closed place (OE *loca stede* → Luckestethel 1317 → Lostede 1348 → Luxsted 1778).

Luton. Lēofa's farmstead (OE *Lēofan tūn* → Leueton' 1240 → Lyeueton' 1313 → Luton c.1600). Lēofa was also the owner of land at LEAVELAND.

Lydd (pronounced Lid). At the slopes (OE *æt þāra hliðum* → ad Hlidum 774 → Hlide c.1100 → Lide 1226 → Lyde, Lide 1253 → Lhide 1313 → Lydde 1610). The town has developed on a slope.

Lydden (near Dover). 'Shelter valley': valley which is sheltered (OE *hlāo denu* → Hleodæna c.1100 → Ledene 1205 → Lyedene 1304 → Lydden 1610). The village lies in a valley surrounded by hills. The same original meaning is found in the names of Lydden on Thanet (Ledene 1205, Lyden 1278), and Lydden Valley near Deal (Lydene 1278).

Lyddendane Farm (Hastingleigh). Lēofwynn's valley (OE *Lēofwynne dene* → Lyuynden' 1292 → Lyuenedane 1327). Lēofwynn was a Saxon woman.

Lymbridge Green. (Place) associated with Lēofmǣr (OE *Lēofmǣring* → Lemering' 1254 → Limering 1257 → Lymeryng' 1328). The present place name appears to be a corruption of these forms.

Lyminge (pronounced Limminje). District around the Limen (OE *Limen gē* → Liminge 697 → Leminges 1086 → Lymynge 1610). The Limen was the Saxon name for the Eastern Rother.

Lympne, River (pronounced Limm). This is the old name for the Eastern Rother, derived from the Saxon name for the river, Limen. This in turn was derived from a British word, *lem*: elm-tree, and the river is recorded as Liminel c.1180 → Lymmene, Lymene 1279 → Lymme 1474.

Lympne (pronounced Limm). The place derives its name from that of the LYMPNE river and was known to the Romans as *Portus Lemanis*, being one of the forts of the 'Saxon Shore' built towards the end of the third century AD. The Roman fort stood on the now-vanished arm of the Eastern Rother, which entered the sea at HYTHE. Lympne is recorded as Lemannis c.425 → of Liminum 805 → Limene 1291 → Lymen 1396 → Limne 1475 → Lymne 1480.

Lynch, The. Rising ground (OE *hlinc* → Lynch' 1292 → Lynche 1332).

Lyndhurst. Lime-tree wooded hill (OE *lind hyrst* → lind hyrste 973 → Lindhirst 1254).

Lynsore (pronounced Linsore). 'Rise's bank': bank or border of rising ground (OE *hlinces ōra* → Linchesora 845 → Lynchesore 1292). Lynsore Bottom and Court lie at the foot of steeply rising ground.

Lynsted (pronounced Linsted). Lime-tree place: place marked by a lime (OE *lind stede* → Lindestede 1212 → Lyndestede 1253 → Linstede 1262 → Lynsted 1610).

Lypcatt Wood (Whitstable). It derives its name from the family of Lipyeatt who owned land in Whitstable during the 18th century.

Lywood House (Boughton Monchelsèa). Woodland clearing (OE *lēah wudu* → Lewode 1425).

M

Mace Wood (High Halden). It was originally known as May's, deriving its name from the family of Reginald May of High Halden (1609). Mace Farm, Cudham, is recorded as Maze Farm in 1778, taking its name from that of Henry de Mars of Cudham (1339).

Macklands. Maca's land (OE *Macan land* → Makeland' 1201 → Mekelande 1275 → Makelonde 1327). Maca, whose name is also found in connection with MACKNADE and MAXTON, was owner of a stretch of marshy ground (OE *brōc*) at the now lost place of Makinbrooke in Herne.

Macknade. Maca's head (-shaped hill) (OE *Macan hēafod* → Macheheue, Machehevet 1086 → Macheuet c.1100 → Makenhauede 1315). Maca also owned property at MACKLANDS and MAXTON.

Madams Court (Frinsted). Described as Meriams-Court *alias* Madams-Court in 1782, the place derives its name from the family of Radolphus de Meyham (1254).

Madginford. Mæghild's enclosure (OE *Mæghilde worð* → Megeldeuurthe 832 → Magelworth' 1278 → Maggelworth 1319 → Magilworthe 1380). Change from -worth to -ford is probably due to the place's proximity to the Medway.

Maidstone. The people's stone (OE *mægðe stān* → to mægðan stane c.975 → Medestan, Meddestane 1086 → Maidestan 1159 → Maidestane 1219 → Maidstone 1610). Maidstone is the old capital town of western Kent and appears to have developed in the vicinity of a stone marking an important meeting-place, or moot.

Maitlands. Mead or meadow land (OE *mǣd land* → Medland' 1247).

Malling, East and **West** (pronounced Mawlin). Mealla's people (OE *Meallingas* → Meallingas 942 → æt Meallingan c.1060 → Metlinges, Mellingetes 1086 → Mallinges 1187 → Mauling 1217 → Malling 1610). East Malling seems to have been the original settlement of this tribe, since a charter dated 942-6 refers

123

to *east meallinga gemære*: boundary of the East *Meallingas*. The tribe were also settled at South Malling in Sussex.

Malmains. It is associated with Henry Malemeins (1261) and John Malmayns of Pluckley (1346). Malmains Farm, Alkham, derives its name from the family of Malmaines who held the Manor of Alkham from the 12th to 14th century. Malmains Farm, Waldershare, is connected with the family of Henry Malemeins (1270) and John Malemeyns of Waldershare (1314). Malmaynes Hall, Stoke, is found as Malmayns maner in 1376, taking its name from the 13th century Stoke family of Malemayns.

Malmaynes Hall. See under MALMAINS.

Malthouse. This appears to have been the home of Robert le Maltmakier, a resident of Littlebourne in 1314.

Manston. The place is recorded as Manneston' in 1254, Mannestone in 1284, the name having the original meaning of 'man's farmstead' (OE *mannes tūn*). It is probably identical with Upmanton, found here together with a Nethermanton in the 13th century — Upmanton being the 'up man's farmstead', or farmstead belonging to a man living up on a hill, while Nethermanton was the 'nether man's farmstead' below the hill. Nether Court, adjacent to Manston, is recorded as Nedercourt in 1431 and probably stands on the site of the original Nethermanton.

Maplehurst. Maple-tree wood (OE *mapuldor hyrst* → Mæpulter hirst 804 → Mapol der hest 850 → Mapeldoreshirst, Mapelhirst 1254 → Mapeldurhurst, Mapelherst 1270).

Maplescombe (pronounced Maplescoom). Maple-tree's field: field marked by a maple (OE *mapuldores camp* → Mapledescam, Maplescamp 1086 → Mapeldreskampe c.1100 → Mapeldurescamp 1195 → Maplescampe 1211).

Maplesden (pronounced Maples-dn). Maple-tree's pasture: woodland pasture marked by a maple tree (OE *mapuldre trēowes denn* → Mapelesden c.1185 → Mapeltresdenne c.1210 → Mapeltreesden', Mapelden' 1254 → Maplesdown 1610).

Mapleton Lodge (Westerham). At the orchard (OE *æt pǣm æppeltūne* → Napeltone 1316). This name is the result of final *n* of ME *atten* — 'at the' — being attached to the following word. At some later date the initial letter was changed to *M* to give more sense to the name.

Marble Wood. See under MARL PIT.

Marchurst. There are no early records for this place name, but it appears to be derived from OE *mearc hyrst*: boundary wood.

Mardale House (Rainham). Pool valley (OE *mere dæl* → Merdale 1278). This must at one time have been land flooded by the Medway.

Marden. Boundary pasture (OE *(ge) mǣre denn* → Mæredæn c.1100 → Mereden 1218 → Merdenne 1240 →

Marden 1610).

Marden Beech and **Marden Thorn.** The names refer to trees in the parish of MARDEN and are recorded as Beche in 1292 (← OE *bēce*) and Thorne in 1327 (← OE *porn*).

Margate. Pool gate: 'gate', or cliff-gap where there are pools (OE *mere geat* → Meregate 1254 → Mergate 1258 → Margate 1293).

Mariners. It derives its name from the family of William Maryner of Westerham (1382).

Mark Farm (Snodland). Boundary, march (OE *mearc* → Merke 1327).

Market Heath. The place is probably associated with the family of John Marcote of Brenchley (1377).

Marley. Pool clearing: clearing beside a pool (OE *mere lēah* → Merley 1278). There is still a small pool here. Marley Court and Marlow Farm, Lenham, share the same original meaning, being recorded as Merlea 1086 → Merleye 1232 → Marleye 1316.

Marlings. The name is possibly associated with Thomas, described in 1258 as 'filius Johannis de Meling' . . . Craye Paulin' — the son of John de Meling' of St. Paul's Cray.

Marlow Farm. See under MARLEY.

Marl Pit. Self-explanatory (OF *marl-iere* → le Marlere 1283 → the Merles 1525). Marble Wood, Ashford, was originally land where marl — a rich soil often used as a fertilizer — was found, and is described in 1632 as

'land in Bethersden caled Marle holden of the manor of Wall in Ashford'. The manor of Wall refers to Wall Farm near Ashford.

Marriage Farm (Wye). Boundary ridge (OE *(ge)mǣre hrycg* → Marreg', Marrege c.1250). The farm lies on the parish boundary of Wye and Crundale.

Marshall Wood (Ulcombe). It is associated with John Marchal (1332), a resident of Tong in the neighbouring parish of Headcorn. Marshalls, Tenterden, derives its name from the family of Marshall who owned the Old House in Tenterden during the 17th and 18th centuries. The surname is also found in connection with Marshall's Farm, Hollingbourne and Marshall's Farm, Lenham. Mount Mascal and Vale Mascal, North Cray, recorded as Mount-Marsh in 1690, ultimately derive their name from the family of Marscal or Marchal (1348).

Marshborough. Mæssa's mound or tumulus (OE *Mǣssan beorg* → Masseberge 1086 → Maseberga c.1100 → Messeberghe 1237 → Mersebergh' 1348).

Marshgate. Gate on to marshland (OE *mersc geat* → Mersgate 1270).

Marshside. It is associated with the family of Wlmari de Marisco of Chislet (c.1225), whose surname means 'dweller by the marsh' (OE *mersc*).

Marsh Street. Marsh (OE *mersc* → Mershstrete 1471).

Martin. Pool farmstead: farmstead

near pools (OE *mere tūn* → Meretum 861 → Mereton' 1270). There are still pools in this area. Marten Farm, Newchurch, appears as Mertumnescirce c.1100 → 'pool farmstead's church' (OE *mere tūnes cirice*). The church must be a reference to that in NEWCHURCH.

Martinhill Spring. The place derives its name from the family of John Martyn of Ash (1370), the 'hill spring' being on their land here. Martin's Hill, Bromley, is associated with John Marton of Bromley (1603).

Marwood. See under MEREWORTH.

Mascalls. Recorded as Mascall maner in 1484 and as Mascals in 1492, the place takes its name from that of Agnes Mascalle (1327).

Matfield. Matta's open land (OE *Mattan feld* → Mattefeld 1227 → Mettefeld 1275).

Mathurst Green. It is suggested that the name is a corruption of Bathurst, recorded here as late as 1930: a Lancelot Bathurst left an annual charity gift to the parish of Staplehurst in his Will of 1639.

Mattshill. The place derives its name from the family of Richard and William Met of Hartlip (1404).

Maxted Street. Dung place: place where dung is heaped (OE *meox stede* → Mexstede 1338 → Mexsted 1610). The name probably refers to a dung heap, or midden.

Maxton. Maca's stone (OE *Macan stān* → Makeston', Maxton' 1242 → Makestone 1273 → Maxton 1346). Maca also owned land at MACKLANDS and MACKNADE.

Maydeken. Recorded as such in 1586, the name is derived from that of Robert Maidekyn and Clement le Madekyn (1327), members of a family which owned the place until the reign of Henry VI.

Maydensole Farm (Mongeham). The name appears as Maidensole in 1676 and is possibly derived from OE *mægdene sol*: maiden's muddy pool. More likely, however, the name is a late one and simply means 'maiden's hollow' — somewhere where the girls went courting.

Mayney Wood (Smarden). It is associated with Richard de Maynye (1348). Mayney Farm, Stone-cum-Ebony, derives its name from the family of John Maney, owners of the Manor of Owley in neighbouring Wittersham during the 17th century.

May Place (Crayford). It is recorded as May-street in 1480, and as May-Place in 1778. Traditionally, the name is a contraction of St. Mary.

Maystreet. The place takes its name from that of William May (1327).

Maytham (pronounced Maytum). Mayweed meadow: water meadow where mayweed grows (OE *mægða hamm* → Maiham c.1185 → Meyhamme 1242 → Maytham 1357).

Mayton Farm (Sturry). Mayweed farmstead: farmstead where mayweed grows (OE *mægða tūn* → Meytone c.1250 → Mayton 1343).

Mazzards Wood (Bromley). It derives its name from the family of Roger and Thomas Mosard of Bromley (1327).

Meachlands. This was once land belonging to a family recorded in 1327 as atte Micche, in 1332 as atte Muche.

Mead Farm (Stelling). Mead, meadow (OE *mǣd* → Mede 1313).

Mean, The. (Land) owned by the community (OE *(ge)mǣne* → le Meneparishe 1476). The Mean is a large area of land jointly owned by the parishes of High Halstow and St. Mary Hoo.

Medhurst Row. Meadow wood: wooded hill by a meadow (OE *mǣd hyrst* → Medhurst c.1200 → Medehurst 1216 → Medherst 1313).

Medway, River. Its name is composed of a British river-name, *wey*: water, with an Old English word *medu*: mead – hence 'mead water', a reference to the sweetness of the water of this river. It is recorded as fluminis Meduuæian 764 → in flumen Medeuuæge 791 → Medwæg c.894 → Medeweye 1227 → atte Medeweie 1327 → at the Midwaye 1587.

Megrims Hill. See under MERRIAMS.

Melliker. At the soft cultivated piece of land (OE *æt þǣm mildan æcere* → Myldenakre 1270 → Mildenacre 1327). OE *mild* has produced the dialect word 'mild', used of soft soil which is easily worked. The place name may be compared with

that of HARDACRE.

Mensden (pronounced Mensdn). Man's woodland pasture (OE *mannes denn* → Mannesdenn' 1240 → Menesdenne 1313 → Mensden 1743).

Meopham (pronounced Meppam). Settlement of the *Mēapas*: the mopers, or sulking ones (OE *Mēapa hām* → Meapaham 788 → Meapham 939 → Mepeham 1086 → Mapeham 1231 → Meapeham 1270). This appears to have been a tribal nickname.

Meresborough. Pool (OE *mere* → Mere 1197). 'Borough' is a late affix to the name, and means 'manor', probably with reference to Meres Court here.

Mereworth (pronounced Merryworth). Mǣra's enclosure (OE *Mǣran worð* → Meran worð 843 → Mǣreweorðe c.960 → Marovrde 1086 → Merewurth 1179 → Mereworthe 1253). Marwood near Lympne derives its name from natives of Mereworth who settled here during the 14th century and who are recorded as de Mereworthe.

Merrals Shaw. It is described as Mirrald's Ground and Mirralds wood in 1698, taking the name of some former landowner in this area. The affix 'Shaw' is from OE *scaga*: a copse.

Merriams. The place derives its name from the family of Robert Meriham (1396). Their surname may also have produced the name of Megrims Hill, Sandhurst, which is recorded as Mearams Hill in 1790, Meagrim Hill c.1815.

Merry Hill (Meopham). It is associated with the family of William
le Myrye of Meopham (1270).

Mersham (pronounced Murzam).
Settlement of the *Mǣrsas*, or famous
ones (OE *Mǣrsa hām* → Mersaham
858 → Mærseham c.1060 → Mers-
eham 1086 → Mersham 1191). This
was probably a tribe of victorious
warriors.

Mersham Hatch. See under HATCH
HILL.

Merston. Marsh farmstead: farmstead on marshy land (OE *mersc
tūn* → mersc tun 774 → Meriston',
Merston' 1242 → Merston 1265).

Merton Farm (Canterbury). Pool
farmstead: farmstead close to pools
(OE *mere tūn* → Mertone 1327).

Middleton Farm (Longfield). It is
associated with the family of Richard Middleton of Longfield (1387),
the name being derived from OE
middel tūn: middle farmstead — this
may refer to Middle Farm, a mile
away from Middleton Farm.

Midley. Middle island (OE *middel
ēg* → Midelea 1086 → Middelea,
Middelei c.1100 → Middele 1270 →
Mydley 1610). Midley was once an
island of firm ground in the middle
of marshalnd, probably mid-way
between Romney Marsh and Well-
and Marsh.

Milbay's Wood (Nettlestead). The
name appears to be a corruption
of Mildmay: a park belonging to
Mildmay, Earl of Westmoreland, is
found in the neighbouring parish of
East Peckham in 1634; probably

the wood was part of his estate.

Mileham. Mill water meadow: water
meadow in which a mill stands (OE
myln hamm → Meleham 1278).

Milgate. Gate leading to a mill (OE
myln geat → Melegate 1254 → Mel-
gate 1347).

Millhall. Mill corner: corner of land
where a mill stands (OE *myln halh*
→ Melehale 1327 → Melhalefeld
1443 → Millale 1483 → Mylhall
1610). The 1443 form refers to
open land (ME *feld*) associated with
the place.

Mill Leese Shaw. Lea, meadow (OE
lǣs → Lese 1348 → Lesse 1357).
At some time there must have been
a mill here. The affix 'Shaw' is derived from OE *scaga*: a copse.

Milsted. 'Milk place': dairy farm
(OE *meolc stede* → Milstede c.1100
→ Milkstede 1243 → Milsted 1247
→ Milcstede 1278 → Milstede 1313).

Milton (near Canterbury). Mill farmstead: farmstead with a mill attached (OE *myln tūn* → Melentun
1044 → Middeltune 1086 → Mele-
tone 1249). East Milton, near Gravesend, shares the same origin, being
recorded as Melantun c.975 → Mele-
tvne 1086 → Meleton' 1226 → Myl-
ton 1610.

Milton Regis. Middle farmstead (OE
middel tūn → Middeltun 893 →
Middeltone 1086 → Middelton
1200). Called Regis because the
place was originally a royal manor,
being recorded in 1052 as *Middeltun pæs cynges*: middle farmstead
of the king.

Milton Shaw. It derives its name from the family of Sampson de Middelton' (1327), 'Shaw' being from OE *scaga*: a copse.

Minacre Farm (Northbourne). Meadowland (OE *mæd æcer* → Medacre c.1240 → Medde acre 1553). The modern spelling of the name seems to have resulted from proximity to LENACRE COURT in the neighbouring parish of Whitfield.

Mincendane Wood (Eastling). This is probably identical with a Mynchin Lane recorded in Eastling during the reign of Henry VIII, the name being derived from OE *myncen*: nun.

Minching Wood (Kingsdown). Nun's wood: wood belonging to a nunnery (OE *myncene wudu* →Menechewode 1268).

Minnett's Hill. See under MINNIS.

Minnis, The. (Land) belonging to the community (OE *gemænnes* → Meunessa 1204 → La Mannesse 1226). Minnett's Hill, Frinsted, probably has the same original meaning, being recorded as Minis-hill in 1782.

Minster in Sheppey. Monastery (OE *mynster* → Menstre 1270 → Mynster 1610). It is referred to c.1100 as Sexburgamynster: Seaxburh's monastry, the foundation being established c.675 by Seaxburh, widow of Eorconbeorht, King of Kent 640-664.

Minster in Thanet. South monastry (OE *sūð mynster* → Suðmynster 696 → Mynster 1610). Called 'south' to distinguish it from the monastry at Minster in Sheppey.

Misleham. Mistletoe meadow: water meadow where mistletoe is found (OE *mistel hamm* → Mestillehamme 1278 → Mystelhame 1313 → Mistelhamme 1384).

Moatlands. Moat, defensive ditch (ME *mote* → Moote 1437 → le Mote 1439).

Modest Corner. It derives its name from the family of John Mode of Tonbridge (1327), the name presumably once being Modes Corner.

Molash (pronounced Mow-lash). 'Speech ash': ash-tree by which speeches are delivered at assemblies (OE *mæl æsc* → Molesse 1226 → Malesse 1240 → Molasshe 1313).

Molland Farm (Ash). Bargaining, or agreement, land: land for which rent is paid in lieu of service (OE *māl land* → Molland' 1226 → Molande 1251 → Mollonde 1327). This origin is also shared by Great Molloms Wood, Cudham, which is recorded as Moland in 1359; and by the now lost place of Molland in Cliffe, which appears as Mollonde in 1332, Molland in 1778.

Molloms Wood, Great. See under MOLLAND FARM.

Monday Boys. The affix is derived from the French *bois*: wood, recorded here as Boys in 1327; the wood appears to have been owned by William and Robert Monde (1450), who also gave their name to Monday House in neighbouring Pluckley.

129

Mongeham, Great and **Little** (pronounced Munjem). Settlement of Mundel's people (OE *Mundelinga hām* → Mundelingeham 761 → Mundlingham 833 → Mundingeham 1086 → Muningeham 1195 → Monigeham 1261 → Mongham 1610).

Monkdown Wood (Boxley). Recorded as a 'wood called Monkedoune' c.1500, the name is derived from OE *munuca dūn*: monks' hill, the place once belonging to Boxley Abbey.

Monks Horton. Filthy, or muddy farmstead (OE *horh tūn* → Hortun 1016 → Hortone 1086 → Horton c.1200 → Horton Monachorum 1610). This last form means 'Horton of the monks', since the estate once belonged to Horton Priory here.

Monkton. Monks' farmstead or manor (OE *munuca tūn* → Munccetun 961 → Monocstvne 1086 → Muneketon 1213 → Monketone 1253 → Monkton 1610). Monkton Court, Eythorne, shares the same original meaning, being recorded as Moneketone in 1346, Monketone in 1357. Monkton has developed on the site of a manor given by Queen Eadgiva in 961 to the monks of Holy Trinity in Canterbury.

Moor, The. Self-explanatory (OE *mōr* → More 1258). This is also the origin of the names of Moor Street, Rainham, and Moor Wood Benenden.

Moorcocks. It derives its name from John, Ralph, Richard and William Morcok' of Mereworth (1320).

Moorden. Moorland pasture (OE *mōr denn* → Morden' 1240 → Moredenne 1313 → Mordenn 1343).

Moorstock. Moorland place (OE *mōr stoc* → Morestok' 1240 → Morstoke 1293 → Mostock Wood 1539).

Mordenden Wood (Hollingbourne). Mōda's farmstead (OE *Mōding tūn* → Modinton 1218 → Modynton 1367 → Motynden 1535). It seems probable that neighbouring Morning Dawn, for which there are no records, is a corruption of the same name. The personal name, Mōda, is also found in connection with MOTTENDEN and MOTTINGHAM.

Morehall. Moreland hall: hall built on a moor (OE *mōr heall* → Morhall 1250 → Morhalle 1346).

Morghew. Morning gift (OE *morgen giefu* → Morghenes 1371 → Morgheve 1454 → Morgeve 1548). The charming name of 'morning gift' was applied to a piece of land customarily given by a husband to his wife on the morning following their marriage.

Morning Dawn. See under MORDENDEN.

Mortimers. The place is associated with Hugh de Mortimer, a rector of Cliffe in the mid-13th century.

Mote, The. Moat, defensive ditch (ME *mote* → La Mote 1266 → The moat 1690).

Motley Hill (Rainham). At the gritty island (OE *æt þǣre motten ēge* → Mottene 1270 → Motteneye 1376). This was once a true island of firm ground standing in marshland.

Mottenden. Mōda's woodland pasture (OE *Mōding denn* → Modinden 1236 → Motinden 1251 → Modindenn 1275 → Muttenden 1610). Mōda, whose tribal settlement was at MOTTINGHAM, had a farmstead at MORDENDEN.

Mottingham. Settlement of Mōda's people (OE *Mōdinga hām* → Modinga hema 862 → Modingeham 1044 → Motingham 1610). Mōda himself owned property at MORDENDEN and MOTTENDEN.

Mount, The. Mount, hill (OE *munt* → Muntes 1218 → Monte 1272 → Munt 1278 → Mounte 1346). This was the meeting-place of the Loningborough Hundred. Mount Castle, Lenham, derives its name from the family of William Monte of Lenham (1270). Mount Cottages, Wrotham, has taken the name of William Mounte of Wrotham (1314).

Mountain Street. It seems to have derived its name from the family of de Opmanton' (1348), whose name in turn was derived from OE *upp manna tūn*: 'up men's farmstead', or farmstead belonging to men living high up — Mountain Street is probably on the site of this settlement. Mountain Farm, Marden, was originally a 'monks' farmstead' (OE *munuca tūn*), being recorded as Monketon in 1535. Mountain Wood, Newnham, has the same origin and appears as Muneketon' 1202 → Munckton 1578 → Mounton 1592.

Mount Mascal. See under MARSHALL WOOD.

Mouseden. Moss pasture: woodland pasture where moss grows (OE *mēos denn* → Meosden 759).

Mowshurst (pronounced Mouseurst). First recorded in 1347, as Mousherst, the original meaning of this place name appears to have been 'moss wood': wooded hill where moss grows on the trees (OE *mēos hyrst*).

Munsgore. There are no records for this name, but the last element is certainly derived from OE *gāra*: wedge-shaped piece of land. The first element is probably a personal name.

Murrain Wood (Thornham). It appears as Moriene in 1226, the name being derived from ME *moryne*: murrain, disease, plague.

Murston. Moorland's farmstead: farmstead situated on moorland (OE *mōres tūn* → Moreston' 1198 → Moristune c.1220 → Morston 1346 → Murston 1610). The now lost place of Murston in Hollingbourne derived its name from the 14th century family of de Morstone, natives of Murston: their name survives in a corrupt form in Musketstone, Hollingbourne.

Murzie Farm (Marden). Pool's island: island in the middle of a pool (OE *meres ēg* → Mereseye 1278 → Merseye, Mereseye 1367).

Musketstone. See under MURSTON.

Mussel House (Leysdown). Mouse hollow: hollow infested with field mice (OE *mūs hol* → Mowseholl c.1560).

131

Mustards. The place is associated with the family of Thomas Smith Musterds (1679).

Mutrix. It takes its name from that of Alfred Motryk (c.1250).

Mystole (pronounced My-stole). Recorded as Mystole in 1610, and as Mistole in 1690, this appears to have been the site of a cattle shed, or stable, the place name being derived from OE *meox steall*: dung stall.

N

Nackholt. At the oak thicket (OE *æt þǣm āc holte* → ME *atten oc holt* → Ocholte 1272 → Acholt 1307 → Nacolte 1390). This last form shows how the *n* of ME *atten* – 'at the' – became erroneously attached to the following word, producing the present place name.

Nackington. Nata's hill (OE *Nating dūn* → Natyngdun 993 → Latintone 1086 → Natinduna c.1100 → Nacindoñ 1199 → Natingdon' 1247 → Nakynton 1415 → Nackington 1610).

Nagden, Nagden Marshes. Recorded as Necgdon Marsshe, Negdon M'sshe in 1535, and as Nagden *alias* Negdon in 1790, the name is possibly a reference to the small hill lying to the south-east of Nagden and is derived from OE *nagg dūn*: small, sturdy hill.

Nailbourne. This is the Kentish dialect word for a small stream which periodically dries up, the name perhaps being derived from ME *atten el burn*: 'at the eel stream'.

Napchester. Nǣp's wooded hill (OE *Nǣpes hyrst* → Napisherst 1198 → Napesherst 1275 → Napserst 1347 → Napcester 1451 → Napchester 1799). It has been suggested that final -hurst was dropped from this place name in favour of 'chester' because of a "craving for gentility" by local residents.

Nash. At the ash-tree (OE *æt þǣm æsce* → ME *atten asshe, atte nasshe* → Nesshe 1332 → Nash Court 1690). This last form refers to Nash Court in Nash. The same original meaning is also shared by Nash Court, Boughton-under-Blean and Westwell; Nash Street, Northfleet; Nashes, Penshurst; and Nash's Farm, Luddenham.

Nashenden Farm (Rochester). Small house pasture: woodland pasture on which stands a small house (OE *hȳscen denn* → Hyscen, Hyscan denes mearce 995 → Essedene 1086 → Hescindena c.1100 → Hnessendenne 1185 → Nessenden 1226). The 995 form means 'boundary of the small house pasture'.

Neavy Downs. The name is possibly associated with the family of William le Neve of Wingham (1313).

Nellington Wood (Speldhurst). Recorded as Nelehampton in 1628 and as Nealhampton in 1778, the name is derived from the family of William Nelehame (1240), owners of a farmstead (ME *tone*) here.

Nepicar House (Wrotham). Turnip land: cultivated land on which turnips are grown (OE *nǣp æcer* → Nepacre 1292 → Nepakere 1327).

Nether Court. See under MANSTON.

Nethergong Farm (Chislet). At the river-bank way, or path (OE *æt pǣm ōfer gange* → Ouergange 1278 → Overgonge 1393). The present name is the result of final *n* of ME *atten* – 'at the' – being erroneously attached to the following word, producing Nover- instead of Over-. The Nethergong used to be the name of a stream draining into the Chislet Marshes by which the farm is situated.

Nethersole Farm (Womenswold). Nether, or lower muddy pool (OE *niðera sol* → Nethersole 1270). The name appears to be a reference to one of the pools in Womenswold.

Nettlestead. Nettle homestead: homestead at a place where nettles grow (OE *netel hāmstede* → an Netel hæm styde 889 → Netlestede c.975 → Nedestede 1086 → Netlestede 1212 → Nettelsted' 1226 → Netlested 1610).

Newage. Recorded as Newegate in 1240, the origin of this place name is probably OE *nīwe geat*: new gate.

New Ash Green. This is a new development, taking its name from neighbouring ASH, near Wrotham.

Newbury. New manor, or borough (ME *newe burgh* → Neuburgh 1342 → Newebourgh 1349 → Newborughe 1535).

Newchurch. Self-explanatory (OE *nīwe cirice* → Nevcerce 1086 → Niwancirce c.1100 → Newechirche 1198 → Newchurche 1610). The original 'new church' appears to have stood on the site of the 13th century Church of SS Peter and Paul.

Newcourt Wood (Charing). New mansion (ME *newe* + F *court* → Newecort 1292 → Newecourt 1327). Newhall Farm, All Hallows, has approximately the same meaning, being recorded as Newhalle in 1384 (← ME *newe halle*: new hall).

Newenden. At the new woodland pasture (OE *æt pǣm nīwan denne* → Neuuenden 1072 → Newedene 1086 → Niwendenne c.1100 → Newenden' 1226 → Newenden 1610). Newenden Farm, Smarden, shares the same original meaning, being found as Neowinden' in 1278, Newyndenne in 1332.

Newhall Farm. See under NEWCOURT WOOD.

Newhook. See under OLDHOOK.

Newhouse (Leysdown). New hall (ME *newe halle* → Newhall 1553).

134

Newhouse, Lynsted, has approximately the same meaning, appearing as New-house in 1690. Newhouse, Penshurst, is recorded as Newhouse *alias* Harts in 1778, being confused with HARTSLAND close by. Newhouses, Edenbridge, appears as Newhouse in 1768. Newhouse Farm, Thanington, seems to be the oldest 'new house' of all, the name being found as Newehuse in 1270.

Newhurst. This is a late name, first appearing in 1720, and has the meaning of 'new wood'.

New Hythe. New landing-place (OE *nīwe hȳð* → La Newehethe 1254 → Niwehethe 1316 → Neuheth 1323 → New hyth 1610). The 'old landing-place' on a tributary of the Medway here is recorded as Ealdehethe in 1292 (← OE *eald hȳð*).

Newington (near Hythe). At the new farmstead (OE *æt pǣm nīwan tūne* → Neventone 1086 → Niwan tune c.1100 → Neweton 1201 → Neuton *juxta* Heth (Hythe) 1285 → Newington 1535). Newington near Ramsgate shares the same origin and appears as Niwan tun in 943, Newenton' c.1250. Newington near Sittingbourne was originally known as 'the new farmstead' (OE *nīwe tūn*), being built on the site of an earlier building dating back to Roman times, and is recorded as Newetone 1086 → Niwantune c.1100 → Neweton' 1223 → Newington c.1550.

Newland (Charing). Self-explanatory (OE *nīwe land* → Neweland 1264). The same original meaning, referring to ground newly cleared for cultivation, is shared by Newland, Romney; Newlands, St. Mary's Hoo; Upper and Lower Newlands, Teynham; Newlands, St. Lawrence; and Newlands Wood, Hollingbourne and Hothfield.

Newlands, Upper and **Lower.** See under NEWLAND.

Newman's Hill (Brasted). It derives its name from the family of John le Newman (1313).

Newnham. At the new settlement (OE *æt pǣm nīwan hāme* → Newenham 1177). The same meaning occurs in the names of Newnham Court, Boxley, and Newnham Farm, Wickhambreux.

Newsole Farm (Coldred). New (formed) muddy pool (OE *nīwe sol* → Newesole 1262 → Newsole 1291).

Newstead, Little. New place (OE *nīwe stede* → La Newestede 1285 → Newstede 1362). Newstead Farm here may be on the site of the 'new place'.

Newstreet Farm (Great Chart). Self-explanatory (ME *newe strete* → Neuwestrete 1278 → Newestrete 1347).

Nichol's Wood (Cranbrook). It is associated with the family of William Nichole of Cranbrook (1278). The same surname is also found in connection with Nickle Farm, Chartham, once the property of John Nichole (1278).

Ninn Lodge (Great Chart). At the lodging, or inn (OE *æt pǣm inne* → ME *atten inne, atte ninne* → Attenynne 1278 → Nynne 1338).

Nizel's Heath. New buildings (OE *nīge gesella* → Nigheselle 1327 → Nyselle 1346 → Niselle 1348 → Nysells 1525).

Nod Wood (Lydd). There is a 'house called Nodde' recorded in the parish in 1569, the name possibly being derived from OE *hnodde*: lump, a reference to some hillock in the neighbourhood.

Nonington (pronounced Nunnington). Nunna's farmstead (OE *Nunning tūn* → Nunningitun c.1100 → Nonyngton, Noningetun' 1282 → Nonyngton 1610).

Nord Corner. Together with Nord Farm here, the place takes its name from that of the family of John of Northe (1327).

Northbourne (pronounced Norburn). North stream (OE *norð burna* → Nortburne 618 → Norborne 1086 → Northburne 1240). This may originally have been the name given to the stream which flows to the north of DEAL.

Northdown. North hill (OE *norð dūn* → Northdoune 1334 → Northdown 1690). Updown House here was originally a site 'upon the hill' (OE *uppan dūn*), and is recorded as Oppendon' in 1254, Oppedoune in 1348.

Northfleet. North creek or inlet (OE *norð flēot* → to Flyote c.975 → Norflvet 1086 → Nortfliete 1176 → Northflet 1201 → North fleet 1610). Called 'north' to distinguish this creek from that at SOUTHFLEET.

Northgate. Self-explanatory (OE *norð geat* → Norgate 1087 → Nortgat' 1231 → Northgate c.1275).

North Lands Shaw. North land: land to the north of the parish (OE *norð land* → Nordland 1232). The affix 'Shaw' is from OE *scaga*: a copse.

Northstead. North place (OE *norð stede* → Nortstede 1278 → Northsted 1351).

Northumberland Heath. Recorded as Northumberlond hethe in 1529, the place derives its name from the small stream just to the south of it, which was originally known as the North Humber and is recorded as Northumbre in 1292. The stream was probably much wider than it is now and gave its name to the land bordering it: north (of the) Humber land. 'Humber', a common name for streams in early times, is derived from the Old Welsh *hu*: good, well, together with a British word meaning 'river' derived from the Latin *imber*: a shower.

Northwood (Herne). Wood to the north of the parish (OE *norð wudu* → Northuuda 832 → Nordevde 1086 → Northwode 1253). Northwood, St. Lawrence, shares the same origin, appearing as Norwood in 1614. Norwood — an abbreviated form of Northwood — is found at Eastchurch, Meopham, Milton Regis, Newchurch and Wormshill.

Norton. North farmstead (OE *norð tūn* → Nortone 1086 → Northtune, Nordtune c.1100 → Nortuna 1114 → Norton' 1254). The same original meaning is found in Norton Court, Chart Sutton, which is just north of of the parish. Norton Green near Stockbury was originally a 'north woodland pasture' (OE *norð denn*), and is recorded as Northdene 1258 → Northdenne 1270 → Nordene 1347 → Northdean *alias* Norton Green 1782.

Norton Green. See under NORTON.

Norwood. See under NORTH-WOOD.

Nouds. Recorded as Nowds in 1690, the name appears to be a manorial one, derived from that of some former landowner in the area.

Nower, The. At the bank, or border (OE *æt þæm ōre* → ME *atten ore* → Owre 1240 → Nore 1348). This is a wood in Brasted which is situated on sharply rising ground.

Nunfield House and **Farm** (Newington). So called because they stand on the site of a priory of Benedictine nuns.

Nurstead (pronounced Nustid). Nut place: place where nuts are found (OE *hnutu stede* → Notestede 1086 Hnutstede c.1100 → Nuttestede 1204 → Nutstede 1242).

O

Oad Street. Old street or road (OE *eald strǣt* → Holdestrete 1254 → Oldestrete 1313). The place name nust refer to a Roman road, since OE *strǣt* is derived from the Latin *via strata*: a metalled or paved way.

Oakenden. Oak-covered pasture (OE *ācen denn* → Akynden' 1278).

Oakenpole Wood (Doddington). 'Oaken fold': fold near an oak-covered place (OE *ācen falod* → Okenefold 1220 → Okenfolde 1327). There are no later forms to show when, or why, -fold changed to -pole.

Oakleigh. Oak clearing: clearing marked by an oak (OE *āc lēah* → ac leage 774 → Acle 1185 → Ocle 1265). The same original meaning is shared by Oakley House, Goudhurst, recorded as Okle in 1348; and by Ockley near Hawkhurst, recorded as Occle in 1254, Oklee in 1340.

Oakwood Farm (Tunstall). Self-explanatory (OE *āc wudu* → Okwode 1387).

Oare (pronounced Oar). Shore (OE *ōra* → Ore, Ora 1086 → Ora 1161 → Ore 1226). Ores Farm, Chislet, has the same origin being recorded as Ore in 1227, Ores in 1242.

Obeden. The name is probably connected with the family of Wills. Habynden of Smarden (1450).

Ockley. See under OAKLEIGH.

Odgiam, Little (pronounced Odjum). Udda's settlement (OE *Uddan hām* → Uddanhom 843 → Odenhām 1278 → Odenham 1313). Odiam Farm here shares the same origin.

Odiam Farm. See under ODGIAM.

Offham (pronounced Uffum). Offa's settlement (OE *Offan hām* → Offaham 942 → Ofeham 1086 → Offeham 1202 → Offenham 1278 → Ofham 1292).

Olantigh Park (pronounced Ollantay). Holly enclosure: enclosure marked by a holly bush (OE *holegn tēag* → Olenteye 1270 → Holmthege, Holitege 1307 → Olentegh' 1313 →

Olantigh 1607).

Oldbury. Old stronghold (OE *eald burh* → Ealdebery 1302 → Eldebery 1334 → Aldebery 1347). The name refers to a Roman stronghold on Oldbury Hill.

Old Hay, Great and **Little.** Originally the place was known as 'the hedged enclosure' (OE *haga*), and appears as Haya in 1226, Haye in 1256. Later it was called 'the old hedged enclosure' (ME *elde haye*), and in this form appears as Eldehey, Eldehaye in 1278, Oldehay in 1379.

Oldhook Grove. Together with adjacent Newhook and Hook Quay, the name is derived from OE *hōc:* hook, or spur of land, and appears as Hoke in 1278. The names of Oldhook and Newhook are self-explanatory, while Hook Quay must refer to some landing-place here in Eastchurch.

Oldlands. Self-explanatory. The place is described as 'the olde Lande' in 1572, the reference being to land which was no longer used for crop-growing.

Oldridge Wood (Littlebourne). Hollow ridge: ridge bordering a hollow (OE *hol hrycg* → Holregge c.1220 → Holdrich 1547).

Old Soar. Recorded as Sore-lands in 1480, and as Sore *alias* Hores in 1520, the place derives its name from the family name of John le Suur (1254) and Roger le Soure of Wrotham (1292).

Old Wives Lees. Old wood (OE *eald wudu* → Ealdewode 1278 → Eldewode 1327 → Old wywes lease 1610 → Oldwives Lease 1690 → Oldwoods-lees c.1750). 'Lees' is derived from OE *lǣs*: lea, meadow.

Omenden. Umma's woodland pasture (OE *Umming denn* → Humindenn' 1254 → Homyndenn' 1270 → Humyndenne 1292 → Omyndenne 1334).

Ommerden, Little. Recorded as Omendenneshok in 1370, this seems originally to have been a spur of land (OE *hōc*) belonging to the settlement at OMENDEN, five miles away.

Ores Farm. See under OARE.

Orgarswick (pronounced Awgerswick). Ordgār's farm (OE *Ordgāres wīc* → Ordgaresuuice c.1100 → Orgareswyke 1253 → Orgareswyk 1278 → Orgarswyke 1610). Ordgār seems also to have been associated with a church here, since Ordgarescirce (← OE *Ordgāres cirice*) is recorded together with the original farm c.1100.

Orlestone (pronounced Awlstun). Ordlāf's farmstead (OE *Ordlāfes tūn* → Orlavestone 1086 → Ordlauestone c.1100 → Ordlaueston 1208 → Ordlaweston' 1240 → Orlaston 1610).

Orpington. Orped's farmstead (OE *Orpeding tūn* → Orpedingtun 1042 → Orpendingtune c.1060 → Orpinton 1086 → Orpington' 1207).

Osierland Wood (Boxley). Recorded early in the 16th century as Hosiersland, the name appears to be a manorial one.

Ospringe (pronounced Osprinje). Gods' spring (OE *ōsa spring* → Ospringes 1086 → Ospringe c.1100 → Ospring 1200 → Osprenge 1610). This would have been a spring dedicated to heathen gods.

Osterland. Oyster land: land by which oysters are caught (OE *oster land* → Osterlande 961 → Osterland' 1240 → Oysterland 1558). The place lies on the Medway estuary.

Otford (pronounced Oat-fud). Otta's ford (OE *Ottan ford* → Ottan forda 773 → Otteford 832 → Otefort 1086 → Otteford 1210 → Otford 1610). The personal name is also found in connection with OTHAM, OTTINGE, and the now lost place of Ottanhyrst in Twyford.

Otham (pronounced Oatum). Otta's settlement (OE *Ottan hām* → Oteham 1086 → Otteham 1253 → Ottham 1610). Otta's tribal settlement was at OTTINGE.

Otterden. Woodland pasture of Oter's people (OE *Ōteringa denn* → Otringedene 1086 → Ottrindænne, Ottringedene c.1100 → Oteringdene 1253 → Otringden 1291 → Ottinden c.1550).

Otterham Creek. The place has taken the early name of the stream on which it stands – 'the swollen one', derived from OE *āttor*: poison, swelling – and was originally 'the water meadow by the swollen stream'. It is recorded as Eterhamme, Atterhamme c.1225 → Etterhamme 1292 → Etterham 1442 → Otterham *alias* Attrum 1782.

Otterpool, Upper. Otter's pool (OE *otores pōl* → Oteres pole 1035 → Obtrepole 1086 → Otrepol c.1100 → Oterpole 1253).

Ottinge (pronounced Ottinje). Otta's people (OE *Ottingas* → Ottyngg', Hottinge 1304 → Ottynge 1348). Otta had a settlement at OTHAM; his ford was at OTFORD.

Ottridge. Its origin may possibly be the old name of the River LEN, since the place is recorded as Wotring in 1285, the name being derived from OE *wōh ðring*: 'crooked press', descriptive of a narrow, winding stream. Ottridge lies in the valley of the Len.

Ouseley. 'Ooze clearing': clearing where the ground is marshy (OE *wāse lēah* → ME *wos leghe* → Wosele 1313). The initial *W* was dropped from this place name some time after the 14th century.

Out Elmstead. Ūhhelm's farmstead (OE *Ūhthelmes tūn* → Vttelmestun' 1226 → Hutelemeston' 1270 → Outhelmeston' 1313 → Outtelmeston 1502 → Outelmeston 1790). 'Out' has become separated from the original place name through confusion with Modern English 'out', meaning outside, without. The present name form has been influenced by ELMSTEAD, six miles away.

Outridge. It derives its name from the Brasted family variously recorded as Huthred (1270), Huttred (1278) and Vghtred (1313), a name derived from the Old English personal name Ūhtred. The present place name has developed from the genitival form Ughtred's.

Ovenden (pronounced Uvven-dn). Hofa's woodland pasture (OE *Hofing denn* → Houyndeñe 1327 → Hofyndene 1338 → Hovynden 1450 → Hovinden 1499).

Oveny Green. Above (on the) island (OE *ufan ēg* → Oueney 1313 → Oueneye, Oveneye 1338). The name may be a reference to land above the lakes formed by the Darent at Sundridge.

Overland Farm (Ash). Bank land: land limited by a bank or border (OE *ōfer land* → Eureland' 1226 → Ouerlaunde 1264 → Ouerland, Overland 1278).

Oversland. This was originally land belonging to the family of Clement Oueray of Boughton-under-Blean (1367).

Overy Street. Over the river (OE *ofer ēa* → Overe street 1315 → Overy Street 1442 → Overie 1548). This is a reference to a place lying across the River Darent.

Owens Court (Selling). Oven (OE *ofen* → Ofne 1247 → Ouene 1381). Owens Court was once the site of a furnace, or oven. The present name has arisen through confusion between the medieval form Ouene, or Ovene, and the personal name Owen.

Owley. Owl corner: corner of land frequented by owls (OE *ūle halh* → Oulehale 1327 → Oulehalle 1332 → Olehale 1347). The present name is a corruption of these forms.

Oxenden. Recorded as Oxenden farm in 1790, the place name is probably derived from OE *oxena denn*: pasture for oxen. This is the original meaning of Oxenden Wood, Adisham, which appears as Oxinden' 1278 → Oxindenne 1347 → Oxenden 1535. Oxenden Wood, Chelsfield, seems originally to have been the site of an enclosure for oxen (OE *oxena gehæg*), since it is found as Oxeneye in 1270. Oxenden Corner, Chislet, derives its name from the family of Thomas Oxenden, owners of land in the neighbouring parish of Reculver during the reign of Henry VI.

Oxenhill Shaw. See under OXNEY.

Oxen Hoath. Ox land: shortened piece of land on which oxen graze or are penned (OE *oxa snād* → Toxnode 1278 → Oxnode 1377 → Oxenheth 1378 → Oxenode 1408 → Oxynhothe 1495 → Oxen-heath 1690). The 1278 form has resulted from the Old English word *æt*: 'at' being made part of the following word. From the early 15th century the land here is referred to as heathland (← OE *hǣð*). Oxen Hoath Mill close by is recorded as Oxnode Melle in 1377, Oxynhothis Myll in 1495, taking its name from the original place.

Ox Lane. See under OXROAD FARM.

Oxley Wood (Lenham). Described as woodland called Exetheghe during the 13th century, the place name may possibly be derived from OE *exen tēag*: oxen enclosure.

Oxney (near Deal). Enclosure for

oxen (OE *oxena gehæg* → Oxena gehæg 1038 → Oxenæ 1240 → Oxenia 1242 → Oxeneye 1270 → Oxney 1610). This original meaning is shared by Oxenhill Shaw, Otford, which is recorded as Oxeneye in 1278. Oxney Wood, Nonington, was originally a pasture for oxen (OE *oxena denn*), and appears as Oxinden' 1278 → Oxindenne 1338 → Oxenden 1535. Final -denn in this place name seems to have been replaced by 'wood' sometime during the 17th century.

Oxney, Isle of. Oxen island: island where oxen are kept (OE *oxena ëg* → on Oxnaiea 724 → Oxeneya 1212 → Oxney 1610). This is still a true island, separated from the Kentish mainland by two branches of the eastern Rother. Pagan altars found on the island depict the sacrifice of oxen to the gods.

Oxroad Farm (Elham). Ox clearing: clearing where oxen are penned (OE *oxa rod* → Oxrode 1242 → Oxerode 1347). The same original meaning is found in the name of Ox Lane, Tenterden, which appears as Oxerode in 1270.

Ozengell Grange (St. Lawrence). Hill of Ōsa's people (OE *Ōsinga hyll* → Osingehull' 1240 → Osingehelle c.1250 → Osyngelle 1357 → Osyngell Grang' 1535).

P

Paddlesworth (near Dover). Pæddel's enclosure (OE *Pæddeles worð* → Pellesorde 1086 → Peadleswurthe c.1100 → Padeleswurth' 1240 → Padleswrth' 1242 → Padlesworth 1610). Paddlesworth near Snodland shares the same original meaning, being recorded as Peteleswurthe, Peadleswyrðe c.975 → Pellesorde 1086 → Pædlesuurtha c.1100 → Padelesworth 1341.

Paddock Wood. Paddock, small enclosure (OE *pearroc* → Parrok 1279 → Parrocks 1782). The change from Parrock to Paddock is a phonetic one. Paddock near Challock has the same origin and appears as Parvocke in 1461. Parrock Farm and Parrock Hall, Milton, are recorded as Parrocke in 1242, la Parrock in 1253.

Pagehurst, Great and **Little.** 'Patch wood': wooded hill near a patch, or irregularly-shaped piece of ground (OE *pæcce hyrst* → Pechehurst 1258 → Pecchhurst 1278 → Pecherst 1313 → Pakhurst 1327 → Pacheherst 1393). This is also the origin of Pagehurst Cottage, Benenden, found as Pecherst in 1346.

Pain Street. The name is derived from that of Thomas and William Payn (1327). Paine's Farm, Goudhurst, is associated with the family of Payn (1348); and Paine's Farm, Shoreham, with Richard Payn (1313).

Painter's Forstall. Recorded as Paynters in 1535, the place takes its name from the family of Robert le Peyntour (1278). The affix is a dialect word used of land in front of farm buildings. Painter's Wood, Westerham, is found as Painters in 1544, the name being a manorial one.

Palmer's Hill (Hawkinge). It is associated with the family of William Palmer (1327). The family name is also found in connection with Palmershill Farm here. Palmers, Penshurst, derives its name from the family of Robert le Palmere (1301).

Palmstead, Little. Pear homestead: homestead where pears are grown (OE *peru hāmstede* → Perhamstede 747 → Permested' 1226 → Pernested' 1270 → Permestede, Permysted 1271). Called 'Little' to distinguish

143

the place from Great Palmstead Farm here.

Palstre Court (Wittersham) (pronounced Pawlster). Point, or spit (OE *palester* → Palstre 1032 → Palestrei 1086 → Palstre 1226). The name probably refers to land bordering the small tributary stream close by.

Panthurst. Recorded as Paunthurst in 1407 and as Pantiers in 1455, this was originally a wooded hill (ME *hurst*) associated with the family of Henry le Paneter of Sevenoaks (1292).

Paramour Street. It is described as Paramore Street in 1526 and takes its name from the family of Paramour or Paramor who are recorded in the Ash area from the 14th century onwards.

Paris Corner. This is a manorial name, derived from that of John and William Parys (1348).

Park. This word (from ME *parke*: parkland, derived from OE *pearroc*: small enclosure) is found in the names of Park Farm, Appledore, Hawkhurst, Leigh and Wormshill; Park House, Boxley and Leigh; and Park Wood, Bilsington.

Parkenden. Small enclosure pasture: woodland pasture adjoining a small enclosure (OE *pearroc denn* → Parcdenne c.1225 → Parkdenne 1327 → Parkenden 1578).

Parker's Green. It is connected with the family of William le Parker of Hadlow (1292). Parker Farm, Warehorne, is similarly associated with John le Parker of Warehorne (1310).

Parmiters. The place is named after the family of Parmeter who owned land in Eastling during the 18th century.

Parrock Farm and **Hall.** See under PADDOCK WOOD.

Pastead Wood (Halling). Pear place: place where pears grow (OE *peru stede* → Perstede 1334). Pested Farm, Challock, has the same meaning and appears as Perstede in 1292.

Pastheap. 'Pear steep place': steep place where pears grow (OE *peru stēap* → Parstepe 1270 → Persteape 1292 → Pastepe 1327).

Patchgrove Wood (Wrotham). This appears to be a comparatively late name, first appearing early in the 18th century as Patchgrove.

Patrixbourne. Stream (OE *burna* → Borne 1086 → Burna 1172 → Patricburñ 1215 → Patrickeburn 1228 → Patrikkesbourne 1253 → Patrickesborne 1610). The place has taken the name of William Patricius, or Patrick, owner of the manor here during the reign of Stephen.

Pattenden, Great and **Little.** Peata's woodland pasture (OE *Peating denn* → Patinden' 1254 → Patyngdenn' 1292 → Petyndenne 1327 → Patindenne 1334). Pattenden in Goudhurst, five miles away, shares the same original meaning.

Pattens Lane. The place derives its name from the family of Benjamin Petyn, or Potyn, of Rochester (1294).

Pauls Farm (Leigh). Poll, head (ME *polle* → Polle 1254). The name originally described a mound or hillock here, the present form obviously being the result of confusion with the personal name Paul.

Pay Street. The place appears to be associated with the family of Henry Peys (1348) who came from the Folkestone area.

Pean. Pound, enclosure (OE *pund* → Pende 1304). Peen Barn, East Sutton, shares the same origin, being recorded as Pynde in 1278, Pende in 1465.

Pearce Barn. It derives its name from the family of William Pers of Tenterden (1474).

Pearmain. Recorded as Peremannesmed (Peremann's meadow) c.1380, the place is associated with the family of John Periman (1347).

Peartree Wood and **Lane** (Shorne). Self-explanatory (OE *pyrige* → Pyrye 1345). Peartree Farm, Bilsington, was originally a 'pear farmstead: farmstead where peartrees grow' (OE *pyrige tūn*), and is recorded as Piritun' in 1256. This is also the meaning of Periton Court, Westwell, which appears as Perriton in 1276.

Peckham, East and **West** (pronounced Peckum). Peak settlement: settlement by a peak, or prominent hill (OE *pēac hām* → Peccham c.975 → Pecheham 1086 → Pecham 1189). West Peckham – recorded as West Pekeham in 1202 – is situated on the slope of a fairly high hill. East Peckham – recorded as East Pecham in 1293 – is low-

lying and is probably a later settlement, or an extension of the original one at West Peckham. Peckham near Ulcombe takes its name from the family of Reginald Peckham, natives of Peckham who possessed the manor here during the reign of Henry VI. This family also owned East Fairbourne in the neighbouring parish of Harrietsham during the reign of Elizabeth I.

Pedding Farm, Great (Ash). Pydda's people (OE *Pyddingas* → Pedinge 1251 → Peddinges, Peddynge 1287 → Peddynge 1304). This tribe were also settled at the now lost place of Peddynge Wood in Doddington, recorded as Peddynge in 1304.

Pedham Court (Eynsford). Pit settlement: settlement close to pits (OE *pytt hām* → Petham 1203 → Putham 1313 → Pettham 1334). The 'pits' may have been traps for large animals.

Pedlinge (pronounced Peddlinje). Pydel's people (OE *Pydelingas* → Pedling' 1240 → Pedelynge 1292 → Pedlynge 1304).

Peen Barn. See under PEAN.

Peening Quarter. Enclosed place (OE *pynding* → le Pendynge 1440 → Pinyon Quarter 1790).

Pegwell Bay. The name first appears in 1799 and is probably derived from ME *pigge well:* 'pig spring'. Pigwell near Lydd has this meaning, being recorded as Pigwell wall in 1433, pyg Well in 1530.

Pell Bridge. This place name, together with Pell House, Biddenden, and Pells Farm, Kingsdown, contains a dialect word 'pell' used of a deeper spot in a shallow stretch of water. The word is derived from OE *pōl*: pool. Pell Bridge is in an area drained by several streams.

Pembles Cross. The place takes its name from the family of William le Pemel of Egerton (1309).

Pembury. Stronghold of the *Pepingas*, or look-out men (OE *Pepinga burh* → Peppingeberia c.1100 → Pepingebir' 1205 → Peapyngeberi 1309 → Peuenburye *alias* Pemburye 1575).

Penenden Heath (pronounced Pennendn). Pinna's woodland pasture (OE *Pinning denn* → Pinnedennam 1086 → Pinnendene 1087 → Pynendenn 1275 → Pinenden c.1350). The personal name is also found in connection with PINDEN.

Penn Court (Hollingbourne). Pound, enclosure (OE *pund* → Pende 1332 → Pendecourt 1434). Penn Farm, Sundridge, has the same original meaning and appears as Pende in 1327.

Penshurst (pronounced Penzurst). 'Pen's wood': wooded hill within a pen or enclosed place (OE *pennes hyrst* → Penesherst 1072 → Pennes herst c.1100 → Peneshurst 1203 → Pensherst 1610). Between 1263 and 1346 the place appears as Penecestre, or Penchester, a name adopted by Stephen de Penecestre who possessed the manor towards the end of the 13th century.

Pepperness. 'Pepper headland': headland where the sand or gravel resembles peppercorn (OE *pipor nœss* → Pipernæsse 1023 → Pepernessa 1328 → Pepper Nesst 1675 → Pepperness 1696).

Periton Court. See under PEARTREE WOOD.

Perry Court (Preston). Pear-tree (OE *pyrige* → Perie, Pirie 1086 → Pirie c.1100 → Pyrie, Perie 1242 → Pery 1610). Pear-trees were also responsible for the names of Perry Court, Wye; Perry Farm, Chartham and Preston; Perry Hill, Lewisham; Perry Street, Chislehurst and Northfleet; and Perry Wood, Knockholt and Selling.

Perry Street. See under PERRY COURT.

Pested Farm. See under PASTEAD WOOD.

Petham (pronounced Pettum). Pit settlement: settlement close to pits (OE *pytt hām* → Pettham 961 → Piteham 1086 → Pettham 1226). As with PEDHAM COURT, the 'pits' were probably animal traps.

Petlands. Pit land: land on which there are pits or hollows (OE *pytt land* → Petlands 1504).

Petleys, Lower Petleys. Pit clearing: clearing marked by a pit (OE *pytt lēah* → Pitle, Petlee 1301 → Petle 1366).

Pett. Pit or hollow (OE *pytt* → Pytte c.1100 → Pette 1325). The same meaning is found in the names of Pett Bottom; Pett Farm, Bridge; Pett Farm and Littlepett, Stockbury; Pett Place, Charing; Pett

Street, Wye; Pett Wood, Bapchild; and Petts Wood near Chislehurst.

Pett Bottom, Petts Wood. See under PETT.

Petteridge. Pætla's ridge (OE *Pætlan hrycg* → Pætlanhryge 747 → Pætlan hyrcg 942 → Petteregge 1232).

Petting Grove. Recorded as Pitting'ue in 1240, the origin of this name appears to have been a grove associated with a pit or hollow (OE *pytting grāf*).

Pevington. Pēofa's farmstead (OE *Pēofing tūn* → Piventone 1086 → Piuentune, Piuingtune c.1100 → Pevinton' 1242 → Pyvington 1346 → Pevington 1610).

Phen Farm (Wrotham). It derives its name from the family of atte-fenne or atte Venne – 'dweller by the fen' (OE *fenn*) – who are recorded in the Wrotham area in the 13th and 14th centuries.

Phillis Grove. The place is associated with the family of John le ffylye (1278), the name being derived from the genitival form ffylyes.

Philpott's Cross. It is named after the family of Thomas Philpott of Hawkhurst (1507). Philpots, Hildenborough, is similarly named after the family of Philipott who owned this estate during the 14th century.

Picardy Street. Recorded in 1562 as Pycardswell, and in 1569 as Pyccarde Streete, the place doubtless takes its name from some local family named Pycard or Pyccarde.

The present form appears to have been influenced by Picardy in France.

Pickelden Farm (Chartham). Pīc's woodland pasture (OE *Pīcing denn* → Pykyndenne 1327 → Pikynden' 1338). The personal name is also found in connection with PICKENDEN WOOD and PICKERING STREET.

Pickenden. Pinca's woodland pasture (OE *Pincing denn* → Pynkyndenn' 1272 → Pinkyndenn' 1307). Alternatively, the name may originally have referred to a pasture frequented by finches (OE *pinca*).

Pickenden Wood (Goudhurst). Pīc's woodland pasture (OE *Pīcing denn* → Pikindon' 1240 → Pykyndenne 1313 → Pykynden' 1347). Pīc had another pasture at PICKELDEN.

Pickering Street. It derives its name from the Maidstone family variously recorded as Pikynge (1327), Pykynge (1346) and Pykyngges (1377). This family name appears to be derived from OE *Pīcingas*: Pic's people.

Picketts. The place is associated with the family of William Pigott of Chiddingstone (1567). Piggott's Wood, Hever, also derives its name from this family.

Pick Hill (Tenterden). 'Point slope': slope running down from a point or peak (OE *pīc hielde* → Pikhilde 1491).

Pickhurst. 'Point wood': wooded hill near a point or peak (OE *pīc*

147

hyrst → Pikehurst 1289 → Pykeherst 1292 → Pikherst c.1325).

Pickles. Goblin (haunted) (OE *pūcel* → Poukel 1327 → Pickle, Puckle wood 1698). Puckle Hill, Shorne, probably shares a similar origin.

Piggott's Wood. See under PICK-ETTS.

Pigsbrook Wood (Great Chart). The place is recorded as Lower Pig-broockes 1617 → Upper Pigbrookes 1618 → Pigbrucks 1683, possibly deriving its name from the family of Thomas Pykebroke (1348). Alternatively, this may once have been marshy ground where pigs were kept (ME *pigge broke*).

Pigwell. See under PEGWELL BAY.

Pikefish. It is associated with the family of Richard Pykeuys of Yalding (1327).

Pilbeams. The place derives its name from the family of Peltebem, recorded in the Chiddingstone area during the 14th century.

Pile Gate. Recorded in 1610 as Pylgate, the name possibly refers to a gate by which piles of wood were stacked, being derived from OE *pīl geat*: pile, or stake, gate.

Pilesheath. This was originally heathland belonging to the family of Richard Puyl (1254).

Pilgrims' Way. This is the name given to the route used by pilgrims to the tomb of St. Thomas à Becket in Canterbury Cathedral. The Way, running along the foot of the North Downs from the Surrey border to Folkestone, is believed to follow the course of a British trading route.

Pimp's Court (East Farleigh). Swelling (OE *pinpre* → Pinpa, Pinpe 1086 → Pinpe, Pympe 1242 → Pympe 1278). The 'swelling' is probably the rounded hill on which Pimp's Court stands.

Pinden. Pinna's valley (OE *Pinning dene* → Pinindene c.975 → Pinnedene 1086 → Pinidene 1216 → Pinden, Pynden 1522). Pinna had a woodland pasture at PENENDEN.

Pineham. Pin, or peg settlement (OE *pinn hām* → Piham 1086 → Pinham 1232 → Pynam 1292). This appears to have been a settlement within some kind of enclosure.

Pinkhorn Green. It is recorded in 1327 as Peancrone, and in 1343 as Pencrone, and may possibly have the original meaning of 'Pineca's fallen trees, or debris' (OE *Pinecan hruna*). Pinkhorn Green is very close to Headcorn, which has a similar origin.

Pinks. Described as Pinkes-croft in 1680, the place derives its name from the family of Pinke (1218), residents of neighbouring Tong. Pinks Corner, Minster, is associated with John Pynck (1619).

Piper's Pen. It appears c.1460 as Pypersford and is probably a manorial name. Little Pipers Wood, Little Chart, is connected with the family of William Pypere or Pipere (1348).

Pippins. The place derives its name from the Brenchley family of Richard Pyppyn (1346).

Pipsden. Pipp's woodland pasture (OE *Pippes denn* → Pippesden' 1240 → Pippesdeñe 1327 → Pyppysden 1559).

Pitfield. Pit's land: open land on which there are pits or hollows (OE *pyttes feld* → Pettesfeld' 1240 → Pettefelde 1313 → Pettesfeld 1347).

Pitstock Farm (Rodmersham). Peas place: place where peas grow (OE *pise stoc* → Pistok' 1254 → Pistocke c.1290 → Pystock 1572).

Pitt Wood (Adisham). Wood in which there are pits or hollows (OE *pytt wudu* → Petwode 1332 → Petwod 1535).

Pixwell. Recorded in 1799 as Pigsole, the name is probably derived from ME *pigge sole*: muddy pool where pigs wallow.

Pizien Well. It appears in 1473 as Pyssyngwelle, and in 1782 as Pizeinwell, the name referring to the small stream here which served in medieval times as an open sewer.

Plaistow (pronounced Plasstow). See under PLAXTOL.

Plaxtol. Play place (OE *plegstōw* → Plextole 1386 → Plaxtol 1650). Plaistow near Bromley shares the same original meaning of a place where villagers gathered for sport and recreation, and is recorded as Pleystowe in 1278, Playstowe in 1467. In many Kentish parishes the name 'pleystole' or playstool

used to be given to a piece of land on which miracle and other plays were performed: the spelling of Plaxtol appears to have been influenced by this word.

Ploggs Hall (Capel). It is associated with the family of Richard Plog (1240).

Pluckley. Plucca's clearing (OE *Pluccan lēah* → Pluchelei 1086 → Plucelea, Plukele c.1100 → Pluckele 1270 → Plukley 1610).

Plumford. Plum-tree enclosure (OE *plūme worð* → Plumwurth 1236 → Plumbworth 1316 → Plumforde 1347 → Plomford 1535). Change of final -worth to -ford is quite common in place names.

Plumpton Farm (Wye). Plum-tree farmstead: plum orchard (OE *plūme tūn* → Plumton' 1272).

Plumstead. Plum-tree place, orchard (OE *plūme stede* → Plumstede 969 → Plvmestede 1086 → Plumsted 1206).

Plumstone Farm (Monkton). It has the same original meaning as PLUMSTEAD, being recorded as Plumsted, Plomstede c.1250, Plumstede in 1357. Later change of -stede to -stone is probably a fanciful corruption.

Plurenden. Plera's woodland pasture (OE *Plering denn* → Plerinden' 1226 → Plerindenn 1260 → Plerynden *alias* Plunden 1790).

Podberry Wood (Eastwell). Pot stronghold (OE *pott burh* → Pottebiri 1294 → Pottebery 1305 →

Potbury 1548). Excavations in this area have revealed a large number of potsherds: perhaps the original residents of Podberry likewise found fragments of pottery in an earthwork here, and named the place accordingly.

Poison Down and Wood. Though there are no records of this name, it is almost certainly a corruption of the name of the now lost place of Pising here in East Langdon. This derived from OE *pysingas*: 'the short, fat people', and is recorded as Pesinges 1086 → Pisingis 1179 → Pesinge 1232 → Pysing 1313.

Poldhurst Farm (Harbledown). Water-logged land (OE *pōlra* → Polre 1292 → Poldre 1332 → Polders 1535). Change of final -ers to -hurst is quite common in the development of place names.

Polebrook Pool ground: marshy ground where there are pools (OE *pōl brōc* → Polebroc 1240 → Polbroke 1347). The place is close to the River Eden.

Polefields. 'Polled land': open land which has been closely cropped (ME *pollede feld* → Polledefeld' 1283).

Polehill Wood. See under POLLYFIELD.

Pole Wood (Chilham). Polled, or pollarded, wood (ME *pollede wode* → Polledewode 1338).

Poles, High and Low. Recorded in 1722 as Highpolesfarm, the name possibly has some connection with pools in this well-watered area.

Pollard's Barn. It is described in 1464 as Pollards, the name appearing to be a manorial one.

Pollyfield. Pool hill: hill above pools (OE *pōl hyll* → Polehull' 1240 → Polhelle 1332 → Polehelle 1346). Change of final -hill to -field was probably done to distinguish this place from Polehill Wood in neighbouring Boxley, which has the same original meaning as Pollyfield.

Polly Shaw. Pool enclosure: hedged enclosure near a pool (OE *pōl hæg* → Polhey 1292 → Polley 1528). The affix 'Shaw' is from OE *scaga*: a copse.

Ponshall. Poplar's corner: corner of land marked by a poplar (OE *popules halh* → Popeselle, Popessale 1086 → Poplesheale c.1100 → Popeshale 1278 → Popshall 1799).

Poors. It derives its name from the 14th century Sheppey family of Por, or Poor.

Pootens. The place is described in 1347 as Potonesmede (Potone's meadow), taking its name from the family of de Potone of Westerham (1327).

Popestreet Farm (Godmersham). Associated with Peter and William le Pope (1313), it is recorded as Popestreet in 1690. The surname is also found in connection with Pope House, Smarden, and Pope's Hall, Hartlip.

Poppington Farm (Selling). It appears as Popindane in 1321, the name probably being derived from OE *Popping dene*: Poppa's valley.

Port Farm (Chislet). Beautiful portal, or entrance (OE *fæger port* → Fayreport c.1225 → Faireport 1240 → Feyrporte, Porta 1270 → La Porte 1375 → Port 1502). The farm lies close to the Great Stour, its name apparently a reference to some fine harbour here.

Porter's Lane. It is associated with the family of Hugh le Porter of Ospringe (1270). This surname also occurs in connection with Porter's Farm, Kemsing; Porter's Wood, Brenchley; and Porters Wood, Goudhurst.

Posiers. The place derives its name from the 14th century Borden family of Posere, or Poser.

Postern. Described in 1347 as 'porta de la Posterne ad Burgā de Tonebrugg' — gate of the postern to the Manor of Tonbridge — the name is derived from OF *posterne*: a back, or side entrance.

Postling (pronounced Pozlin). Postel's people (OE *Postlingas* → Postinges, Pistinges 1086 → Postlinges 1211 → Postlinge 1253 → Postling 1610).

Potman's Heath. See under POTTEN STREET.

Potten Street. It derives its name from the family of Potyn, found in St. Nicholas-at-Wade during the 14th and 15th centuries. Potten Farm, Bethersden, is connected with the family of Potten, recorded here in 1661; while Potten Farm, Sellindge, takes its name from that of the Poteman family of Sellindge, recorded in 1327. Potman's Heath, Wittersham, is probably to be associated with the family of Potyn, who are recorded in the Wittersham area between the 14th and 16th centuries.

Potters Corner. Recorded as such in 1620, the place is named after a landowner in the Ashford area.

Pouces. It is connected with the family of Thomas Poucyn of Minster (1310).

Poulders, Great and **Little** (pronounced Pole-ders). Water-logged ground (OE *pōlra* → Polr 1220 → Polre 1237 → Poldre 1269). This is still a well-watered district.

Poulhurst. The place name is recorded as Poueshurst in 1254 and as Powesherst in 1338, and contains as a final element OE *hyrst*: wooded hill. The first element appears to be a personal name, but lack of earlier forms prevents definition. Neither are there any records after the 14th century to show how the name developed to its present form.

Poulton (pronounced Poletun). Pool farmstead: farmstead by pools (OE *pōl tūn* → Poltone 1086 → Poltune c.1100 → Poltone 1226). The same origin is shared by Poulton, Aldington, and by Poulton Farm, Woodnesborough.

Pound House. See under POUNDS BRIDGE.

Poundhurst. Pound wood: wooded hill by a pound or enclosure (OE *pund hyrst* → Pundhurste 1240 → Pundherst 1278 → Poundherst' 1325).

Pounds Bridge. Recorded as Powndesland c.1400, this seems to have been land owned by the medieval family of atte Punde, or atte Pounde — 'dweller by the pound' (OE *pund*). This name is found in connection with Pound House, Sellindge.

Pratt's Bottom and **Grove.** They derive their name from the family of Stephen Prat (1332).

Preston (near Faversham). Priests' farmstead, or manor (OE *prēosta tūn* → Preostatùn 946 → Prestetone 1086 → Prestone 1253). Preston near Wingham has the same origin, being recorded as Prestetun 1086 → Prestetune c.1100 → Preston 1204. Priests also held farmsteads, or manors, at Preston Farm and Hill, Shoreham; Preston Farm, St. Lawrence; Preston Hall and Little Preston, Aylesford; and at the now lost place of Preston in Tenterden.

Priestwood. Priests' wood: wood belonging to a monastic establishment (OE *prēosta wudu* → Prestewude 1240 → Prestwode 1338). Priestwood Green here has taken its name from the original place.

Priviss Wood (Selling). Originally known as Privet's, the place derives its name from the family of John Priuet, or Privet (1313).

Provender. It is recorded as Provenders in 1782 and is named after the family of John de Provender who owned the place during the reign of Henry III.

Puckle Hill. See under PICKLES.

Puckston Farm (Stodmarsh). Goblin's farmstead (OE *pūceles tūn* → Pukeleston 1198 → Pukelestun, Poukestone c.1225 → Pokeston' 1278). Perhaps the name is a reference to a farmstead which seemed cursed by demons.

Punish Wood (Snodland). Pufa's ash-tree (OE *Pufan æsc* → Povenesse 1242 → Pouenasse c.1300 → Pouenesshe 1313 → Pawnassh 1465).

Purr Wood (Godmersham). Clean, unblemished, wood (OE *pūr wudu* → pur wuda 824 → Purwod 1535). This probably refers to a wood which had not been touched, or cut in any way.

Putland's. The place is named after the family of Putland who owned the nearby manor of MASCALLS at the beginning of the 18th century.

Puttenden Manor (Shipbourne). Putta's woodland pasture (OE *Putting denn* → Putinden' 1175 → Puttenden 1258). Putta also owned woodland at PUTT WOOD.

Puttocks Down. Kite hill: hill where kites gather (OE *puttoc dūn* → Puttakedowne 1384 → Puttokkysdowne 1417).

Putt Wood (Ospringe). Putta's wood (OE *Puttan wudu* → Putewude 1164 → Putwude 1240 → Putwode 1313). Putta's pasture was at PUTTENDEN.

Q

Quarrington. Cūðhere's farmstead (OE *Cūðhering tūn* → Cudrinton' 1254 → Codrintone 1304 → Quedrinton' 1313 → Quetheryntone 1337 → Gwederyngton 1381).

Queenborough. The original place name was Bynnee, derived from OE *binnan ēa*: within the river, a reference to the old site at the mouth of the West Swale. Between 1361 and 1377 Edward III built a castle here to protect the important sea passage and renamed the site Queen's Borough in honour of his wife, Philippa. It is recorded as Quenesburgh 1367 → Queneburgh' 1376 → Queenborow 1610.

Queen Court (Ospringe). This was originally a royal estate, probably owned by Anne of Bohemia, queen of Richard II, and is recorded as Quencort 1405 → Quenecourt 1473 → Quenecourte 1535. Queen Court, Rainham, was the property of Eleanor, queen of Henry III, and appears as Quenescourte in 1376.

Queen Down Warren. It is recorded as Quenedowne in 1535 and as Queendown in 1598, the place presumably being the property of the Crown at some time.

Queningate. At the queen's gate (OE *æt þǣm cwēne gatum* → ad Quenegatum 762 → cwene gaton 993 → Quenegate 1254 → Quenyngate 1278). This is one of the old gates into the city of Canterbury.

Quex Park. Recorded as Queax in 1677 and as Quekes in 1690, the place derives its name from the family of Stephen and Robert le Queke of Minster (c.1250).

Quinton Farm (Milton Regis). It appears as Qwyntanstreet in Minster in 1530, taking its name from that of a local family variously recorded during the 14th and 15th centuries as Quyntyn, Queynte, Quinte and Quinton.

R

Rabbit's Cross. The place is associated with the family of Thomas Rabbet of Boughton Monchelsea (1613).

Radfield. Hrōda's open land (OE *Hrōdan feld* → Rodefeld' 1254 → Roddefeld 1270 → Rodefield 1349 → Radfelde 1556).

Rainham (pronounced Rainum). Settlement of the *Rœgingas*: the ruling, or powerful men (OE *Rœginga hām* → Rœginga hàm 811 → Rænham c.1100 → Reneham 1176 → Reynham 1240). Rainham is described as a royal town in a charter of 811.

Ramhurst. Ram wood: wooded hill where rams graze or are penned (OE *ramm hyrst* → Ramherst 1313 → Ramhurst 1347).

Ram Lane, Ram's Hill. See under RAMSGREEN.

Ramsden. Ram's pasture: woodland pasture where rams graze (OE *rammes denn* → Ramesdeñ 1200 → Rammesdenn' 1346 → Ramisden' 1347).

Ramsgate. Hrǣfn's gate, or cliff-gap (OE *Hrǣfnes geat* → Ramisgate, Remmesgate c.1225 → Ramesgate, Remisgate 1278 → Ramesgate 1357).

Ramsgreen. It derives its name from the family of John Ram of St. Mary's Hoo (1369). This surname also occurs in connection with Ram's Hill, Horsmonden, and Ram Lane, Westwell.

Ramslye. Raven's clearing: clearing frequented by ravens (OE *hrǣfnes lēah* → Ramesleye 1271 → Remeslegh 1314 → Rammyslee 1333).

Randle Wood (Shorne). Circular, round in shape (OF *rondelle* → Rondale 1147 → Rundalle 1226 → Roundale 1362). The name probably refers to a hill here.

Rankham Wood (Pembury). Raven valley: valley or coombe frequented by ravens (OE *hrǣfn cumb* → Ranecombe 1292 → Ranecumbe 1314 → Ravenescombe 1392).

Ranscombe. Raven's valley: valley or coombe frequented by ravens

154

(OE *hræfnes cumb* → Rainescumbe 1199 → Rennescumbe, Ramescumb' 1203 → Rammescombe 1392).

Ratling (pronounced Rattlin). 'Rubbish slope': slope where there is rubbish or rough growth for burning (OE *rȳt hlinc* → Rytlinge c.1100 → Retlinga 1176 → Rytling 1287 → Rattelyng 1393 → Ratlyng 1453).

Ravensbourne, River. Rendel's stream (ME *Rendeles burne* → Randesbourne 1360 → Rendesburne 1372). The present name is a late corruption of these original forms.

Rawlinson. Recorded as Rallynson in 1564, and as Ralynsonne in 1566, the place appears to have derived its name from a family living in the Newenden area during the early 16th century.

Rayham. At the island water meadow (OE *æt pǣre ēg hamme* → ME *atter eyhamme, atte reyhamme* → Reyhamme 1254 → Reyham, Ryhamme 1270). Rayham lies on flat, marshy ground on the Isle of Sheppey.

Ray Wood (Charing). At the island (OE *æt pǣre ēge* → ME *atter eye, atte reye* → Reye 1270). Ray Wood and Raywood Farm here must be on the site of an island formed by the stream close by.

Reach Court (St. Margaret's-at-Cliffe). Ridge (OE *hrycg* → Reche 1292 → Regge 1327 → La Regge 1346 → Ryche 1535).

Reading Street (Tenterden). Clearing-dwellers (OE *Hrydingas* →

Reedinges 1216 → Ryding' 1254 → Redynges 1372 → Reding 1690). Reading Street, St. Peters, is recorded as Redyng in 1399 and possibly has the original meaning of 'clearing, ridded place' (OE *hryding*).

Reason Hill (Linton). It takes its name from that of the family of John Reisoun of Linton (1327).

Reculver (pronounced Ray-culver). Great beak, or headland (B *ro-gulbā* → Regulbium c.425 → Racuulfe c.730 → æt Ræculfo 825 → Reaculfe c.890 → Rocolf 1086 → Raculvre 1276 → Reculuer 1610). Regulbium, recorded c.425, was the Romano-British name for this point on the north Kentish coast.

Redborough. The family name of Redborough' is recorded here in 1522: either the place name is a manorial one, or it is derived from OE *rēad beorg*: red mound.

Redbrook Street. Described in 1790 as Redbrooke-street, the origin of the name is probably 'reed marsh: marshy ground where reeds grow' (OE *hrēod brōc*). Redbrook Wood, Worth, certainly has this meaning, being recorded as Ridbroke, Ryedbroke c.1250. Redbrooks Wood, Saltwood, appears as Redebroc c.1140 → Redbroc 1154 → Redebrock' 1270 → Radbrooks 1790, and may either have the meaning of 'red marshy ground' (OE *rēad brōc*) or 'reed marsh' (OE *hrēod brōc*).

Rede Court (Strood). Cleared, or ridded, land (OE *rīed* → Rede 1270 → Rede Court 1535). Reed Court, Marden, has the same original meaning of land cleared of trees and undergrowth, appearing as Rede in 1232.

Redham Mead. Reed settlement: settlement by a place where reeds grow (OE *hrēod hām* → Hreodham 778 → Riedham 1251 → Redeham 1257). The affix is from OE *mǣd*: mead, meadow.

Red Hill (Appledore). Recorded in 1565 as Read hill, the name is probably self-explanatory and refers to red clayey soil. Red Wood, Luddesdown, has the original meaning of 'at the red wood' (OE *æt þǣm rēadan wuda*) and appears as Redenewode 1345 → Readwode 1381 → Redde wod 1538 → Redd wood 1572. Red Wood Lees, Petham, appears to share the same origin, with the addition of 'lea' (OE *lǣs*: meadowland).

Redleaf House (Penshurst). The house stands on the site of parkland recorded as Redleaf in 1279, the name being derived from OE *rēadlēaf*: red-leaved, referring to the colour of tree foliage here.

Redoak. See under BLADBEAN.

Redsole. Reed pool: muddy pool where reeds grow (OE *hrēod sol* → Readesole 1327 → Redesole 1334).

Redsteadle Wood (Ash). Although there are no records for this name, it appears to contain the Kentish dialect word 'steddle', the framework of a timbered building.

Red Wood. See under RED HILL.

Reed Court. See under REDE COURT.

Reinden Wood (Hawkinge). Roes' woodland pasture: pasture where small deer graze (OE *rǣgena denn* → Reindene 1262 → Reyndenn 1270 → Rayneden 1539).

Remmingtons. Horsemen's woodland pasture (OE *rǣdemanna denn* → Redmundenne c.1270 → Radmyndenne 1348 → Rymington 1632). The place is very close to HORSMONDEN, which was also a pasture used by horsemen, or horse-keepers.

Renville. Trimmed, or cut off open land (OE *pryme feld* → Trimfeld' 1240 → Thremfelde 1332 → Renfelde 1535). The present name has resulted from the corruption of -field to -ville.

Reynold's Wood (Otterden). It derives its name from the family of Roger Reynold of Otterden (1371). This surname is also found in the names of Reynolds Place, Horton Kirby; Reynold's Farm, Hawkhurst; and Reynolds's, Brasted.

Rhee Wall (pronounced Ree). At the river (OE *æt pǣre ē* → ME *atter ee, atte ree* → Ree 1293 → Rewal c.1450). The Wall, the Roman *Rivi Vallum*, was built to contain WALLAND MARSH to its south and west.

Rhodecommon Wood (Selling). Clearing (OE *rod* → Rode 1247). Rhodecourt Farm here shares the same origin, -common and -court being late affixes to the original place name.

Rhoden Green. Clearing pasture:

156

woodland pasture beyond a clearing (OE *rod denn* → Roddene 1254 → Roddenne 1332). Ridding Farm, Lenham, has approximately the same meaning, being recorded as Riddeden' 1226 → Ryddenne 1292 → Ridenne 1334 (← OE *rīed denn*).

Rhodes Farm (Lyminge). Clearing (OE *rod* → Rode 1327). Rhodes Minnis here is recorded as Mennesse-gate in 1327, and has the meaning of 'gate on to land owned by the community' (OE *gemænnes geat*).

Rhodes Minnis. See under RHODES FARM.

Richborough. The name appears to be derived from the British word *rūt*: a ditch or trench, with an affix *-up-*, and is recorded as Routoupiai c.150 → Rutupis c.425 → Rutubi portus, Reptacæstir c.730 → Rætte c.1100 → Ratteburg 1197 → Retes-brough c.1350 → Richborow 1610. 'Borough' is derived from OE *burh*: stronghold. Richborough was the great Romano-British fortress of *Rutupiæ* which guarded the main port of Roman Britain.

Richdore. Recorded as Dore in 1535, the place appears to have taken the name of Hugh le Riche (1240) to distinguish it from ANSDORE nearby.

Rickwoods. It is described as 'tenement called Ricard' in 1487, and as 'tenement called Rykards' in 1543, and is probably on the site of a tenement, or house, belonging to the 15th century family of Ricard.

Ridding Farm. See under RHODEN GREEN.

Rides, Old and **New.** Clearing, ridded place (OE *rīed* → Rid' 1239 → Ryde, Ride 1327 → Rede 1535 → Rydes 1679).

Ridge Row. Ridge (OE *hrycg* → Regge 1226). Ridge Farm here shares the same origin. Ridge Wood, Chilham, appears as Rugge in 1338; and Ridge Wood, Meopham, is Regwode in 1381, the name being derived from OE *hrycg wudu:* wooded ridge.

Ridgeway Farm (Herne). Self-explanatory (OE *hrycg weg* → Rigweye 1226 → Regge way 1485). Shorne Ridgeway was also originally a way or track across a hill ridge, and is recorded as Regedweya in 1250, Regweye in 1332. There was also a now lost Ridgeway in Woodchurch.

Ridge Wood. See under RIDGE ROW.

Ridinggate. At the red gate (OE *æt þæm rēadan gate* → Reada gata 1038 → Radegate 1240 → Redingate 1282). This was one of the old gates into the city of Canterbury.

Ridley. Reed clearing: clearing where reeds grow (OE *hrēod lēah* → Redlege 1086 → Riddelee 1198 → Redligh 1275 → Redlegh, Reddeley 1278 → Ridley 1610).

Rigshill. Rīca's muddy pool (OE *Rīcan sol* → Rikesole 1278 → Rykesole 1313 → Riggesole 1367 → Rygsole 1535).

Ringlecrouch. Recorded as Crouche

157

in 1327, and as Cruche in 1347, the place appears to have taken its name from a cross (ME *crouche*), the arms of which were enclosed within a decorated ring: 'ringle' is a dialect word for a ring or circle, so the cross would have been known as the 'ringle cross'.

Ringlemere. Hringwynn's pool (OE *Hringwynne mere* → Ryngwynm'e 1278 → Ryngylmere 1431 → Ringlemere c.1545). Hringwynn's farmstead (OE *Hringwynne tūn*) was on the site of neighbouring Ringleton, and is recorded as Ringetone 1086 → Ringuentun c.1090 → Ringeton 1200 → Ringelton 1264 → Ringleton 1610. In both place names, ME *hringel*: a little ring or circle, appears to have crept in to alter the original forms. This Saxon lady's property appears to have been close to a pool or other round natural formation which gradually became associated with the places long after Hringwynn herself had been forgotten.

Ringleton. See under RINGLE-MERE.

Ringwould (pronounced Ring-wolde). Forest of Hreðel's people (OE *Hreðelinga weald* → Rœdlig-wealda 861 → Rudelingewealde 1216 → Ridelingweald 1274 → Redelingwelde 1311 → Ringeweld 1476 → Ringewold 1502). Contraction of this place name had already begun in the 12th century, since it is recorded as Ringwald in 1185.

Ripe, East and **West.** Edge, strip (OE *ripp* → Ripp 741). The Ripes, a stretch of land running out towards the sea near Lydd, also has this original meaning.

Ripney Hill (Minster). Rippa's island (OE *Rippan ēg* → Ripenay 1192 → Rippen' 1205 → Rypeneie 1226 → Rippene 1329). This would have been an island of firm ground in marshland.

Ripple. Strip of land (OE *rippel* → Ryple 1087 → Rippell' 1226 → Ripple 1235). The same original meaning is shared by Ripple near Hollingbourne (Ripple 1301); Ripple near Westwell (Riple 1240, Ripple 1292); and Ripple Farm, Crundale (Little Ripple 1728).

Ripton Farm (Ashford). Rǣpa's farmstead (OE *Rǣpan tūn* → Rapen-tone 1086 → Rapintune c.1100 → Repeton 1267 → Rapetun 1275 → Rypton 1471). Alternatively, this may have been the farmstead of a captive or slave (OE *rǣpa*), or one which was worked by Britons.

Risden. Brushwood pasture (OE *hrīs denn* → Rissesdenn' 1240 → Risden bridge 1507).

Riseden. Brushwood pasture (OE *hrīs denn* → Rysdenne c.1225 → Risseden 1278 → Risden' 1347).

Rishfords. Rush ford: ford where rushes grow (OE *rysc ford* → Risse-forde 1253 → Ryshford 1270 → Rissheford 1346 → Rishfords *alias* Rushfords 1782). The place lies on a tributary stream of the Beult.

River. The name was originally OE *burna*: stream, and is recorded c.1100 as Burnan. Late in the 12th century the Old French *rivere*: river, took the place of the earlier English name, and River is found as Riv-eria 1199 → River 1227 → La

Ryvere 1228. River Minnis here takes its affix from OE *gemænnes*: land owned jointly by the community, and appears as Manesse in 1203.

Riverhead. The place is described in 1778 as 'Rotherhith, or Rethered, now called Riverhead'. The original meaning of this name is 'cattle landing-place' (OE *hrīðer hȳð*), and it appears as Reydrythe 1292 → Readride 1313 → Retherhead 1619 → Retherhed *alias* Riverhead 1656. The present name is due to the place's position at the head of the River Darent.

Robhurst. Bubba's wooded hill (OE *Bubban hyrst* → Bubehurst 1254 → Bubherst 1278). The change in initial letter appears to be the result of confusion with the personal names of Bob and Robert.

Rochester (pronounced Rochister). Its Romano-British name was Durobrivæ: 'stronghold at the bridges' (← B *duro brīvā*) – the British stronghold was enclosed by Roman walls, and the bridges crossed the Medway. In early pronunciation the first syllable in the place name, which is recorded as Durobrivis c.730 and as Dorobrevi in 844, was unstressed, the accent being on the second syllable. Bede, copying down the name c.730, mistook its meaning to be 'Hrofi's fortified camp' (OE *Hrofes cæster*), and in this form Rochester developed as Hrofæscæstre c.730 → Hrofescester 811 → Rovecestre 1086 → Rochester 1610.

Rockhills. The place appears to be associated with the family of de la Rokele, owners of the Manor of

Beckenham during the reign of Edward I.

Rodmersham (pronounced Roddmersum). Hrōðmær's settlement (OE *Hrōðmæres hām* → Rodmæresham c.1100 → Rodmaresham 1197 → Rodmersham c.1210).

Rogers Wood (Biddenden). It derives its name from the family of Robert Roger of Biddenden (1357).

Rogley. Rough clearing (OE *rūh lēah* → Rogelegh', Rugel' 1254).

Rolvenden (pronounced Rovvinden). Hrōðwulf's woodland pasture (OE *Hrōðwulfing denn* → Rovinden 1086 → Ruluindænne c.1100 → Ruluindena 1187 → Rulfindenn' Rulvenden' 1226 → Rolvindenn' 1242 → Rolvenden 1610).

Rolvenden Layne. Recorded in 1251 as Leyne, this was a large tract of arable land, the name probably being derived from 'lain' – *i.e.* that which has lain fallow. The word 'laine' is still used in dialect speech of such land.

Romacres. Wide piece of cultivated land (OE *rūm æcer* → Romekere 1327).

Romden. Wide woodland pasture (OE *rūm denn* → Rumden' 1240 → Romdenn' 1346 → Romden 1690).

Romney, Old and **New** (pronounced Rumney). The name is derived from OE *æt þære rūman ē*: 'at the spacious, or wide, river', recorded in 895 as Rumenea, and in 914 as Rumenesea. This appears to have been an early name for Romney

Marsh, whose inhabitants are referred to in 774 as *Merscuuare*, and in 796 as *Merscware* (← OE *mersc ware*: marsh people). Their territory is described in 811 as *regio Merscuuariorum* (region of the marsh people); and earlier, in 697, there appears here the name *Ruminingseta*: 'fold of the dwellers by the spacious river'. The present place names appear as Rumney, Old Rumney in 1575, and as Romney, Old Romney in 1610.

Romney Street. It possibly derives its name from the family of Roger Romeyn (1327).

Roodlands. The name appears as Rodlande in 1348, and may either have originally meant 'clearing land' (OE *rod land*), or 'rood land': land measuring one rood, or rod (OE *rōd land*).

Rooting (pronounced Rootin). Rōta's people (OE *Rōtingas* → Rotinge 1086 → Rotinges 1237 → Rotynge, Roting' 1278).

Roper Lane. See under LONGROPE WOOD.

Ropersole Farm (Barham). Rook's pool: pool frequented by rooks (OE *hrōces pōl* → Roxpoll 1444 → Roxpole 1475 → Rockspoole Wood 1589 → Great Roxpoll Wood, Little Roxpoll 1622). There are no later forms to show how the present name evolved. Neither are there any forms for Roxborough Wood in the neighbouring parish of Denton, but the name appears to be derived from OE *hrōces beorg*: rook's mound.

Roseacre Street. Rook's land: cultivated piece of land frequented by rooks (OE *hrōces æcer* → Rokesakere 1258 → Rokesacre 1327).

Rosecourt Barn. Together with Rosecourt Farm here, the place is on the site of a Rose Court, recorded in 1371.

Rosecroft. It takes its name from the family of John Rose of St. Mary Cray (1374).

Roselands Farm (Ulcombe). Described as 'Rose Land called Stone Bridge in Ulcomb' in 1466, and called Roses Farm in 1636, the place derives its name from the family of William Rose (1461).

Rosherville. The place is named after Jeremiah Rosher, who created a popular Victorian pleasure spot here in the mid-19th century.

Rother, River (Eastern). The name is a back-formation from that of Rotherfield in Sussex, where the river rises. The original name of the river was derived from a Celtic word for elm-tree: *lem*, and is recorded as Liminel c.1180 → Lymmene, Lymene 1279 → Lymme 1474. It first appears as the Rother in 1575.

Roughstocks Wood (Ruckinge). Rough stock, or stump (OE *rūh stocc* → Rowstokks, Rowse Stocks 1539).

Roughway. Rough enclosure (OE *rūh (ge)hæg* → Rouheye 1240 → Rouhey, Rogheye 1270 → Rufway 1690). Ruffets Wood, Woodchurch, shares the same original meaning, being recorded as Rogheye in 1313.

Round Street. Recorded in 1630 as Roundstreete, the place has probably taken the name of some local family.

Rowetts. It derives its name from the family of Thomas Rowhede of Eastchurch (1485).

Rowhill Wood (Wilmington). Together with Rowhill Grange and Rowhill Mount here, the place has the original meaning of 'rough hill' (OE *rūh hyll*) and appears as La Ruehille 1294 → Rowehulle 1358 → Rowhull, Roughull 1376.

Rowley Hill (Pembury). 'Row clearing': clearing containing a row of dwellings (OE *rāw lēah* → Raule 1313).

Rowling Court (Goodnestone). Rōla's people (OE *Rōlingas* → Rolling 1247 → Rollinges 1270 → Rullyngge 1278 → Roullyngs 1363 → Rollynge 1421 → Rowling 1648). Rowling House and Farm here are also on the site of the territory of the *Rōlingas*. This tribal name appears again in Rowling Street near Bilsington, recorded as Rolling in 1275.

Roxborough Wood. See under ROPERSOLE.

Royal Military Canal. The canal runs from Hythe to Rye and was constructed at the beginning of the 19th century as part of the land defences during the Napoleonic War.

Royal Tunbridge Wells. See TUNBRIDGE WELLS.

Royton Chapel. At the island farmstead (OE *æt þǣre ēg tūne* → ME *atter eye tone, atte reye tone* → Reyton' 1223 → Reitun', Reytone c.1250 → Roytone 1332 → Royton chappell 1535). Chapel Farm here is very close to the Great Stour and may be on the site of the original farmstead, built on an island in marshy ground.

Rubery Drove. Rough mound (OE *rūh beorg* → Ruweberg' 1240 → Rewbergh 1382). The affix 'Drove' is a dialect word used of a wide path along which cattle are driven.

Ruckhurst Wood (Goudhurst). It has been suggested that the place is named after William Rookherst, "a gentleman of Scotland", who built a mansion in Goudhurst some time during the reign of Henry I. However, this place name may possibly be derived from OE *hrōc hyrst*: rook wood, wooded hill frequented by rooks.

Ruckinge (pronounced Ruckinje). Hrōc's people (OE *Hrōcingas* → Hrocing 805 → Hrocinges 1066 → Rochinges 1086 → Rokinges 1211 → Rukynges 1242 → Rokinge 1253 → Rucking 1610). Ruckinge Grove, Herne, which is recorded as Rokinggraue in 1278, appears originally to have been a grove (OE *grāf*) associated with this tribe.

Ruffets Wood. See under ROUGHWAY.

Ruffin's Hill (Aldington). It is associated with Robert Ruffin and Henry Ruffyn of Aldington (1278) and appears as Ruffins Hill in 1619.

Rugmore Hill (Yalding). Rugga's

161

pool (OE *Ruggan mere* → Ruggem'e 1292 → Ruggemere 1313 → Rugmerehyll 1503 → Rugmere Hill 1782).

Rumney Farm (Stansted). It derives its name from the family of Romeney, natives of ROMNEY, who settled in the parish in the 14th century.

Rumshott Wood (Sevenoaks Weald). Wide, roomy, shed (OE *rūm scydd* → Romesedde, Romeshede 1254 → Rumshedde 1359 → Rumshet 1485 → Rumpsted *alias* Rumpshot 1778). This last form refers to Rumstead Farm here.

Rumstead Farm. See under RUMSHOTT WOOD.

Rumsted Court (Hucking). Cut off place (OE *prim stede* → Thrūsted' 1240 → Thromstede 1338 → Thrumstede 1348 → Thrumsted c.1375). The name probably refers to a clearing where trees had been cut down, leaving only the stumps.

Runham, Upper and **Lower.** Wide water meadow (OE *rūm hamm* → Rumham c.1225 → Runham 1270). The place is on low-lying ground beside the River Len.

Runsell Farm (Bethersden). 'Running pool': muddy pool near running water (OE *ryne sol* → Rynsole 1254 → Rynsoll 1527). The name is a reference to the small stream which rises close by.

Rusham Farm, Great and **Little** (Wingham). Rush meadow: water meadow where rushes grow (OE *risc hamm* → Reseham, Risseham

1278 → Rissehame 1357).

Rushbourne. Rush stream: stream by which rushes grow (OE *risc burna* → Risseburn' 1240 → Rissheborne 1270 → Rissebourne 1313 → Risshebourn' 1347). This appears to have been an early name for the Sarre Penn which flows into the River Wantsum.

Rushenden. Rush-covered hill (OE *riscen dūn* → Rissendon' 1192 → Rysindun 1275 → Rissendene 1278 → Risshendoune 1327 → Rissindun 1329).

Rushett. Recorded in 1782 as Rushitt, the place name is probably derived from ME *rishette*: rushy place. The same meaning is to be found in The Rushetts, Tonbridge, which appears as Rishette in 1279.

Rushfield Shaw. Rush land: open land on which rushes grow (OE *risc feld* → Risshefeld 1289). The affix 'Shaw' is from OE *scaga*: a copse.

Rushmere. Rush pool: pool by which rushes grow (OE *risc mere* → Ryssm'e 1258 → Risshemere 1346). Rushmore Wood, Lenham, also has this original meaning, appearing as Rysshemere c.1250.

Rushmore Wood. See under RUSHMERE.

Russell's Wood (Penshurst). It is associated with the family of Simon and William Russel (1278). This surname is also found in the names of Russel Farm, Stourmouth, and Russels, Rainham.

Rusthall (pronounced Rustawl).

Originally known as 'rust spring' (OE *rust wielle*) because of the rust-coloured water of the chalybeate mineral springs in this area, the place is recorded as Rustuwelle c.1180. By the middle of the 13th century a hall or building of some kind had been erected here, and the name appears as Rusthalle in 1264. There is still a large spring close to Rusthall House.

Ruxley. Rook's clearing: clearing frequented by rooks (OE *hrōces lēah* → Rochelei 1086 → Rokeslea 1175 → Rokeslega 1211).

Ryarsh (pronounced Ree-ash). Rye field: stubble field on which rye has been grown (OE *ryge ersc* → Riesce 1086 → Reiersce c.1100 → Reyhersse, Ryersse 1253 → Rehersh, Reyershe 1278 → Ryersh 1610).

Rye House (Dunton Green). At the island (OE *æt pǣre ēge* → ME *atter eye, atte reye* → Reye 1278 → Rye 1374). Rye House, on the site of an island of firm ground, is very close to the River Darent in an area which is still liable to flooding.

Rye Street. Rye land: open land on which rye is grown (OE *ryge feld* → Reyefeld 1371). There are no later forms to show at what date -field was dropped in favour of Street.

163

S

Sackettshill. It is associated with John and Walter Zaket of St. Peters (c.1250). This surname, in a later form, is also found in connection with Sacquett's Place, Swalecliffe, named after a John Sackett who was resident in the neighbouring parish of Blean during the 17th century.

Sacquett's Place. See under SACKETTSHILL.

St. Alban's Court (Nonington). Recorded as St. Albons in 1610, this was originally the manor of EASOLE, granted to the Abbot of St. Alban's in Hertfordshire in the 12th century.

St. Blaise's Well (Bromley). There was formerly an oratory dedicated to St. Blaise close to the chalybeate spring here: the saint's name is preserved in St. Blaize Avenue in Bromley.

St. Clere. Named after the family of Isolda Seyntclere of Ightham (1346), the place is recorded as Saintcleres in 1592, St. Cleres in 1690.

SS Cosmus & Damian in the Blean. See under BLEAN.

St. Dunstan Without. The place takes its name from that of its church which originally stood outside, or 'without' the village, and is recorded as de scō Dunstano 1254 → Eccl'ia Scī Dunstani 1291 → villa de Scō Dunstano 1292 → Sancti Dunstani 1316 → St. Dunstons 1610.

St. Edith's Farm (Kemsing). So named because St. Edith is believed to have been born in Kemsing. St. Edith's Well, in the centre of the village, has produced the name of EATWELL SHAW.

St. James's Farm (Grain). The farm is recorded as St. James in 1690, taking its name from the Church of St. James in Grain.

St. John the Baptist. This is the old alternative name for MARGATE: the church is dedicated to St. John the Baptist, and is recorded as Scī Joh'is 1291 → Sancti Johannis 1431 → St. Johns 1610.

St. John's (Sutton-at-Hone). The

164

manors of Sutton-at-Hone and Hawley were granted to the Knights Hospitallers of St. John of Jerusalem during the reign of King John. This Order also gave its name to the now lost manor of St. John's Ash, in Ash. St. Johns, Swingfield, was the property of the Order during the reign of Henry II.

St. Julians. Recorded as Julyanhyll in 1498, and as Jelianhill in 1514, this was originally a hill on the property of a medieval family named Julyan. The present name is a fanciful corruption.

St. Lawrence. The place is named after its parish church and appears as de Sancto Laurencio 1253 → Sancti Laurencii 1346 → St. Laurence 1610.

St. Margarets. It was originally known simply as 'hills' (OE *hyllas*) and is recorded as Helle c.1100 → Helles 1193 → Hilles Sanct' Margaret 1472 → Scē Margarete de Hilles 1484 → St. Margarets 1610. The parish church of Darenth is dedicated to St. Margaret.

St. Margaret's-at-Cliffe. The Norman church, less than a mile from the steep cliff here, has given its name to the village, recorded as Sancta Margarita 1086 → Cliue c.1100 → Seinte Margerete 1240 → Clyue scē Margarete 1270 → St. Margarets at Clyffe 1610.

St. Martin's Plain. It derives its name from the Church of St. Martin in Cheriton.

St. Martin's New Romney. Adjacent to the parish of New Romney, the place is named after the church here.

St. Mary Cray. Lying on the River Cray, the village has taken the name of its church and appears as Sudcrai 1086 → Seynte Mary Crey 1270 → St. Marie Craye 1610. The Domesday form means 'south of the Cray'.

St. Mary in the Marsh. The place derives its name from its church recorded as Seinte Marie Chirche in 1258. The area here was once low-lying marsh (OE *mersc*), hence the descriptive affix.

St. Mary's Hoo. The place name has the original meaning of Church of St. Mary on the spur of land (OE *hōh*), and is recorded as Scē Marie de Ho 1240 → beate Mar' de Hoo 1249 → Seynte Maryho 1292 → St. Maryes 1610.

St. Nicholas-at-Wade. The affix 'Wade' is derived from OE *(ge) wæd*: ford, or wading-place, referring to a crossing on some stream here by which the Church of St. Nicholas was built. The village is recorded as Villa Sancti Nicholai 1253 → St. Nicholas by Wade 1456 → St. Nicholas at Wade 1458. The original ford appears as *gewæd* in a charter of 943.

St. Paul's Cray. Taking its name from its church, beside the River Cray, the place is recorded as Craie 1086 → Craye Paylin 1258 → Paulinescreye 1270 → Craypaulyn 1278 → Paulscray 1610.

St. Peters. This was originally the borough, or manor, of the Church of St. Peter, and appears as borgha scī Petr' 1254 → scī Petri 1270 → St. Peters 1610.

Salmans. Recorded in 1505 as Salmannys, the place derives its name from the family of Thomas Salamon (1313).

Salmstone. Salesman's, or trader's farmstead (ME *salemannes tone* → Salemoneston' 1194 → Salemanneston 1225 → Salmoneston 1275 → Salmanston 1318).

Salters Heath. This was originally heathland owned by the family of Robert Salt'e — 'the salter' — of Chevening (1270).

Saltwood. Self-explanatory (OE *sealt wudu* → æt Sealtwuda 993 → Saltode 1086 → Saltewda 1161 → Saltwood 1610). The name is a reference to early saltworks close to a wood here.

Sandgate (pronounced Sangate). Sand gate, or cliff-gap (OE *sand geat* → Sandgate 1256).

Sandhill Farm (Tonbridge). Self-explanatory (OE *sand hyll* → Sandhelle 1332).

Sandhurst. 'Sand wood': wooded hill where the soil is sandy (OE *sand hyrst* → Sandhyrste c.1100 → Sandhurst 1230). The same origin is shared by the various Sandhursts in the parishes of Hollingbourne, Lamberhurst and Westwell. Saunder's Cross, Shoreham, also has this meaning, being found as Sendhurst in 1278, Sandherst in 1313. The present name is a corruption.

Sandling (pronounced Sannlin). Sand rise: rising ground where the soil is sandy (OE *sand hlinc* → Sandlinke 1293 → Sandlyng 1466). Sandling Farm and Park, Saltwood, share the same original meaning, being recorded as Sandlynk' in 1327, Sandlyng in 1488.

Sandown Castle. Sand hill (OE *sand dūn* → Sandoñ 1199 → Sandowne 1295).

Sandpit Cottages. Self-explanatory (OE *sand pytt* → Sandepitte 1278).

Sandway. Way across sandy soil (OE *sand weg* → Sandweie c.1250 → Sandweye 1327).

Sandwich (pronounced Sandwidge). 'Sand farm': farm on sandy ground (OE *sand wīc* → Sondwic 851 → Sandwic c.1000 → Sandwice, Sanuuic 1086 → Sandwich 1610).

Santon Farm (Preston). Sigewynn's farmstead (OE *Sigewynne tūn* → Sywent' 1154 → Seuwenton' 1254 → Sowyntone 1302 → Sewyntone 1347 → Sawynton 1483). Sigewynn was a Saxon woman.

Sappington Court (Petham). Sapling hill: hill on which saplings grow (OE *sæping dūn* → Sapindon' 1218 Sapyndone 1332 → Sependon 1431 → Savington 1690).

Sarre. It takes its name from a British river-name for the stream which joins the Wantsum here, derived from the Latin *serāre*: to close, or shut — a reference perhaps to dams along the stream. Sarre is recorded as ad Serræ, Seorre 761 → Syrran c.1100 → Serres 1184 →

Serre 1253.

Satmore. Shoat, or trout, pool (OE: *sceota mere* → Shottemer' 1275 → Sottemere 1307).

Saunder's Cross. See under SANDHURST.

Saunders Wood (Cranbrook). It derrives its name from the family of William Sandre of Cranbrook (1381).

Savage Wood (Wormshill). The place is associated with the family of Arnold Saluage, or Salvage (c.1250). Savage Farm, Hunton, is similarly connected with the family of William le Sauuage of Hunton (1270).

Saxby's Hill (Brenchley). It is named after a 17th century Brenchley family recorded as Saxbie, or Saxby.

Saynden Farm (Staplehurst). Burnt woodland pasture (OE *sænget denn* → Sænget den 830 → Sengdenne 1232 → Sendenn 1275).

Saywell's Banks. The place appears to take its name from that of Richard Sefoghel of Wormshill (1351).

Scadbury Park. Thief, or criminal, stronghold (OE *sceaða burh* → Scadhebir' 1254 → Scathebury 1292 → Scadbery 1300). This same meaning, of a disused fortification used by criminals, also occurs in the name of Scadbury Farm, Southfleet, recorded as Scadebery 1327 → Scathebery 1332 → Scadbury 1690.

Scalers Hill (Cobham). Recorded as Skarelettes in 1572 and as Scareless Hill in 1770, the name appears to be a manorial one.

Scarborough. Cleft stronghold: stronghold by a cleft or gap (OE *sceard burh* → Scardeburg' 1278 → Scarborow 1610). The place is close to a steep chalk pit.

Scathes Wood (Ightham). It derives its name from the 14th century family of atte Scathe — 'dweller by the boundary' (OE *sceað*).

Scene Farm (Hythe). Sandy ground (OE *sende* → Seende 1292 → Sende 1304).

Scotland Hills (Canterbury). Recorded as Scotland during the 13th century, the name denotes land on which a tax or payment of some kind was made: the phrase 'going scot free' preserves the old meaning of scot. Scotland Lane, Cobham, shares this meaning and appears as Skottlandes in 1572.

Scotney Castle. The name appears as Scotney in the late 16th century and is derived from the title of the barons de Scotini, natives of Scotigny in northern France, who possessed large areas of land in Kent until the reign of Edward III. Scotney near Lydd is also associated with this family name, being originally the property of Walter de Scoteny (1270). It is recorded as Scoteney in 1449.

Scrivington. The place was once a farmstead (ME *tone*) belonging to the family of Reginald Scroffyn of Speldhurst (1292), and would originally have been known as Scroffyntone.

Scrubcut Wood (Tenterden). Scrub cot: cot, or cottage, close to shrubs (ME *shrubbe cote* → Shrobecot' 1254 → Shrobbecotte 1338 → Shrubcoat 1690).

Scuttington Manor (Tonge). Scuna's farmstead (OE *Scuning tūn* → Sconingtune c.1220 → Sconyngton 1298 → Scouyngton 1409 → Scuttington 1782).

Seabrook. Sea marsh: marshy ground near the sea (OE *sǣ brōc* → Seabrooke 1585).

Seacox Heath. Recorded as Sicocks hoth in 1507, this was once heathland owned by the family of Simon Sikoc (1323).

Seal. Hall, building (OE *sele* → Lasela 1086 → Sela c.1100 → Sele 1233 → La Seele 1292). Seal Chart nearby was originally rough commonland (OE *cert*) belonging to Seal.

Seal Chart. See under SEAL.

Seasalter (pronounced See-salter). Sea saltern, or salthouse, place (OE *sǣ sealtærn steall* → Sealterna steallas 786 → Sealternsteall 863 → Seseltre 1086 → Sesaltre c.1230 → Sesaltir 1269 → Seasalter 1610). This was originally a place where sea salt was processed.

Seaton. Occupied land: land already having an owner (OE *seten* → Setene, Seten 1292 → Setone, Seton 1327). Seaton's Wood, Crundale, has the same origin and appears as Setene in 1226, Seytun in 1275.

Seed. Separation, boundary (OE *scēað* → Shede, Shethe 1327 → Schede, Sethe 1334 → Shede 1347). The name refers to a land boundary, or division.

Selgrave. 'Miry place pit': pit, or grave, near a miry place (OE *syle græf* → Sylgrave 1236).

Sellindge (pronounced Sellinje). See under SELLING.

Selling (pronounced Sellin). Halldwellers (OE *sellingas* → Setlinges 1086 → Sellinge 1087 → Selleng 1226). This name, denoting a group of people living communally, is also the origin of Sellindge, which is recorded as Sedlinges 1086 → Sellinge, Sedling c.1100 → Sellinge 1219 → Sellindg 1610.

Selson. 'Shelf's farmstead': farmstead on shelving ground (OE *scylfes tūn* → Siluestone c.1225 → Selveston 1283 → Shelfhystoun' 1327 → Seluistone 1347). The present name is a contraction of these forms.

Selstead. Mire place (OE *syle stede* → Silstede 1330 → Celsted, Selsted c.1540).

Sepham Farm (Shoreham). Sodden or soppy water meadow (OE *sypan hamm* → Sepeham 1270 → Sepham 1346). The farm is close to the Darent and one of its tributaries.

Settington. Sidewynn's farmstead (OE *Sidewynne tūn* → Sedewenton 1263 → Sedewynton', Sedwinton' 1278 → Sedewyntone 1332). Sidewynn was a Saxon woman.

Sevenoaks. At the seven oaks (OE *æt þǣm seofan ācum* → Seouenaca c.1100 → Sevenac, Sevenacher 1200 → Seuenok 1610 → Sevenoaks c.1800). Sevenoaks Weald close by was originally known simply as 'the forest' (OE *weald*), and is recorded as Walda in 1535. Its proximity to Sevenoaks has produced the present form.

Sevenscore. Recorded in 1440 as Sevendelys, this seems to have once been land divided into seven parts, or doles (ME *seven deales*). 'Score', a dialect word meaning a field or pasture, was substituted for 'deals' in the place name some time after the 16th century.

Sevington. Sǣgifu's farmstead (OE *Sǣgife tūn* → Seivetone 1086 → Sayeueton' 1221 → Sewenton', Sewinton 1242 → Seveneton 1267). Sǣgifu was a Saxon woman.

Sextries Farm (Nackington). Recorded as Sextry in 1507 and as Sextrye in 1572, this was once a manor belonging to the Monastry of St. Augustine in Canterbury, its name resulting from the fact that it was used as a sacristy.

Shade, The. See under SHODE, THE.

Shadoxhurst. The first element in this place name is obscure, but may well be a personal, or family name. The second element is OE *hyrst*: a wooded hill, and the place is recorded as Schettokesherst 1239 → Sadhokesherst 1267 → Shattokesherst 1271 → Shadoxherst 1610.

Shalley Wood (Hurst). It derives its name from the family of Shelley who owned the Manor of Hurst

from the 15th century.

Shalmsford Street (pronounced Shaamsfud). Shambles ford: ford by a shambles, or place of slaughter (OE *scameles ford* → Essamelesford 1086 → Scamelesford c.1100 → Shamelesford 1226). The ford crossed the Great Stour, which must have been used as a drain to take away the blood from this primitive butcher's shop.

Sharden's Farm (Minster). Dung pasture: woodland pasture where dung is gathered (OE *scearn denn* → Sherendeñ 1197 → Scharindenn' 1226 → Sharnden 1399).

Sharfleet Creek. See under SHARP NESS.

Sharnal Street. Dung spring: spring near a dung heap, or midden (OE *scearn wielle* → Ssarnwelle 1327 → Sharnwelle 1332). The present name is a contraction of these forms.

Sharp Ness. Sharp headland (OE *scearp næss* → Scerpenesse, Sarpenesse 1204 → Sharppenesse 1359 → Sharpnesse 1408 → Harfleet *alias* Sharpness 1782). This last form refers to Sharfleet Creek here, originally 'sharp creek, or inlet' (OE *scearp flēot)*.

Sharstead Court. See under SHAWSTEAD.

Shatterling. The place name appears to be derived from an early local name for the River Wingham, half a mile away, which was probably known as 'the shattering, or clattering one', a description derived from ME *schater*: to shatter, to dash against something. Shatterling is recorded as Scat'ling 1240 → Shaterlynge 1304 → Chatterling 1678.

Shawstead. Shard place: place where shards, or potsherds, are found (OE *sceard stede* → Scharstede 1240 → Sharstede 1292). Sharstead Court, Doddington, shares the same original meaning and is found as Scharstede 1254 → Shartstude, Sharstede 1292 → Sharsted 1610.

Sheaf Wood (Rolvenden). It is associated with the family of Richard Sheafe of Rolvenden (1647).

Shearnfold Wood (Goudhurst). Dung land: open land where dung is collected (OE *scearn feld* → Scarnfeld c.1270 → Sharnfeld 1329).

Shears Green. Recorded as Scherrifs-grene in 1357 and as Scherresys-grene in 1358, this was once a green, or common, belonging to the estate of a sherrif (OE *scīrgerēfa*), the king's chief executive for the shire. The present place name is a contraction of the 14th century forms.

Sheep Court (Waltham). Nook, corner of land (OE *scēat* → scæt 811 → Sytecurt 1327 → Shytecourt 1346). The substitution of *p* for *t* in this name appears to have been made for reasons of taste.

Sheerland. Shire land: land not in private possession, but belonging to a district (OE *scīr land* → Sherlond' 1307 → Schirlande 1318 → Shurland 1790).

Sheerness. Bright headland (OE *scīr*

nœss → Scerhnesse 1203 → Shernesse 1221 → Shirenasse 1462 → Sheerness 1690).

Sheldwich (pronounced Selwidge). 'Shield farm': farm which is shielded, or protected from the elements (OE *scild wīc* → Scilduuic 784 → Sceldwik 1198 → Sheldwych 1254). Alternatively, this farm may have been in some way shielded from attack by raiders.

Shelford Farm (Hackington). Scufel's ford (OE *Scufeling ford* → Scufeling forde 859 → Scolyforde 1275 → Sholyford' 1334 → Shulford 1431). The place is not far from the Great Stour.

Shelleys. The name is derived from that of Thomas de Schelvelegh of Knockholt (1323) and his descendant, Thomas Shelleghe (1365).

Shell Ness. Shell headland (ME *shell nesse* → Shelnasse c.1575).

Shelve, Old and **New.** Shelving ground (OE *scylf* → to Scylfe 960 → Estselve, Westselve 1086 → Selves 1199 → Shelue, Shelve 1226). The east and west sites referred to in Domesday later became Old and New Shelve.

Shelvin. Shelf-dwellers: dwellers on shelving ground (OE *scylfingas* → Seluinges 1240 → Sheluinge 1265 → Sheluyng 1327). Another group of shelf-dwellers occupied a slope at the now lost place of Shelving in Woodnesborough, recorded as Selinges 1086 → Shelvyng 1346 → Shelving 1799. Shelvingford and Shelving Wood, Hoath, are on a similar site, and appear as Scheluyngg'

SHELVINGFORD – SHINGLEWELL

c.1250 → Schellinge 1287 → Sheluinge 1317. 'Ford' and 'wood' are late additions to the name.

Shelvingford. See under SHELVIN.

Shepherd's Barn. It takes its name from the family of Jordain le Shepherde (1313). This occupational surname also occurs in connection with Shepherd's Close, Patrixbourne, and Shepherd's Lane, Dartford.

Shepherds Hill (Sheldwich). Sheep wood: wooded hill where sheep graze (OE *scēap hyrst* → Shepehurst 1251 → Shipherst 1322). In this name, final -erst has become corrupted to -erds.

Sheppey, Isle of. Sheep island: island on which sheep are kept (OE *scēap ēg* → Scepeig 696 → Sceapig 832 → Scape 1086 → Ile of Shepey 1610).

Sherenden. Dung pasture: woodland pasture where dung is gathered (OE *scearn denn* → Scharndenn' 1278 → Scharynden 1445 → Sherenden Wood 1557). Shirrenden near Horsmonden shares the same origin, being recorded as Scarenden in 1044, Sharyndene in 1330.

Sherlocks, Sherlock Cottages. The name is derived from that of the family of Robert Schirloc of Speldhurst (1240).

Shernden. Dung pasture: woodland pasture where dung is gathered (OE *scearn denn* → scearn dæn 973 → Scherndñ 1254 → Shardenne, Scharenden' 1270). Shernden Farm, Capel, has the same original meaning and appears as Sharenden in 1270,

Scharndenne in 1332.

Shernfold Farm (Loose). Together with Shernfold Pond here, the place takes its name from that of the family of Galfridus de Sharnworth' (1313). Change from final -worth to -fold is quiet common in the development of place names.

Shillingham Hole. The name is a late corruption of that of the old manor of Shillingheld in Chilham. This was close to the site of an earthwork and appears to have had the original meaning of 'slope of the shield-bearers, or warriors' (OE *scillinga hielde* → Cherinchehelle 1086 → Schellingehelde 1087 → Sillingehall 1162 → Shilingheld 1247 → Shillingheld 1284).

Shingleton Farm (Eastry). The withered, or shrunken, people (OE *Scrinclingas* → Scrinlinge 1163 → Sringlinges 1176 → Scringlingis 1242 → Schrynclyng, Scrynclinge 1270 → Shrinklyng' 1316). This appears to have been a tribal nickname, perhaps given to a group of elderly warriors past their fighting prime.

Shinglewell. Shingled spring: spring covered over by a roof of shingles (ME *shynglede welle* → Chinglede Welle 1240 → Shingledewell 1316). Perhaps the spring was a holy one, or an early 'wishing well'. Singleton near Great Chart was originally a farmstead roofed with shingles (ME *shyngle tone*), being recorded as Singleton in 1513, Shingleton in 1638. The now lost place of Schingeldhall in St. Mary in the Marsh derived its name from a hall whose roof was similarly made of shingles — thin strips of wood used as a cover-

171

ing – the name appearing as Schingledehall in 1253, and as Schingeldhall in 1387.

Shipbourne (pronounced Shibbun). Bright, or clear, stream (OE *scīr burna* → Sciburna c.1100 → Siburñ 1199 → Sibburn', Sipburn' 1226 → Schireburn 1240 → Schyburne 1270 → Shipburne 1292). Late in the 13th century the place name appears to have been altered to give it the meaning of 'sheep stream' – the River Bourne here is the original stream.

Shipway Cross. This was the meeting-place of the old Lathe, or county division, of Shipway, the name of which was derived from OE *scēap weg*: sheep way, or path, and is recorded as Shepweye in 1227, Shypwey in 1254.

Shirley Moor. Shire clearing: clearing belonging to the shire, or district (OE *scīr lēah* → Sirle 1199 → Shirle 1240 → Sherlee 1347 → Shyrlemore 1535). Shirley Moor is a large area of marshland.

Shirrenden. See under SHERENDEN.

Shoddington. Shooting, or projecting, hill (OE *scēoting dūn* → Sotindun 1206 → Shotindun 1264 → Schotingdon' 1270 → Shottington 1560). The name must refer to the elevated site of the place. Shottenden Hill in Chilham is very high, and shares the same original meaning as Shoddington, being recorded as Sotindona c.1175 → Shotindun' 1253 → Shotingdon' 1270 → Shotyndon' 1327.

Shode, The. The Shode and the Shade are both river-branches, the name being derived from the Old English verb *scēadan*: to divide, or separate.

Sholden (pronounced Showlden). 'Shovel hill': hill shaped like a shovel (OE *scofl dūn* → Shoueldune 1176 → Schueldene, Schoueldone 1253 → Soldon 1284 → Sholdon 1346).

Shooter's Hill. Shooter's slope: slope used by archers (ME *scheteres helde* → Schetereshull' 1240 → Shetereshelde 1292 → Shetersselde 1374 → Shetershill 1406 → Shoters hill 1533). This may originally have been a slope where archers practised; but the name may have a more sinister meaning, referring to robbers who frequented this area close to WATLING STREET. Hasted refers to Shooter's Hill at the end of the 18th century as being "of much danger and dread to travellers, from the narrowness of the road over it, and the continual lurking nests of thieves among the woods and coppices with which this hill was much overspread".

Shoreham (pronounced Shore-am). 'Score settlement': settlement by a score, or cut (OE *scoru hām* → Scorham 822 → Sorham 1210 → Shorham 1240). The 'score' probably refers to the deep bed cut by the stream which flows into the Darent here.

Shorncliffe. Recorded as Shornclyff in 1585 and as Shorn Clife in 1666, the original meaning of this name appears to have been 'at the scored, or cut, cliff' (OE *æt pǣm* *scorenan clife*), the cliff being scored by two stream valleys here.

Shorne. (Land) scored, cut (OE *scoren* → Scorene c.1100 → Shorna 1158 → Scorene, Sorne 1166 → Shorne 1240). The name appears to be a reference to the steep hill here.

Shorne Ridgeway. See under RIDGEWAY.

Shortwood. Self-explanatory (OE *scort wudu* → Sortewud' 1226 → Shortewode 1270).

Shottenden Hill. See under SHODDINGTON.

Shrofield Farm (Lee). Pit thicket: thicket by a pit or cave (OE *scræf holt* → Shrafholt 1240 → Shrofholte 1386 → Schroffold 1489 → Shroffolt, Shroffold 1491).

Shuart (pronounced Show-art). Skirt: piece of land 'skirted' or cut off (OE *scyrte* → Shert 1226 → Schyerthe 1273 → Shoart 1778). There was another such piece of land at the now lost place of Shoart in Hackington, recorded as Shurte in 1319, Shoart in 1790.

Shulland Wood. See under SHURLAND.

Shurland. Shire land: land not in private possession, but belonging to a district (OE *scīr land* → Shirland' 1240 → Sherlond 1467 → Shorland 1690). Shulland Wood, Newnham, shares the same definition, being recorded as Shyrland in 1236, Schirlond in 1334.

Shuttlesfield, Little. This place name, together with that of Great Shuttlesfield Farm nearby, may be derived from an early local name for the Nailbourne Stream, half a mile away, which was possibly known as 'the Shuttle' – the separator or divider (OE *sceaðel*), giving Shuttlesfield the original meaning of 'the Shuttle's open land' (OE *sceaðeles feld*). The name is recorded as Sedelesfeud' 1240 → Shadlesfeld' 1329 → Shedlesfelde 1347.

Sibertswold. Swīðbeorht's forest (OE *Swīðbeorhtes weald* → æt Swyðbrihteswealde 940 → Sibrighteswealde 944 → Swyðbeorteswald 990 → Siberteswalt 1086 → Sibertswood 1610).

Sibton Wood Park. Sibba's farmstead (OE *Sibban tūn* → Sibbetone 1210 → Sibeton' 1278). Sibba was also the owner of a stream (OE *Sibban burne*) at the now lost place of Siborne in the Hundred of Street. The personal name also occurs in connection with SUBDOWN.

Sidcup. 'House top': hilltop with a house upon it (OE *sǣte copp* → Cetecopp' 1254 → Setecoppe 1301 → Sedecoppe 1332 → Sidycope 1407).

Sights. There are no forms for this name, but it is probably derived from OE *siht*, a short form of *seohter*: drain, ditch.

Sillibourne Farm (Wye). Chalky stream: stream running through chalky soil (OE *cielce burna* → Chelcheburn' 1272 → Chelchebourne 1390). There are no later records to show how the name developed to its present form.

Siloam. Miry water meadow (OE *syle hamm* → Sylehā 1226 → Sylhamme 1304 → Silham 1359).

Silverden. Selebeorht's woodland pasture (OE *Selebeorhting denn* → Selbrythenden', Sebritendenn' 1278 → Selbrittendenne 1290 → Selfbrichtindeñe 1327). This was the meeting-place of the Selbrittenden Hundred, the present name being a contraction of the forms given.

Silver Locks. It is associated with the family of Agnes Silverlock of Marden (1473).

Simmonds Wood (Southborough). It derives its name from the local family of Symond (1348). Simmond's Hole, Cliffe, is connected with the family of William Symund of Cliffe (1293), the 'Hole' being a hollow or dip on their land here.

Singledge. Recorded as Sænling c.772 and as Senglyngge in 1313, the origin of this name appears to have been a tribal nickname, *Sænlingas*: 'the lazy, or late ones'.

Sinkertweazel (pronounced Sinkertweezle). Languid river-fork (OE *sylce twisla* → Selketinsele c.1160 → Selketwesell *alias* Sylkeatwesell 1548). The name is a reference to the slow-moving waters of the two streams which join to form a fork here.

Singleton. See under SHINGLEWELL.

Sinkhurst Green. Recorded in 1563 as Sinkeherste den, the origin of this place name is probably 'wooded hill, or hurst, by low-lying ground' (ME *sinke hurst*). There is a stream here and several pools, so *sinke* may have referred to marshy ground in the area.

Siseley (pronounced Sisslee). Sissa's clearing (OE *Sissan lēah* → Sisele c.1230 → Sisely 1285 → Sesselee 1313 → Seseley 1507).

Sissinghurst. Saxon's wooded hill (OE *Seaxing hyrst* → Saxingherste c.1180 → Saxsinghurst 1278 → Syssingherst 1610). So called to distinguish this land from that owned by Angles at nearby ANGLEY.

Sittingbourne. Stream of the slope-dwellers (OE *sīdinga burne* → Sidingeburn 1200 → Sidingburne c.1230 → Sithingeburne 1262 → Sittingborne 1610). Sittingbourne stands on the lower slope of a ridge close to Milton Creek.

Skeynes (pronounced Skaynes). Recorded as Skaines in 1677 and as Skeynes in 1683, the name is a manorial one.

Skid Hill (Cudham). 'Slip of wood pasture': pasture where slips of wood, or billets, are collected (OE *scīd denn* → Schidden 1377 → Skidhill 1589).

Skinners Hill (Meopham). It derives its name from the family of William Skynnere (1347). Skinner's, Edenbridge, recorded as Skinners in 1638, is associated with the family of Henry le Skynnere (1327).

174

Slade. Low, flat valley (OE *slæd* → Slade 1294). Slades Green near Crayford shares the same meaning and appears as Slade Green in 1561.

Slades Green. See under SLADE.

Slaughterhouse Point. See under SLAYHILLS.

Slaybrook. This name, together with that of the Slay Brook, a stream, is recorded as Slerebroc in 1240 and as Slarebrok in 1389. The last element in the name is obviously OE *brōc*: marshy ground; the first may have some association with the dialect word 'slare': to smear, or slime.

Slayhills Marsh. Slaying, or slaughter, hill (OE *slege hyll* → Sleyhulle 1205 → Slayhelle 1313). The marsh, on the Medway estuary, has given its name to Slaughterhouse Point close by. It has been suggested that the description refers to animal sacrifices made to the sea gods by early mariners before beginning a voyage. But the name may equally well describe some long-forgotten battle which took place here before the estuary silted up to form the marsh.

Slede Ooze. Flat valley marsh (OE *slæd mersc* → Sledemers c.1225). The place lies on the Medway estuary, 'ooze' having replaced the 'marsh' of the original place name.

Slipmill. Mill by a slippery place (OE *slæp myln* → Slepmilne, Slepmelle 1313).

Smallbridge. The name is self-explanatory, being recorded as Smallbrydge in 1542.

Smalldane. Small, or narrow, valley (OE *smæl denu* → Smaldane 1348).

Smallhythe. Small landing-place (OE *smæl hȳð* → Smalide c.1230 → Smalhede 1289 → Smalhithe 1377 → Small hith 1610). Smallhythe lies on the stream known as the Reading Sewer, which takes its name from READING STREET, and was a prosperous harbour until late Tudor times.

Smarden. Fat, or grease, pasture (OE *smeoru denn* → Smeredænne c.1100 → Smeredenn 1229 → Smarden 1610). The name refers to rich pastureland here, resulting in a good supply of butter and milk.

Smartwell. This appears to have been a spring (ME *welle*) on land owned by the family of Thomas Smart (1278).

Smeed Farm. See under SMEETH.

Smeeth (pronounced Smeethe). Smithy, forge (OE *smiðða* → Smiða 1018 → Smeth 1245 → Smethe 1254). Smeed Farm, Hastingleigh, is also on the site of an early forge, being recorded as Smethe in 1332. Smeeds Farm, Monks Horton, was the home of Augustin le Smethe – 'the smith' – of Monks Horton (1327).

Smersole. 'Grease mire': miry pool in rich pasturage (OE *smeoru sol* → Smeresole 1332 → Smersole 1347). The name has the same reference as SMARDEN.

Smithfield Shaw. Smooth open land (OE *smēðe feld* → Smythfeld 1532). The affix 'Shaw' is from OE *scaga*: a copse.

Smockham Farm (Tunbridge Wells). Recorded as Smocham in 1191, this may originally have been a small settlement where smocks or shifts were made (OE *smocc hām*).

Smugley. Creeper clearing: clearing where creepers grow (OE *smuge lēah* → Smoghele 1275 → Smowelegh' 1292). Alternatively, 'creeper' may refer to one or another of the two streams which merge here.

Snakebrook. The only reference to this place name comes in 1735, when it is recorded as Snagsbrook. The final element is from OE *brōc*: marshy ground; the first is probably a personal name.

Snargate. Snare gate: gate where snares are set (OE *sneare geat* → Snergathe c.1197 → Snargate c.1210 → Sneregate 1258 → Snaregate 1292). There was another such gate – probably an opening in a hedge or fence set with traps – at Snargate Street, Dover.

Snarkhurst Wood (Hollingbourne). Recorded in 1645 as Snockhurst, the name is descriptive of the noticeable hilltop in the wood and contains the dialect word 'snook', used of a projecting point of land, derived from OE *snōc*. 'Hurst' is from OE *hyrst*: a wooded hill.

Snave. The name may possibly be derived from an early local name for the stream on which Snave lies, which appears to have been called 'the tripper, or faller' (OE *snæfe*). There are many streams in this area, giving a plurality to the original name, recorded as Snaues 1218 → Snaves 1234 → Snave 1610.

Snoad. Detached piece of land (OE *snād* → Snode c.1300). This original meaning also occurs in the names of Snoad Farm, Otterden; Snoadhill, Bethersden; Snoad's Hole, Linton; and Snoad Wood, Staplehurst.

Snoadstreet. It is associated with the family of John Snoth of Throwley (1475).

Snodhurst. Wooded hill by a piece of detached land (OE *snād hyrst* → Snad hyrst 822 → Snodhurste 1243).

Snodland. Snodda's land (OE *Snodding land* → Snodding land 838 → Snodingcland 964 → æt Snoddinglande c.1060 → Esnoiland 1086 → Snodiland 1242 → Snodlande, Snodilonde 1253 → Snodland 1610).

Snotsdale Wood (Downe). Snot's valley, or dale (OE *Snotes dæl* → Snettesdele 1297 → Snettesdale 1337).

Soakham Farm (Wye). 'Dispute valley': valley over which there is dispute or conflict (OE *sacu cumb* → Sacecumb 824 → Sacumbe 1254 → Socombe 1346). Right of the possession of the land here appears to have caused conflict among the early settlers.

Solefield. Muddy pool land: open land marked by muddy pools (OE *sol feld* → Solefeld 1410).

Solesdane Wood (Chilham). Together with neighbouring Soleshill Farm, the place is recorded as Sole in 1327, the name being derived from OE *sol*: muddy pool. The endings -dane (valley) and -hill are late additions.

Sole Street (Cobham). Muddy pool (OE *sol* → Sole 1327 → Solystrete 1448 → Solestreate 1572). Sole Street, Crundale, has the same origin and is found as Sol in 824, Sole in 1346. Sole Street, Selling, is on the site of several muddy pools, being recorded as Solis 1211 → Soles 1261 → Sole 1327. Soles Court, Nonington, is the same, being Soles in the Domesday Book (1086) and throughout the 13th century. Sole Street Farm, Denton, appears as Sole in 1254.

Soles Court. See under SOLE STREET.

Solton (pronounced Sole-tun). 'Muddy pool farmstead': farmstead close to muddy pools (OE *sol tūn* → Soltun 1038 → Soltone 1086 → Solton' 1226).

Somerden Green. Summer pasture (OE *sumor denn* → Sumerden' 1218 → Somerden 1610). This was the meeting-place of the Somerden Hundred.

Somerfield Court (Sellindge). Summer land: open land used during summer (OE *sumor feld* → Sum'feld 1251 → Somerfeld 1313).

Soper's Lane. Recorded as Soperslane in 1507, the place, together with neighbouring Soper's Lane Farm, is on the site of a lane or path across land owned by the family of Soper. This medieval surname is also found in connection with Sophurst Wood, Brenchley, recorded as Sopers in 1652. The present form is the result of final -ers being corrupted to -hurst.

Sophurst Wood. See under SOPER'S LANE.

Souledge Farm (Stelling). South ditch: ditch to the south of the parish (OE *sūð dīc* → Suthdich' 1313 → Southdyche 1346 → Southage 1790).

Southborough. South borough, or manor (ME *suth burgh* → bo. de Suth' 1270 → la South Burgh 1450 → le Southborgh 1488). This was originally a borough of TONBRIDGE.

Southenay. South of the river (OE *sūðan ēa* → Suthene 1249 → Sutheneye 1313 → Sotheney 1346). The place lies to the south of the East Stour.

Southernden (pronounced Southern-den). Swīðrēd's woodland pasture (OE *Swīðrēding denn* → Swytheryndenn' 1292 → Switheryndeñe 1327 → Swytherden' 1338). The personal name also occurs in connection with SURRENDEN.

Southfield House (Dartford). South land: open land to the south of the parish (ME *suth feld* → Southfelde 1452).

Southfleet. South creek or inlet (OE *sūð flēot* → Svdfleta 1086 → Suthflite 1089 → Suthflete 1218). Called 'South' to distinguish this place from NORTHFLEET.

Southfrith Lodge (Tonbridge). South woodland (OE *sūð fyrhðe* → Sutfrith 1295 → Suthfrith 1325 → Southfrith 1610).

South Green. Recorded c.1435 as Southgreney, this would originally have been a common, or green, to the south of the parish.

Southpark Wood (Boughton Malherbe). It appears in 1552 as Southparke, the name referring to parkland south of the parish. South Park, Penshurst, has the same meaning, being described as le Southpark in 1414.

Speldhurst. Chip wood: wooded hill where chips, or splinters, are gathered (OE *speld hyrst* → Speldhirst 765 → Speldhurst 1226). The now lost place of Speldhurst in Biddenden had the same original meaning, appearing as Speldhurst in 1218.

Spelmonden. Player's woodland pasture (OE *spilemanning denn* → Speluyngden' 1292 → Spelmendenne 1313 → Spelmyndenne 1332 → Spelmonden 1610). OE *spilemann* denoted a jester or musician: one who played.

Spilshill (pronounced Spillzill). Chip buildings: collection of buildings roofed with chips or spinters of wood (OE *speld gesella* → Speldgisella 814 → Speldeshelle 1327 → Speldesell' 1347 → Spilshill 1610).

Spittal Wood (Kingsdown). It is named after the spital, or hospital, of St. Mary to which the Manor of Kingsdown once belonged. This old word for a hospital is also found in Spitalfield Lane, New Romney, which marks the site of a hospital recorded here in 1380.

Spitz Bridge. Together with neighbouring Spitzbrook, it lies on a stream described as the Spyttes River in 1595, which has given its name to the two places. There are no early forms to explain why the stream was so called unless the name is related to the Old English verb *spittan*: to spit.

Spitzbrook. See under SPITZ BRIDGE.

Spong Farm (Elmstead). Recorded in 1334 as Sponge, the name probably has the same meaning as the old dialect field-name 'spong', or 'spang', used of a long, narrow piece of land.

Spoonlets Pond. See under SPUNDEN.

Spout House (Leeds). The building appears to be on the site of a waterspout, or conduit (ME *spoute*) which is recorded here as Spotte in 1270.

Spratsbourne Farm. See under SPRATS HILL.

Sprats Hill (Newnham). It derives its name from the family of Godefridus Sprot (1231). Sprats Wood, Chartham, is similarly associated with the family of William Sprot of Chartham (1270). This surname is also found in connection with a stream (bourne) in Spratsbourne Farm, Cranbrook, and occurs again in Spratt Cottage, Bethersden.

Sprattling Street. The place takes its

name from that of the family of Adam Spratlyng' (1292).

Sprivers. Recorded as Sprewers, Sprewerys in 1546, the name is derived from that of John Speruer (1310) and his descendant, Robert Spriver (1447).

Spunden. Chip pasture: pasture where chips, or wood shavings are found (OE *spōn denn* → Sponden' 1254 → Spondenne 1313). Spoonlets Pond, Goudhurst, is on the site of a clearing where chips of wood were either collected or stacked (OE *spōn lēah*), being recorded as Sponlee c.1200 → Sponlegh c.1270 → Spounle 1278.

Stace Wood (Smarden). It is associated with the family of Thomas Stace of Smarden (1292).

Stacklands Wood (Kingsdown). Recorded as Stokfeld in 1338, this seems originally to have been open land on which there were stocks, or tree-stumps (OE *stocc feld*).

Stalisfield (pronounced Starsfield). Stall's land: open land containing a cattle stall (OE *stealles feld* → Stanefelle 1086 → Stalisfeld 1172 → Stalesfelde 1253 → Stalesfield 1610).

Stallence. It appears in 1323 as Stonlondesmed — 'stony land's mead, or meadow' — and in 1332 as Stonylonde — 'stone land'. The present name appears to be a contraction of SUTTON VALENCE, the parish to which Stallence belongs.

Stammerden Wood (Horsmonden).

Stone-man's, or stone mason's, woodland pasture (OE *stānmanning denn* → Stamendon 1275 → Staminden' 1278 → Stamyndenne 1327).

Standard Hill (Newington). Recorded in 1598 as Standerhill, Standerd, this would seem to be a hill on which a military standard was raised at some time. Alternatively, it may once have had a standard — a single tree left standing when a coppice is cut down — upon it.

Standen (near Benenden). At the stony woodland pasture (OE *æt pǣm stānihtan denne* → Stanehtandenn 858 → Stonekindenn' 1240 → Stoneghyndenn 1278 → Stoneghindenne 1314). The present name is a contraction of these forms. The same origin is shared by Standen near Biddenden, recorded as Stankyndenn' in 1334. Upper and Lower Standen, Hawkinge, has the original meaning of 'stone pasture: woodland pasture where the ground is stony' (OE *stān denn*), and appears as Stonden 1275 → Stondenne 1327 → Standen' 1332.

Stanford. Stone ford: ford with a stony floor (OE *stān ford* → Stanford 1035). The same meaning is found in the names of Stanford Bridge Farm, Pluckley (Stonford 1278); Stanford Lane, East Peckham (Stanford 1226); and Stanford's End, Edenbridge (Stanford' 1248).

Stangate. Stone gate: gate on stony ground (OE *stān geat* → Stangate 1232).

Stangrove Park. Stone grove: grove where the ground is stony (OE *stān grāf* → Staingraue 1270 → Stane-

179

grove 1275 → Stangraue, Stangrave 1378).

Stanham Farm (Dartford). Stone meadow: water meadow where the ground is stony (OE *stān hamm* → Stanham 1270 → Stanham, Stonham 1292). The meadow bordered the Stanham River here.

Stansted. At the stony place (OE *æt þæm stān stede* → Stansted' 1231 → Stanestede 1278 → Stansted 1610).

Staple. Post, staple (OE *stapol* → Stapl', Staples 1205 → Staple 1240). Other posts – probably used to mark the boundary of land – were at Staple Farm, Hastingleigh, recorded as Stapele in 1313, Staple in 1348; and at Staplestreet, Hernhill, which appears as Staple in 1313.

Staplehurst. 'Post wood': wooded hill marked by a post, or staple (OE *stapol hyrst* → Stapelherst 1226 → Stapelhurst 1254).

Staplestreet. See under STAPLE.

Star Hill (Chevening). It derives its name from the family of Paget and Richard le Ster of Sevenoaks (1313).

Statenborough. At the steep mound (OE *æt þæm stēapan beorge* → Estenberge 1086 → Stepenberga c.1100 → Stapinbergh' 1240 → Stapenbergh c.1325). There are no later forms to show how the present name evolved.

Stedehill Wood (Harrietsham). Together with Stede Court here, it derives its name from the family of Roger Stede of Harrietsham (1450).

Stede Quarter, Biddenden, is named after a local landowner, Edmund Steed, who died in 1664.

Steels Wood (Stockbury). It is associated with the family of Maurice atte Steghele of Stockbury (1296). This surname, meaning 'dweller by the stile' (OE *stīgel*), is also found in connection with Stile Farm, Chilham, the family of ate Steghele being recorded here during the 14th century.

Stelling (pronounced Stellin). Stealla's people (OE *Steallingas* → Stellinges 1086 → Steallinge, Stellinges c.1100 → Stelling 1240).

Stile Farm. See under STEELS WOOD.

Stilstead House (East Peckham). Shrub or thicket place (OE *pȳfel stede* → Tywelested' 1258 → Tyuelestede 1270 → Tylstede 1338 → Tilstede 1404 → Spilsted 1782).

Stock, Little. Stump, stock (OE *stocc* → Stocke 1254 → Stokke 1347). Perhaps the bridge here, recorded in 1240 as Stokbrigg', was made from, or had its foundations laid on, tree stumps.

Stockbury. Swine pasture of the Stoke people (OE *Stocinga bær* → Stochingaberge 1086 → Stocingabere c.1100 → Stokingebir 1208 → Stokebyry 1243 → Stockbery 1610). This was a pasture belonging to STOKE, eight miles to the north.

Stockfield Wood (Lower Hardres). The place appears to have taken its name from the family of Henry de Stoke of Hardres (1315), being

180

originally their open land (ME *feld*). The family name atte ffelde – 'dweller by the open land' – is recorded in Lower Hardres in 1343.

Stockham. Stock settlement: settlement by stocks, or tree stumps (OE *stocc hām* → Stocham 1275 → Stokham 1357 → Stockham Bushes 1539). The affix 'Bushes' in this last form is derived from ME *busheppes*: 'of the bishop'.

Stocking Lane. The name is a corruption of the now lost place of Stokenbury, near the site of which Stocking Lane runs. Stokenbury had the original meaning of 'place-dwellers' stronghold' (OE *stocinga burh*) and appears as Estochingeberge 1086 → Stotingeberga c.1100 → Stokingbiry 1278 → Stokynbury 1486.

Stocking Wood (Sheldwich). This was originally a field, described in 1198 as Stocket, the name meaning 'collection of stocks, or tree stumps' (ME *stocket*). The present form is a late corruption.

Stodmarsh. Stud marsh: marshland where a stud, or herd of stallions, is kept (OE *stōd mersc* → Stodmerch 675 → Stodmersche 686 → Stodmerse 1198 → Stodmersh 1610). The place lies by the marshes of the Great Stour.

Stogarts & Drapers Wood (Strood). Described in 1698 as Stockgate wood, Drapers wood, the first form refers to a gate made of stocks or stumps (← OE *stocc geat*), while the second is taken from the family name of Draper. The two names have since become one.

Stoke. (People) of the place (OE *stoces* → Stokes 738 → Stoche c.975 → Stoches 1086 → Stoke 1610). The swine pasture of the people of Stoke was at STOCKBURY.

Stonar (pronounced Stownar). Stony bank (OE *stān ōra* → Stanoure 1225 → Stanore 1227 → Stonore 1280).

Stone (near Dartford). Stones (OE *stānas* → of stane c.975 → Estanes 1086 → Stanes 1226 → Stone 1610). Stone near Faversham has the original meaning of 'at the stone' (OE *æt þǣm stāne*) and is recorded as Stane c.1100 → Stanes 1259 → Stone 1312. Stone-cum-Ebony, sharing its name with the village of EBONY in the Oxney Hundred, also marks the site of a stone, perhaps a boundary marker, appearing as Stane c.1185, Stone in 1274.

Stoneacre. Stony piece of cultivated land (OE *stān æcer* → Stonacre 1254 → Stoneacre 1327).

Stone Bridge. Self-explanatory, the name appearing as Stonebrugge in 1334.

Stone Castle (Stone). It takes its name from that of Alan de Castello of Stone (1278), and is recorded as Stone-castle in 1346, Stone Castell in 1494.

Stonecrouch. Stone cross (ME *stane crouche* → Stone Crouch 1559 → Stonecrouch 1690).

Stone Down. Hill (ME *done* → Downe 1370 → Downe Court 1452 → Down Court 1790). The change from Down Court to Stone Down is a late one.

Stoneham. Stony water meadow (OE *stān hamm* → Stonhame 1306). The place is close to the Beult and one of its tributaries.

Stoneheap Farm (Northbourne). Stone house (OE *stān ærn* → Stonrene, Stonren 1247 → Stonerenne 1278). The present name may have resulted from the fact that the farm buildings were built close to the ruins of the old stone house.

Stone Hill (Sellindge). Recorded as Stoneheld in 1250, the name is derived from OE *stān hielde*: stony slope. Stonehill, Wilmington, shares the same origin and is found as Stonihelde in 1327, Stoneheld in 1450.

Stone House (St. Peters). Together with Stone Farm here, it derives its name from some noticeable stone in the vicinity, being recorded as Stone c.1250. Stonehouse Farm, Frindsbury, appears as Stonehouse farme in 1632, the name being self-explanatory.

Stoneings. It is probably to be associated with the family of Robert de Stanhengh' (1254).

Stonelake. Stony watercourse (OE *stān lacu* → Stanlak' 1240 → Stonelake 1512). There are many streams in this area near Chiddingstone.

Stonepit. Stony pit or hollow (OE *stan pytt* → Stanpette 1216 → Stonepette 1338). Alternatively, the name may refer to a small quarry.

Stonereed Shaw. Stony clearing: land cleared, or rid, of stones (OE *stānig rīed* → Stonired 1267). The affix 'Shaw' is from OE *scaga* : a copse.

Stoners Rough Wood (Rainham). It is associated with the family of Nicholas Stonhard of Rainham (1327).

Stone Street. This is the Roman road running from Canterbury to Lympne, its name being derived from OE *stān strǣt*: stone, or paved, Roman road.

Stonestreet Green. It is close to a short stretch of Roman road, the name having the same derivation as that of STONE STREET.

Stonewood. Wood where the ground is stony (OE *stān wudu* → Stonewode 1327).

Storth Oaks. Recorded as la Steerte in 1424, the name may be derived from OE *steort*: tail; spit of land. The affix obviously refers to a group of trees here.

Stour, River (pronounced Stoor). A British river-name derived from the Latin *stauro*, it has the meaning of 'strong, powerful', and is recorded as Stur in 686, Sture in 811. The Little Stour is a late name for a branch of the river: earlier it was known as Wingham creek, or inlet (OE *flēot*), and appears as Wyngeflet in 1343.

Stourmouth (pronounced Stoormouth). Mouth of the Stour (OE *Stūr mūða* → Sturmutha 1089 → Sturmuða 1175 → Sturmuth 1235). This is the point at which the Great and Little Stour rivers join the Wantsum.

Stowting (pronounced Stowtin). Stūt's people (OE *Stūtingas* → Stutinge 1044 → Estotinghes, Stotinges 1086 → Stutingis c.1150 → Stotinge 1240 → Stowtting 1610).

Stray Marshes. Described in 1553 as Straye Marche, the origin of this name appears to be derived from the Old English verb *strēgan*: to strew, or spread out. The old name for the water separating the Isle of Grain from Hoo Hundred was The Stray; and Stray Farm, Lower Halstow – which, like the Stray Marshes, is low-lying and water-logged land – lies beside a ford known as The Stray crossing a branch of the Halstow Creek.

Street End. Self-explanatory. It is recorded as Strethende 1292 → Streteende 1332 → Stretend 1334.

Strettit House (East Peckham). It probably stands on the site of a spot recorded in 1404 as Strodettcrosse: cross, or perhaps crossways, on marshy land overgrown with brushwood (← OE *strōd*). The ground here is still marshy.

Strode Park. See under STROOD.

Strood (pronounced Strude). Marshy land overgrown with brushwood OE *strōd* → Strod 889 → Strode 1158 → Strood 1610). Strode Park and Farm, Herne, share the same original meaning, being recorded as Strode in 1240.

Stubblefield. The original place name was Otershe, derived from OE *āte ersc*: stubble field where oats have been grown. A direct translation of the final element in this name, recorded in 1240, has produced the modern form.

Studdal. Stud forest: forest where a stud, or herd of stallions, is kept (OE *stōd weald* → Stodwalde 1240 → Stodwolde 1338). The present name is a contraction of these forms. An Eststodwolde and a Weststodwolde are recorded here during the 13th century, showing that the place was once two distinct settlements.

Stud Hill (Herne). Recorded as Studhill in 1473, the name is derived from that found in Studds Farm close by, originally the property of William Stud (1327). In 1474 a descendant, George Studde, or Studhill, is recorded.

Stumpshill Wood (Beckenham). Tree stump's hill: hill marked by a tree stump (OE *stumbeles hyll* → Stumeleshull' 1226 → Stomeshulle, Stombleshelle 1327).

Stunts Wood (Horsmonder). It is associated with the family of Sidney Stunt of Horsmonden (1235).

Stuppington. Steep slope's hill: hill which has a steep slope (OE *stūpes dūn* → Stupesdone 1253 → Stopesdone 1321 → Stopindon' 1348). Stuppington Farm, Canterbury, has the same original meaning and appears as Stupesdone, Stopesdone 1270 → Stopyndon' 1327 → Stopyngton 1535. Both places are sited on a slope.

Sturry. District of the Stour (OE *Stūr gē* → Sturigao 605 → Sturrie,

Sturige 675 → Esturai 1086 → Sturrey 1610). Sturry preserves the name of a large district in the county.

Stutfall Castle. Stud fold: fold in which a stud, or herd, is kept (ME *stod folde* → Stotfolde 1327 → Stodfolde 1338 → Stotfold 1347 → Stutfall Cast. 1610). This is the ruin of a Roman stronghold, the stones of which were used to build Lympne Castle close by in 1360. Obviously the ruins were used as an enclosure for horses during medieval times.

Subdown, Little. Though there are no records for this name, it may possibly be identified with a *Sibban-burnan mearce*: 'boundary formed by Sibba's stream', recorded in a charter of 993. The personal name, Sibba, is found in connection with SIBTON.

Summer Field. Summer land: open land used in summer (OE *sumor feld* → Som'feld 1278 → Somerfelde 1313).

Summer Hill. See under SUMMER-LEESE.

Summerleese. Summer lea: lea, or meadow, used in summer (OE *sumor lǣs* → Som'lese 1348). Summer Hill, Headcorn, shares the same origin, being recorded as Somerlese in 1531.

Sundries. It takes its name from that of the family of Richard Saundre of Lynsted (1365).

Sundridge. Private enclosed parkland (OE *sundor edisc* → Sunder-

hirse 1072 → Sondresse 1086 → Sunderhersce c.1100 → Sunderesse 1210 → Sundris, Sundarrisse 1240 → Sundrich 1610). The old parkland in Sundridge is preserved in the names of Sundridge Park and Park Wood here. Sundridge Park, Bromley, has a common origin, appearing as Sundrish' 1295 → Sundresshe 1381 → Sundresh 1421.

Supperton Farm (Wickhambreux). South barley-farm (OE *sūð beretūn* → Suthburton' 1242 → Suthberton' 1278 → Soberton' 1327 → Subbertone 1332).

Surrenden, Old. Swiðrēd's woodland pasture (OE *Swiðrēding denn* → Swiðrædingdænne c.1020 → Sytherinden' 1270 → Suryngdenne 1313 → Surrynden 1535). Surrenden Dering, three miles away, has taken the name of Old Surrenden – the 'old' or original settlement – being distinguished from it by the affix 'Dering', derived from the family name of Richard Dering (1480), a landowner in Pluckley.

Sutton. South farmstead (OE *sūð tūn* → Suttone 1154 → Sutton' 1226). There appear to have been three separate farmsteads in this area, since an Estsuttone and a Westsutton are recorded here with Sutton in 1253.

Sutton, East. South farmstead (OE *sūð tūn* → Svdtone 1086 → Est Sutton 1212 → East Sutton 1265). The farmstead was originally called 'south' because of its position on the estate; the affix 'East' was added to distinguish the place from SUTTON VALENCE, which lies due west.

Sutton-at-Hone. South farmstead (OE *sūð tūn* → Sudtone 1086 → Suttone 1087 → Suthtuna c.1100 → Suttoñ 1199 → Sutton' atte hone 1240 → Sutton at hone 1610). The affix is derived from OE *æt pæm hāne*: 'by the rock', referring perhaps to a boundary stone here.

Sutton Baron. It has the same original meaning as SUTTON, being distinguished by the affix of its parish name, Borden. The place is recorded as Sutton in Borden in 1383, Sutton Barne in 1782.

Sutton Street. 'Strife farmstead': farmstead over which there is strife or contention (OE *strūt tūn* → Strutton' 1254 → Strottone 1327). The present form is the result of confusion with the more common place name, Sutton.

Sutton Valence. It shares the same origin as SUTTON, the affix 'Valence' being derived from the family of Valence who possessed the manor from 1265. The place is found as Suðtune 814 → Svdtone 1086 → Sutton' 1219 → Sutton Valence 1610.

Swadelands. See under SWAY-LANDS.

Swale, River (pronounced Swaal). It is recorded as suuealuue fluminis in 812 and as Sualuæ in 815, the name being derived from an Old English river-name, *swealwa*: 'whirlpool, rushing water; swallow'.

Swalecliffe (pronounced Swakeley). Cliff by the Swale (OE *Swealwa clif* → æt Swalewanclife 949 → Soaneclive 1086 → Swalesclive 1242

→ Swale cliffe 1610). The place is not far from the mouth of the River Swale.

Swan Street. It is associated with the family of Thomas le Swon of Charing (1262). Swan Farm, Goudhurst, is similarly connected with the family of John Swan (1334).

Swanley (near Eastchurch). Peasants' clearing (OE *swāna lēah* → Swanle 1334). Swanley near Sutton-at-Hone shares the same origin, being recorded as Swanleg 1203 → Swanle 1396 → Swanley 1573.

Swanscombe. Peasant's field (OE *swānes camp* → Suanescamp 695 → Svinescamp 1086 → Swanescampe 1166 → Swanescombe 1292 → Swanscomb 1610).

Swansfield Lodge (Stone). This was originally land belonging to the family of John Swon of Stone (1327), the name appearing as Swaneslonde in the 14th century.

Swanton. Peasants' farmstead (OE *swāna tūn* → Svanetone 1086 → Swanetoñ 1215 → Swanton 1346). The same original meaning occurs in the names of Swanton Court, Bredgar and Sevington; Swanton Farm, Bilsington and Littlebourne; and Swanton Valley, West Peckham.

Swarling (pronounced Swawlin). The swordsmen, or warriors (OE *Sweordlingas* → Sweordlingas 946 → Swerlinges 1205 → Swerling 1223 → Suerdlinges 1240). This was originally a settlement of fighting men.

Swatfield Bridge. 'Track ford': ford approached by a track (OE *swæð* *ford* → Syað ford 993 → Swatford 1267 → Swetfordesbregg' 1313). The bridge, spanning the Swatfield River, stands at the original ford where the road from Ashford to Hythe now crosses a stream.

Swattenden. Swæ ðel's woodland pasture (OE *Swæðeling denn* → Swetlingdenn' 1240 → Swetlyndenne c.1260 → Swethyngden 1305).

Swaylands. Swain's, or peasant's, land (ME *sweines land* → Sweyneslonde 1329 → Swaneslond 1332 → Swaynlond 1488 → Swaylandes 1550). Swadelands, Lenham, possibly shares a similar origin, being recorded c.1250 as Swallond (← OE *swāna land*: peasants' land). Alternatively, this may originally have been land frequented by swallows (OE *swealwa land*).

Sweech Farm (Elmstone). Trap, snare (OE *swice* → Sweche 1313 → Swych' 1357). Another place where traps were laid was Sweech Farm, Sturry, recorded as Swech, Suech c.1250.

Sweetlands Corner. Described as Swithlands in 1801, this name may be derived from OE *sūð land*: south land. There is a Suthland recorded in this area in 1278 which is possibly identical with Sweetlands.

Swift's Green. It is associated with the family of William Swyft of Smarden (1356).

Swinford Old Manor (Hothfield). Swine ford: ford across which swine are herded (OE *swīna ford* → Swineford 1226 → Swyneford' 1327).

Swingfield. Swine land: open land on which swine are kept (OE *swīna feld* → Suinafeld c.1100 → Swinefelde 1211 → Swynefelde 1253 → Swynkfield 1610).

Sydenham. Cippa's settlement (OE *Cippan hām* → Chipeham 1206 → Cyppenham 1319 → Sipeham 1327 → Syppenham 1494 → Sidenham 1690).

Syliards. The place derives its name from the family of Seyliard who are believed to have owned it from the time of Stephen.

Symnell. It is associated with the family of Hugh Siminel (1240).

Syndale Bottom. Huge valley (OE *sin denu* → Syndan' 1196 → Sindane 1240 → the Syndane 1375 → Syndale, Syndanes 1380). This was originally the name given to the long valley which extends from Lenham to Ospringe.

T

Tailness Marshes. 'Tail headland': headland on a tail, or spit of land (OE *tægl næss* → Taylnesse 1368 → Talnasse 1535 → Tayleness 1558).

Talmead. It is recorded in 1500 as Oldmede: 'old mead, or meadow'.

Tankerton. Pancrēd's farmstead (OE *Pancrēding tūn* → Tangrenton', Tangrinton' 1242 → Tangyntone 1278 → Tangreton 1346 → Tankerton 1459).

Tanners Cross. It derives its name from the 14th century family of Tannere.

Tapners. Tæppa's brushwood (OE *Tæppan hæs* → Teppanhyse 765 → Teppenese 1274 → Tapenese 1346). Tæppa's farmstead was at TAP-PINGTON.

Tappington Farm (Denton). Tæppa's farmstead (OE *Tæpping tūn* → Tapinton' 1242 → Tapintone 1243). Tæppa also had property at TAP-NERS.

Tarnden. Teorra's woodland pasture (OE *Teorring denn* → Terindenn c.1225 → Teryndenn' 1347 → Terynden 1426). The present name is a contraction of these forms.

Tassell's Wood (Norton). It is associated with the family of Thomas Tassell' (1522).

Tatlingbury. Stronghold of Tætel's people (OE *Tætelinga burh* → Tetlingebir' 1206 → Tetlingbury 1311 → Tetlingbery, Tatlingbyri 1347). The two places named Tattlebury, one at Headcorn, the other at Goudhurst, may originally have been associated with this tribe, but there are no records for either place from which to ascertain their meaning.

Tatnam Bridge. Tāta's water meadow (OE *Tātan hamm* → Tatenhame 1226 → Tatenhamme 1242 → Tatenham 1374). The place is on one of the many streams flowing into the sea near Dymchurch.

Tattlebury. See under TATLING-BURY.

Taylorland. It derives its name from that of John and Thomas Taillour

187

(1327), whose surname is also found in connection with Taylor's Lane, Higham Upshire.

Taywell. Enclosure spring: spring within an enclosure (OE *tēag wielle* → Teywell 1489 → Taywell 1790).

Tedder's Leas. The name is derived from that of Thomas Tyndour (1348), the affix being from OE *lǣs*: lea, meadow.

Teise, River (pronounced Teez). It takes its name from Ticehurst in Sussex, which is recorded as Theise Hirst in 1577: the river appears as Theise in the same year.

Temple Ewell. Spring, source of a stream (OE *ǣwiell* → Æwille c.772 → Ewelle 959 → Templum de Ewell 1213). Temple Ewell, on the Upper Dour, was held by the Knights Templars from the time of Henry II.

Temple Hill (Godmersham). Recorded in 1313 as Temple, the hill appears to have been part of the property of the Knights Templars in this area. Temple Farm, Dartford, which appears as Templars in 1311, le Temple in 1360, was certainly owned by the Order: it held large areas of land in Dartford at the beginning of the 13th century. Temple Farm and Marsh, Strood, also belonged to the Knights Templars, the Manor of Strood being granted to them by Henry II. Temple Farm is recorded as Templeborgh' 1292 → Templestrode maner' 1337 → Le Temple manor 1404 → Templ-ill 1524.

Tenacre. Ten (plots of) cultivated land (OE *tīen æcer* → Tyenacr' 1327 → Tyenakre 1338 → Tenakere 1347).

Tenterden (pronounced Tenderden). Pasture of the men of Thanet (OE *Tenet wara denn* → Tentwardene 1178 → Tentwardenn' 1240 → Tentyrden' 1255 → Tenterden 1610). The men of the Isle of Thanet also owned tracts of marshy ground (OE *brōcas*) in this area, recorded as *Tenet wara brocas* in 968. Tenterden was originally the property of the manor of Minster in Thanet: in the 13th century it is described thus: Tenwardenne pertinet ad manerium de Menstre (Tenterden pertains to the manor of Minster).

Terlingham. Settlement of the *Tyrlingas*: the trillers or songsters (OE *Tyrlinga hām* → Terlingeham 1262 → Terlingham 1270). Another tribe with this nickname – or perhaps a branch of the same tribe – were settled at TRILLINGHURST.

Terry's Wood (Waltham). It is associated with the family of Stephen Terry of Waltham (1313). Terry's Lodge, Wrotham, similarly derives its name from William and Thomas Terry of Wrotham (1452).

Teston (pronounced Teesun). Cleft stone (OE *tær stān* → terstan, cærstan c.975 → Testan 1086 → Testane c.1100 → Teston 1610). The name must refer to a stone or rock which was probably used as a boundary marker.

Teynham (pronounced Tennam). Settlement of the *Tǣnas*: the offspring or descendants (OE *Tǣna hām* → Tenaham 798 → Tenham 801 →

Therham 1086 → Tæneham c.1100 → Tenham 1139). TIMBOLD HILL close by appears to have been associated with a member of this tribe.

Thames, River (pronounced Temms). Dark river (B *tamasā* → Tamesis 51 BC → Tamesa 115 → Tamisa 681 → Temis 683 → Temse 1387). The *h* in this name was inserted, unnecessarily, by 17th century antiquarians.

Thanet, Isle of (pronounced Thannit). Bright island, or fire island. The name is British, surviving in the Old Welsh *tanet*, meaning 'brilliant river'. To the early Romans Thanet was Tanatus, and thereafter its name appears as Thanet 679 → Thænet 732 → Tanet 1086 → Ile of Thanet 1610. The island was probably so called because of a Roman lighthouse or beacon on it, marking the approach to the channel leading to the Roman stronghold at Richborough.

Thanet Wood (Great Chart). It is named after Nicholas Tufton, created Earl of Thanet in 1629, who owned nearby Ripton Farm in Ashford and Etchden Farm in Bethersden.

Thanington. Tǣna's farmstead (OE *Tǣning tūn* → Taningtune 833 → Tenitune c.1100 → Taninton 1203). Tǣna – 'the offspring, or descendant' – may have been a member of the tribe settled at TEYNHAM.

Thong. Thong, band: strip of land (OE *þwang* → Thange 1147 → Thuange, Twonge 1185 → Thonge 1226).

Thornden (near Boughton Malherbe). Thorn-bush pasture: woodland pasture marked by a thornbush (OE *þorn denn* → þorn den 850 → Thorndenn' c.1250). The same original meaning is found in the names of Thornden near Dunkirk (Thorndenne 1240), and Thornden near Rolvenden (Thornden' 1261).

Thorne. At the thorn-bush (OE *æt þǣm þorne* → Thorne 1278). Thorne Farm, Bethersden, takes its name from the thorn-bush which is still growing near the buildings. Thorn Wood, Saltwood, has the same origin as Thorne, appearing as Thorne in 1278.

Thornham. Thorn-bush settlement: settlement close to a thorn-bush (OE *þorn hām* → Turneham 1086 → Thorneham 1174 → Tornham 1218).

Thornhill Farm (Maidstone). Thorn-bush hill (OE *þorn hyll* → Thornhill' 1313 → Thornhelle 1334). Thornhills House here has adopted the old name.

Thornton Farm (Tilmanstone). Thorn-bush farmstead: farmstead by a thorn-bush (OE *þorn tūn* → Thornton' 1240).

Thorn Wood. See under THORNE.

Three Crutches. Recorded in 1695 as The three Crouches, this was once the site of three wayside crosses (ME *crouche*).

Thrift, The. Woodland (OE *fyrhðe* → Vrith, ffrethe 1362 → ffrythe 1376). The same original meaning also occurs in the names of Great and Little Thrift, Chislehurst, recorded as the Frythe in 1387; Thrift Wood, Meopham: the Frithe in 1381; and Thrift Wood, Stansted, home of William Attefrythe — 'dweller by the woodland' — of Stansted (1270).

Thrognall. Recorded as Frognall in 1598 and as Frognal, Frogenhall in 1782, the place is believed to derive its name from William de Frogenhall, a native of Frognal in Teynham, to whom this manor was given by Henry III.

Throwley. Trough clearing: clearing through which runs a trough or pipe (OE *prūh lēah* → Trevelai, Brulege 1086 → Thrulege c.1100 → Trulegh 1236 → Throulegh' 1270 → Throughley 1610). The name appears to refer to the trough-shaped valley below Throwley church.

Thruxted. Recorded as Thruxsted during the 16th century, this place name probably has the original meaning of 'thrush place: place frequented by thrushes' (OE *prysce stede*).

Thundersland Road. This was once land owned by the family of Richard Thunder (1357).

Tickenhurst. Kids' wood: wooded hill frequented by kids, or young goats (OE *ticcena hyrst* → Ticheteste 1086 → Tikenherst c.1250 → Tykenherst 1278).

Tickham. Kids' meadow: water meadow where young goats graze (OE *ticcena hamm* → Tykehamme 1327).

Tiffenden. Tippa's woodland pasture (OE *Tipping denn* → Tepindene 1086 → Tipendene c.1100 → Tippindeñe, Teppindeñe 1327 → Typyndenne 1350). The present name appears to be a corruption.

Tilden (Benenden). Young tree pasture: woodland pasture where young trees grow (OE *telga denn* → Teligden 858 → Teldenn 1311 → Tildenne 1346). The same origin is shared by Tilden, Headcorn (Tyldenne 1312, Teldenne 1338); and by Great and Little Tilden, Marden (Teldenne 1252, Tildenne 1346).

Tile Barn. This place, together with neighbouring Tile Yard Cottages, appears as Le Tylehost in 1535, the name being derived from OE *tigel āst*: tile kiln, or oast. Tile Kiln Lane, Bexley, marks the site of another kiln, being found as le Tylekyll c.1525.

Tilmanstone. Tilman's farmstead (OE *Tilmanes tūn* → Tilemanestone 1086 → Tilemannestune c.1100 → Tilemaneston' 1235 → Tilmaneston' 1242).

Tilt's Farm. See under HIGH TILT.

Timberden Bottom. Timber valley (OE *timber denu* → Timberdena 1175 → Timberden' 1278).

Timbold Hill (Lenham). Fold of Tæna's people (OE *Tæninga falod* → to Teninge faledun 850 → Tengefald 1196 → Teningefeld c.1250). There are no later forms to show how the present name evolved. Tæna — 'the offspring, or descendant' — whose name is also found in connection with THANINGTON, may have been one of the *Tænas* whose settlement was close by at TEYNHAM.

Tinton. Tīda's farmstead (OE *Tīding tūn* → Titentone 1086 → Tidenton 1135 → Tedingthone 1216 → Tydynton' 1292 → Tynton 1346). Tīda also owned a woodland pasture (OE *denn*) here, since Tinton is also recorded as Titindenne c.1275 → Tiddindenn' 1346 → Tydindenne 1347.

Tokeland Wood (Bethersden). It derives its name from the family of Clara Toke (c.1644). Tokeland Wood, Great Chart, is similarly associated with a 16th century family named Toke who owned farmland in this area.

Tollhurst. Heirs' wooded hill (OE *tūnlāfe hyrst* → Tunlafahirst 804 → Tun laf hirste 850 → Toluerherst c.1250 → Tuluerhurst 1254 → Tolueherst 1292). A *tūnlāf* was a person who had inherited a *tūn*, or farmstead.

Tollingtrough Green. Recorded in 1460 as Toltyngtrowgh, this was the meeting-place of the old Hundred of Toltingtrough, sharing the same origin of name: 'at the tilting, or tottering, tree' (OE *tolting trēow*) recorded as Tollentrev 1086 → Toltentrui c.1100 → Totingetre 1187 → Toltingtre 1226.

Tonbridge (pronounced Tunbridge). Farmstead bridge: bridge beside a farmstead (OE *tūn brycg* → Tonebrige 1086 → Tonebrigga c.1100 → Tunbrigg 1206 → Tunbridge 1610). The bridge was an important cross-

ing on the Medway here, guarded by Tonbridge Castle. The spelling of the place name has been altered to avoid confusion with TUNBRIDGE WELLS.

Tonford Farm (Thanington). (Land) between fords (OE *betwēon fordum* → Tuniford c.1215 → Twyniford' 1254 → Tweniford, Tuneford 1278 → Toniford 1313). There are fords crossing the Great Stour close by.

Tong (Eastling). Tongue of land (OE *tang* → Thoong' 1218 → Tonge 1240 → Tange, Tonge 1254). Tong, Headcorn, has the same origin, being recorded as Taunge in 1249, Tonge in 1334; and the topographical description occurs again in the names of Tong Farm, Brenchley; Tong Green, Throwley; Tong Wood, Whitstable; and Tong's Farm, Chislehurst.

Tonge (pronounced Tong). Tongue of land (OE *tang* → Tangas 1086 → Tanga 1160 → Tange 1190 → Tonge 1240).

Torry Hill (Lenham). The name is possibly derived from that of the family of John Terri of Lenham (c.1250).

Tottenden Wood (Benenden). Tota's woodland pasture (OE *Toting denn* → Totyndenn' 1313). The personal name is found again in TOTTINGTON.

Tottington. Tota's farmstead (OE *Toting tūn* → Totintune 1086 → Totington' 1254 → Totyntone 1327). Tota's pasture was at TOTTENDEN WOOD.

Tovil (pronounced Tovvil). Tough, or sticky, open land (OE *tōh feld* → Tobbeffeld 1218 → Toghfeld' 1304 → Toufeld 1313 → Toffelde 1327 → Toffel 1374). The place stands at the junction of the Medway and a tributary stream: at one time the land here must have been sticky and muddy, tough to work.

Townland. This was originally simply a farmstead (OE *tūn*), being recorded as Tune in 1240. The place name later came to mean 'land by the farmstead' (OE *tūn land*), and in this form appears as Tunlande in 1253, Tounlonde in 1327. Town Place, Throwley, also marks the site of an early farmstead, being recorded as Towne in 1262. Another site is now covered by Towns Wood, Wye, described as Tune 1226 → Toune 1327 → Town 1690.

Town Place. See under TOWN-LAND.

Toys Hill. The name is a manorial one, derived from that of some landowning family in the Westerham area.

Tramhatch. Beam hatch: hatch or gate made from wooden beams (OE *pram hæcc* → Thremhecch' 1338 → Thramhacche 1407). Beams, or logs, also provided the framework for a landing-place at the now lost place of Tremhuth, where the road from Sheppey to Harty crosses the Capel Fleet: this is recorded as Tremehethe in 1278, Tremhuth in 1328 (← OE *pram hȳð*: beam landing-place).

Trapham Farm (Wingham). Troppa's settlement (OE *Troppan hām* →

Tropham 1270 → Trapham 1690). Troppa's pasture was at TURPING-TON.

Trench, The. Ditch, trench (OF *trenche* → the Trenche 1541).

Trenley. Round clearing (OE *trind lēah* → Trindlee 1254 → Trindle 1347 → Trendley ponde 1507). Little Trenley here has the same origin. Trenleypark Wood, Littlebourne, is also on the site of a circular-shaped clearing, being recorded as trind lea 948 → Trindele, Trendle 1275 → Tryndley 1278 → Trendele Parke 1425.

Trenleypark Wood. See under TRENLEY.

Trent Wood (Boughton-under-Blean). It derives its name from the family of August Trente (1278).

Trillinghurst. Wooded hill of the *Tyrlingas*: the trillers or songsters (OE *Tyrlinga hyrst* → Therlingehurst 1254 → Terlingeherst 1334 → Trelingherst 1348). This may have been the same tribe which had its settlement at TERLINGHAM.

Trimworth Manor (Crundale). Drēama's enclosure (OE *Drēaman worð* → Dreaman uuyrðe 824 → Dreamwurthe c.1100 → Tremewrth 1218 → Tremworth 1254).

Trottiscliffe (pronounced Trozley). Trott's cliff (OE *Trottes clif* → Trottes clyva 788 → Totescliua c.975 → Totesclive 1086 → Trottescliue 1231 → Trosclyffe 1610).

Trotts Ash. The name appears to be a corruption of Trottesham, recorded here during the late 16th century, which very likely had the original meaning of 'Trott's settlement' (OE *Trottes hām*). This personal name is found in connection with TROTTISCLIFFE.

Trouts. Described as Troutes during the time of Elizabeth I, the place derives its name from the family of Thomas Troutes of Sheppey (1334).

Tubbenden. Tubba's woodland pasture (OE *Tubbing denn* → Tubindenn' 1240 → Tubbingden' 1309 → Tuppingdens 1595 → Tuppendens 1690). Tubba also gave his name to the now lost place of Tubnes in Marden.

Tubslake. Recorded as Tubb's Lane in 1700, the present name is a corruption of the original manorial one.

Tudeley (pronounced Tewdley). Thieves' valley (OE *pēofa dæl* → Tivedele 1086 → Tiuedele, Theudelei c.1100 → Teudeleye 1270 → Thewdele 1313 → Tuydley 1610).

Tudors. It takes its name from that of Theodorius de Stokes (1244) and his descendant, John de Teuder of Stoke (1346).

Tuesnoad. Tīw's piece of detached land (OE *Tīwes snād* → Teuesnode 1292 → Teuwesnod 1332 → Tewesnod 1346). This was a piece of land dedicated to the Saxon wargod Tīw, after whom Tuesday is named.

Tunbridge Wells. The place takes its name from nearby TONBRIDGE, the 'Wells' being the chalybeate

mineral springs discovered here in 1606. The affix Royal was granted to the town in 1909 by King Edward VII.

Tunstall. Farmstead (OE *tūnsteall* → Tunestelle 1086 → Tunsteal, Tunestele c.1100 → Tunstall 1227).

Turkeyhall. The place is probably to be associated with the family of William Turgys or Turgis (1278). Turkey Farm, Marden, derives its name from that of John Turke of Marden (1641).

Turnden. 'Turn pasture': woodland pasture by a turn, or bend (OE *tyrn denn* → Turnden' 1254 → Turndenne 1347). The name may be a reference to the junction of roads here.

Turpington Farm (Bromley). Troppa's woodland pasture (OE *Tropping denn* → Tropinden' 1278 Tropyndenn 1313). The present name is a corruption of these early forms. The personal name, Troppa, is also to be found in connection with TRAPHAM.

Tutsham Hall (West Farleigh). Tutt's settlement (OE *Tuttes hām* → Tuttesham 1248 → Tutesham 1279 → Tutsham 1610).

Twinney Creek. (Land) between rivers (OE *betwēonum ēa* → Twinneneia 1166 → Tuinenea 1190 → Twyney Salts 1598). This is the name of the sea creek to the west of Upchurch.

Twisden Plantation. See under TWYSSENDEN.

193

Twitham (pronounced Twittum). 'Detached land settlement': settlement by land which is cut off (OE *þwīt hām* → Twitham 1199 → Thwitham, Tuitham 1203 → Twytham 1240). This is a reference to land which was cut off by the flooding of the Wingham River.

Twitton. 'Detached land farmstead': farmstead by land which is cut off (OE *þwīt tūn* → Twetton 1292 → Tweton 1555). The place is on sloping ground leading to Twitton Brook, a marshy area which must once have cut off this farmstead from surrounding ground.

Twydall. Double portion, or dole (OE *twidǣl* → Twydele 1240 → Twydole 1313 → Twidall 1690).

Twyford Bridge. (Place) with a double ford (OE *twi-fyrde* → Tviferde 1086 → Twiuerd' 1160 → Twyferd', Twiford' 1226 → Twyforde bridge 1610). The name is probably a reference to the junction here of the Beult and the Teise.

Twyssenden (pronounced Twiss-en-dn). 'Fork pasture': woodland pasture at the fork of a path or stream (OE *twys denn* → Twysdenn' 1240 → Twisdenne 1327 → Twysdenne 1334 → Twysden Borough *alias* Twysenden 1790). Twisden Plantation, Sandhurst, shares the same origin, being recorded as Twysdenn' in 1278.

Tyehurst. Enclosure wood: wooded hill by an enclosure (OE *tēag hyrst* → Teghurste 1292 → Tegherst 1332 → Teyhurst 1362).

Tyland. Recorded in 1535 as Tylond, the place name is probably derived from OE *tēag land*: land by a tye, or enclosure.

Tylerhill. Tile-house slope: slope on which there is a tile-house or kiln (OE *tigelǣrn hielde* → Teghelerehelde 1363 → Tegularynhelde 1432 → Tylorhill 1535). During the 18th century the place was known as Tile Kyln Hill; and in 1292 two tile-makers who must have worked at the kiln here – Philip le Tythelere and Peter le Theghelere – are recorded in the area.

U

Uckfield Wood (Hever). Together with Uckfield Lane here, it derives its name from that of John le Bakere de Vkkefelde (c.1300), a native of Uckfield in Sussex.

Uffington Farm (Goodnestone). Uffa's farmstead (OE *Uffing tūn* → Vffingtun' 1226 → Offingtun' 1282 → Vffyntone 1304). Uffa had a second farmstead at UFTON COURT.

Ufton Court (Tunstall). Uffa's farmstead (OE *Uffan tūn* → Oftun' 1254 → Uffeton 1283 → Ufton 1301).

Ulcombe (pronounced Oolcum). Owl valley: valley frequented by owls (OE *ūle cumb* → Uulacumb 941 → Ulecumbe 946 → Olecvmbe 1086 → Ulecumbe 1233).

Ulley Farm (Kennington). Owl clearing: clearing frequented by owls (OE *ūle lēah* → Wlleg' 1226 → Ullee 1369 → Ulley 1499).

Underdown. Under, or below, a hill (OE *under dūne* → Vnderdoun' 1292 → Vnderdoune 1347). The same original meaning is found in the names of Underdown Farm, Herne, and Underdown Wood, Chislet.

Underhill. Under, or below, a slope (OE *under hielde* → Hondheld c. 1185 → Vnderhulle 1254 → Vnderheld' 1278). Underhill House, Cheriton, has the same origin, appearing as Vnderhelde in 1332.

Underling Green. Under, or below, a pasture (OE *under denne* → Underden Green 1700). The pasture lay on the slope of the small hill just north of the place.

Under River. There are no records for this place name, but it appears to be a description of the village site, on the Hilden Brook which is a tributary of the River Medway.

Upchurch. Church standing high up (OE *uppe cirice* → Vpcyrcean c.1100 → Upechereche c.1150 → Uppechirche 1208 → Upchurch 1610). The church and village are situated on a hill, the church spire once being used as a landmark by seamen.

Updown Farm (Ham). Up (on a) hill (OE *uppe dūn* → Uppedun 1206 → Opedoune 1357).

Updown House. See under NORTH-DOWN.

Up Hill. Wippa's spring (OE *Wipping wielle* → Wyppingwell' 1292 → Wyppinwelle 1357 → Uppingwelle 1539). The present name is a contraction of these forms, with final -well becoming -hill.

Uphousden Farm (Ash). Recorded as Ophosen in 1484 and as Uphousen in 1790, the original meaning of this name was 'at the up, or high, houses' (OE *æt þǣm uppe hūsum*).

Uplands Farm (Westerham). Self-explanatory (OE *uppe land* → Vppeland, Huplaund 1278 → Oplonde 1313).

Upnor. Originally meaning 'at the bank' (OE *æt þǣm ōre*, ME *atten ore*), the name appears as atte Nore in 1292. After this date it was altered to mean 'upon the bank' (ME *uppan ore*), with reference to some building which preceeded the Elizabethan castle here, and is recorded as Upnore in 1374, Upnor Castle in 1690.

Upstreet. Recorded as such in 1690, the name refers to a street or narrow road running up the side of a hill. There was also a now lost Upstreet in Dartford, found as Vpstrete in 1278, Vppestrete in 1292 (← OE *uppe strǣt*).

Upton (Bexley). 'Up farmstead': farmstead built high up (OE *uppe tūn* → Vpton' 1292). Upton, St. Peters, shares a common origin (Vptune c.1225); as do Upton Court, Sibertswold; Upton Farm, Alkham; and Upton House, Worth. The now lost place of Upton in Great Chart was on the site of a high homestead (OE *uppe hāmtūn*), appearing as Vphamton' in 1254.

V

Vale Mascal. See under MARSHALL WOOD.

Valence. It is believed to have derived its name from the family of de Valoniis, or Valons, who were landowners in the Westerham area during the 13th century. Vallance Wood, Stelling, is associated with the family of William de Valloingnes (1235) and his descendants, recorded as de Valoyns in 1346.

Valley, The. Self-explanatory (OF *vallee* → Valeye 1278).

Valleys Shaw. The place possibly takes its name from the family of August Waleys of Ridley (1346). The affix 'Shaw' is from OE *scaga*: a copse.

Venson Farm (Eastry). Vandal's farmstead: farmstead belonging to a Vandal (OE *Wendles tūn* → Wendleston' 1254 → Wenneleston' 1332 → Wendlestone 1346 → Weneston 1417 → Wenson 1675).

Vexour. Rough grass bank: bank on which grows rough or coarse grass (OE *feax ōra* → ffexsore, Hexore 1278 → ffexore 1338 → Fexore 1382).

Vigo (pronounced Vi-go). This is a new village which has been developed at the foot of Vigo Hill, near Meopham. The name appears to be derived from the Spanish seaport of Vigo, captured by the British in 1719 and an important port of call for merchant shipping. Vigo New Village is not far from the Medway port of Gravesend, and the pub sign depicts a seaman of Nelson's time priming a cannon.

Vine Wood. See under VINEY'S WOOD.

Vineyard, The. Recorded as Vyaundys 1370 → Vyander *alias* Viaundez 1435 → Viance, the Vyance 1572, this name is ultimately derived from that of the family of Robert Vyaund (1302), the place once being part of their estate in Cobham. Vineyard Shaw near Farningham appears as Nethere Vynhagh in 1357, a name perhaps derived from OE *fīn hæg*: 'heap enclosure', or hedged enclosure near a heap.

Viney's Wood (Crundale). Heap enclosure: enclosure near a heap of wood (OE *fīn hæg* → ffineghe 1348). *Fīn* — heap of wood — appears to be the origin of the name of Vine Wood, Stalisfield, for which no forms have been found.

Vinters. Together with Vinters Farm here, the place derives its name from the 13th century family of le Vineter: vintner, or wine-seller.

W

Wadd, Little. Forest (OE *weald* → Wold' 1240 → Wealde 1334).

Wadden Hall (Waltham). Wædda's corner of land (OE *Wædding halh* → Wadinhale 1176 → Wadenhal 1247 → Wodenhale 1279). Wædda's farmstead was at WEDDINGTON; his woodland pasture (OE *denn*) was at the now lost place of Waddendene in Bethersden.

Waddling Hill Plantation (Waldershare). There are no records for this name, but it is obviously derived from that of the now lost place of Wadling, three miles away in Ripple, originally OE *Wædelingas*: 'Wædel's people', and recorded as Woldinge 1253 → Wodlynge 1327 → Wadlinge 1338 → Wadling *alias* Watling 1799.

Wade Marsh (St. Nicholas-at-Wade). It probably has the same origin as the parish name: ford, or wading-place (OE *(ge)wæd*); but an alternative derivation may have been from the now lost place of Wardmarsh close by, which had the meaning of 'watch marsh': marshland where watch is kept (OE *weard mersc*) and is recorded as marisco de Warde 1292 → Le Warde 1418 → Wardmarsh 1538.

Wadholt Wood (Coldred). Wlāta's thicket (OE *Wlāting holt* → Platenovt 1086 → Wlatenholte 1270 → Wadynholte 1327 → Watyngholte 1357 → Wadenholte 1377).

Wainscot. There are no early forms, but the name may perhaps be derived from OE *wægnes cot*: 'wagon's cot' – a cot, or shed, where wagons were kept.

Walderchain Wood (Barham). Forest-dwellers' cavern (OE *wealdwara cine* → Waterchine 1263 → Waldirchene 1327 → Walderchyn 1463 → Waldercheyne Wood 1662). This may have been the same tribe of forest people whose land boundary was at WALDERSHARE.

Waldershare. Forest-dwellers' boundary (OE *wealdwara scearu* → Walwalesere 1086 → Waldwereshawe 1240 → Waldwarshare 1278 → Waldershare 1610).

Walderslade. Forest valley (OE *weald*

slæd → Waldeslade 1190 → Walder-slade 1278). The place lies in a flat valley.

Wales Wood (Chilham). It is associated with the family of John Waleys of Chilham (1375).

Walkhurst. Wealca's wooded hill (OE *Wealcan hyrst* → Walcherst, Walke-herst 1313).

Walland Marsh. Wall land: land against a sea wall (OE *weall land* → Waland' 1219 → Walland 1475). The name refers to the RHEE WALL. Wallend, Chislet, probably has the same original meaning, but there are no records for the name.

Wallend. See under WALLAND MARSH.

Wallet Court (Boughton Malherbe). Meeting of ways: junction (OE *wega gelǣte* → Woghelete 1327). The place lies just north of a road junction. Wallett's Court, West Cliffe, appears as Walgate in 1338 and as West Cliffe *alias* Walletts Court in 1799, the 14th century form being derived from OE *weall geat*: 'wall gate', or gate in a wall.

Wall Farm (Ashford). Recorded in 1632 as Wall, the name is probably from OE *weall*: wall, denoting a place close to, or enclosed by, a wall. Wall Farm, Brabourne, certainly has this original meaning, appearing as Walle in 1292; as does Lower Wall Farm and House, Lympne, found as Walle in 1327.

Wallingham. Recorded as Walenge-ham in 1397, the place lies on the site of a British settlement (OE

Wealinga hām). *Wealh* properly meant 'foreigner, Briton', a name given by the conquering Saxons to those of the old race whom they forced into bondage. The word has produced modern 'Welsh', since many Britons chose to escape to the free lands of the Welsh Marches. The now lost place of Wall-inghurst in Frittenden was originally a wooded hill belonging to a Briton (OE *Wealing hyrst*) and is recorded as Walingherst in 1256.

Wallsfoot Sewer (Bilsington). Wall's end (OE *wealles ende* → Wallesende 1248). A change of name to mean 'at the wall's foot' produced the modern form for this sewer, or drain, in old marshland country.

Walmer (pronounced Wall-mer). Britons' pool (OE *Weala mere* → Walemere 1087 → Wealemere c. 1100 → Walmere 1253 → Walmer 1610). This was probably a pool set aside for the sole use of the British Celts who farmed near Saxon settlements around Deal: the Britons often lived apart in their own communities, as is shown by WALL-INGHAM, where they had a settlement of their own, and WALTON, which was a farmstead run by Britons.

Walmer's Hill (Chislet). It derives its name from the family of John Wallemere (1332), a native of Wal-mer.

Walmestone (pronounced Wawms-tun). Wīghelm's farmstead (OE *Wīg-helmes tūn* → Wielmestun c.1100 → Wyhelmestoñ 1205 → Welmestone 1253). The personal name is also found in connection with WIL-

MINGTON and WINTON.

Walsingham. It is named after the family of Walsingham who became owners of the manor of Scadbury (now SCADBURY PARK in this parish) in the mid-14th century.

Waltham (pronounced Waltum). Forest settlement (OE *weald hām* → Wealtham c.1100 → Waltham 1199).

Walton Farm (Folkestone). Britons' farmstead (OE *Weala tūn* → Waleton' 1204 → Waletune 1262 → Walton 1431). Walton House, Eastry, shares the same meaning of a farmstead run by British Celts, and is recorded as Walton in 1302.

Wanden. Dark woodland pasture (OE *wann denn* → Wandenn' 1278 → Wandenne 1327). The name probably refers to a place overshadowed by trees.

Wanshurst Green. Wand's (land covered with) brushwood (OE *Wandes hǣs* → Wendeshase 1254 → Wondeshese 1292 → Wandeshese 1334 → Wanh'st 1348).

Wanstone Farm (St. Margaret-at-Cliffe). Wensige's farmstead (OE *Wensiges tūn* → Wansieston' 1233 → Wenstone 1304 → Wannston 1487).

Wansunt. Want's spring (OE *Wantes funta* → Wantesfonte 1270). The present name is a contraction of this 13th century form.

Wantsum, River (pronounced Wansum). Described in a charter of 944 as ea wantsum: 'winding river', the name is derived from an Old English adjective *wændsum*: winding, which aptly describes its course. Earlier, the river is recorded as uantsumu c.730, wantsume c.890.

Warden. Watch hill: hill on which watch or ward is kept (OE *weard dūn* → Wardoñ 1207 → Wardeñ 1215). Warden Mill, Wateringbury, is recorded as Wardens in 1782, taking its name from that of Roger Wardayn of Wateringbury (c.1450).

Ware. Weir (OE *wer* → War' 1226 → La Ware 1308). The place lies on the Wingham River. Ware Street, Thornham, is also close to the site of a weir, appearing as Were, Ware in 1240 and as Ware in 1321. Wear Farm, Chislet, shares the same derivation, being found as Ware in 1327.

Warehorn. See under WAREHORNE.

Warehorne. 'Weir spur': spur of land close to a weir (OE *wer horn* → Werahorna 830 → æt Werhornan 1032 → Werahorne 1086 → Werehorne 1210). Warehorne is situated on a projection of land, as is Warehorn, St. Nicholas-at-Wade, which is recorded as Werehorn c.1250. At Warehorne, the weir would have been on the River Lympne; at Warehorn, it would have been on the Horn.

Warrington Place (Brenchley). Wǣrburh's farmstead (OE *Wǣrburge tūn* → Warbbutone, Warblintone 1253 → Warblyngton 1314 → Warbelton 1347). Wǣrburh was a Saxon woman.

Washenden. Wæcca's woodland pasture (OE *Wæccing denn* → Wecchynden 1270 → Wachingdenn' 1278 → Wechyngdenn' 1313 → Wachenden 1535).

Watchester Farm (Minster). At the water (OE *æt pæm wætere* → Watere 1348 → Water 1357 → Watchester 1799). The name refers to one of the many streams on the Isle of Thanet. Water Street, Lenham, shares the same origin, being found in 1254 as Attewat'e (← ME *atte watere*: at the water).

Waterditch Farm (Lenham). Self-explanatory (OE *wæter dīc* → Waterdich 1240 → Weterdiche 1278).

Waterham. Water meadow: meadow where the ground is water-logged (OE *wæter hamm* → Wet'hamme 1292 → Waterhamme 1313). Waterham Farm, Wickhambreux, has the same derivation, appearing as Waterhamme c.1250; as does Waterham Shaw, Ospringe, which is found as Waterham in 1500.

Wateringbury. Swine pasture of the *Wōðringas,* or noisy ones (OE *Wōðringa bǣr* → æt Woðringaberan 964 → Otringeberge 1086 → Wotringaberia c.1100 → Watringbury 1610).

Water Street. See under WATCHESTER.

Watling Street. This has the meaning of 'road to St. Albans', since the street (← OE *strǣt*: Roman road) originally ran from London to St. Albans, the early name for which was Wætlingaceaster: fortified camp of the *Wætlingas.* Watling Street, extended by the Romans through Rochester and Canterbury to south-east Kent, appears as Wætlingastræt in 880.

Watt's Cross. The place takes its name from the family of John Watte (1327), the 'cross' referring either to a wayside cross, or to crossroads here.

Way. Self-explanatory (OE *weg* → Weye 1254). Waystreet Farm, Hernhill, has the same meaning of a way, or track, being recorded as La wey in 1240, Weye in 1327.

Waystreet Farm. See under WAY.

Waystrode Farm (Cowden). 'Whey marsh': sour marshy land overgrown with brushwood (OE *hwæg strōd* → Weystrode 1292 → Wheystrode 1328 → Whystrode 1543). The name appears to refer to marshy ground which was apt to ferment in warm weather.

Wear Farm. See under WARE.

Weavering Street. The unstable, or wavering, people (OE *Wæfringas* → Wavering 1189 → Waveringes 1198 → Waveryng̅ 1259 → Weveringe 1330 → Wavering 1782). This may have been a nickname given to a wandering tribe who settled in this area.

Wechylstone. This was the meeting-place of the Washlingstone Hundred, and doubtless shares the same original name meaning: 'watcher's stone', a stone or rock by which look-out was kept (OE *wacoles stān*). The place is recorded as

WEDDINGTON – WESTENHANGER

Wachelestan 1086 → Wakelestan 1175 → Wechelestone 1253 → Wechelstone 1278.

Weddington. Wædda's farmstead (OE *Wædding tūn* → Wedinton' 1254 → Wadyntone 1348). Wædda owned land at WADDEN HALL.

Well. This name, derived from OE *wielle*, ME *welle*: spring, is found in Well Chapel, Ickham; Well Court, Blean; and Well House, Beckenham, Bridge and Kingsdown.

Welling. (pronounced Wellin). Recorded as Wellyngs in 1362 and as Wellyng in 1370, the place derives its name from the family of Radolphus Willing of Bexley (1301).

Wellington Place (Tenterden). Wilfrið's woodland pasture (OE *Wilfriðing denn* → Wylu'denn' 1292 →Wiluryndeñe 1327→Wyl'uindenn' 1346 → Wilfrinden' 1348). The change in name may well be due to the popularity of the Duke of Wellington.

Wellmarsh. Wild, uncultivated marshland (OE *wilde mersc* → Wildemershe 1362).

Well Pen. Recorded in 1456 as Welpende, the name is probably derived from OE *wielle pund*: pound or enclosure by a spring.

Well Street. Spring, source of a stream (OE *æwiell* → Ewelle 1240).

Wenderton Farm, Great and **Little** (Wingham). Wēnðrÿð's farmstead *Wēnðrÿðe tūn* → Wenderton' 1200 → Wendreton' 1270 → Wendirton 1296 → Wendertone 1304). Wēn-

ðrÿð was a Saxon woman.

Westbere. West swine pasture (OE *west bær* → Westbere 1212 → Westbeere 1610). This was originally a pasture lying to the west of the settlement here.

Westbroke Farm and **House.** See under WESTBROOK.

Westbrook. West marshy ground (OE *west brōc* → Westbrok' 1254). Westbrook Farm, Herne, shares the same meaning of marsh to the west of the parish, appearing as Westebrok' in 1270, Westbroke in 1458. Westbroke Farm and House, Lydd, are recorded as Westbrok' in 1292, Westbrooke in 1455.

West Cliffe. See under CLIFFE.

West Court Downs (Sibertswold). Together with West Court Farm here, the place derives its name from a local manorhouse (F *court*), and is recorded as West Corte in 1477, Westcourt in 1535.

Wested. West place: place to the west of the parish (ME *west stede* → Westede 1270).

West End. West place stream (OE *west stede burna* → Westedburn' 1278 → Westend 1525). A stream runs by here, at the western end of the parish.

Westenhanger. Wooded slope of the *Osteringas*, the knotty or lumpy ones (OE *Ostringa hangra* → Witingehanga 1135 → Ostringehangre 1210 → Estringeshangre 1231 → Ostringhangere 1275 → Westringhangre 1316 → Ostenhanger 1690).

203

There seems to have been confusion in the development of this place name caused by the English 'west' and the French 'ouest', apparently thought to be part of the original name.

Wester, Little. Western: lying towards the west (OE *westerra* → Westerey 1254 → Westere, Westery 1292). Little Wester, Wester Hill and Westerhill Farm are all in the western part of the parish of Linton.

Westerham (pronounced Westram). The western settlement (OE *se westra hām* → Westarham 871 → Westerham c.975 → Oistreham 1086 → Westerham 1211). So called because it lies in the extreme west of the county, close to the Surrey border.

Westfield Wood (Ash). West land: open land to the west of the settlement (OE *west feld* → Westfeld 1232). Westfield Wood and Westfield Sole, Boxley, share the same origin, appearing as Westfelde c. 1500; 'Sole' is from OE *sol*: muddy pool. Westfield Farm, Addington, is recorded as Westfield in 1680.

Westgate Court (St. Dunstan Without). On the site of the west city gate of Canterbury, and the meeting-place of the Westgate Hundred, the place is recorded as Westgate in 1115.

Westhawk Farm (Kingsnorth). Recorded in 1690 as West-Hauk and in 1790 as West Halke, the name is probably derived ultimately from OE *west halh*: west corner.

Westhoy. The place lies just to the west of HAYLAND FARM in Smarden, and appears to have the original meaning of 'west of the hedged enclosure', since Hayland Farm is on the site of such an enclosure and is recorded as Haye in 1254.

Westlands. Land to the west of the parish (ME *west lande* → Westlande 1278).

West Marsh. Recorded as such in 1406, the name is self-explanatory.

Westpark Farm (Trottiscliffe). Described between 1283 and 1291 as le West Park, or le Westparc, the farm obviously lies on land which was once parkland to the west of the parish.

Westpherhawk Farm (Smarden) (pronounced Wesperhawk). Hwīt's enclosure (OE *Hwītes pearroc* → Hwithsparroch, Wytsparroc c.1225 → Whitesparok 1379 → Wisperhawke 1782).

Westwell. Spring (OE *wielle* → Welle 1086 → Westwell' 1226). Called 'west' to distinguish this place from EASTWELL nearby.

West Wood (Stockbury). Originally woodland to the west of the parish, it appears as Westwoodes in 1551. West Wood, Lyminge, is described as Westwood in 1546; Westwood Court, Preston, appears as Westwode in 1242; and Westwood Farm, Bexley, is Westwood in 1551.

Wetham Green (pronounced Wettum). Wet water meadow (OE *wǣt hamm* → Weteham 1348 → Wheatham Saltmarsh 1598). The place is on the estuary of the Medway.

Whatsole Street. Wada's muddy pool (OE *Wadan sol* → Wadesol', Wodesole c.1240 → Wadesole 1313).

Wheelbarrow Town. Enclosure of the forest-dwellers (OE *wealdinga worð* → Wealdingworth' 1278). During medieval times final -worth in this name was dropped in favour of -burgh: 'manor'. The present place name is thus a corruption of the Middle English form *Wealdingburgh*, with the explanatory addition of 'Town', derived from ME *tone*: farmstead.

Wheeler's Street. It is possibly to be associated with the family of Elizabeth Wyllard of Headcorn (1602).

Whetstead. 'Wheaten place': place where wheat grows (OE *hwæten stede* → Hwӕtanstede, Hwetenstede 838 → Whetstede 1226).

Whiteacre. Wheat land: cultivated piece of land on which wheat is grown (OE *hwæt æcer* → Watekere 1210 → Whetacre 1253 → Whitacre, Wheteacre 1346).

Whitefield Shaws. See under WHITFIELD.

Whitehall Crossing. Recorded in 1324 as the home of Robert de Wythenhale, the place name has developed from this family name, 'Crossing' presumably being a reference to a ford on the River Cray close by. White Hall, Hoo St. Werburgh, has the original meaning of 'white manorhouse', referring to the colour of the building, and is recorded as le Whitehall in 1436. White Hall, Lynsted, shares the same origin, being found as Whythale in 1292.

Whitehill. White slope (OE *hwīt hielde* → Whytehelde, Whiteheld 1466). The soil here is chalky.

White's Wood (Hawkhurst). Described in 1507 as Whitdownewood, the place takes its name from that of the family of Robert Wyte of Hawkhurst (c.1250).

Whitfield. White (chalky) open land (OE *hwīt feld* → Wytefeld' 1228 → Whitfeld', Whitefeld 1278). Whitfield Sewer, Chislet, shares the same origin, being recorded as Hwitefeld' in 1348, Whitefeld' in 1357. Whitfield in Biddenden is named after the family of Whitfield who lived there during the 17th and 18th centuries. Whitefield Shaws, Detling, shares the same origin as Whitfield and appears as Wytefeld in 1278, Whitefeld' in 1313. The affix 'Shaws' is from OE *scaga*: a copse.

Whitley Forest. The original name seems to have been 'at the white (chalky) hill' (OE *æt þæm hwītan hylle*), since the place is recorded as Whitehell' in 1313. By the 16th century the hill had become cliff, the name appearing as Whytclyffe in 1535. In 1574 it is recorded as Whitley *alias* Whitcliff.

Whitstable (pronounced Whit-stubble). At the white post, or staple (OE *æt þæm hwītan stapole* → Witenestaple 1086 → Witstapel 1184 → Whitstapl' 1226 → Whitstable 1610). This was the meeting-place of the Whitstable Hundred, the white post probably acting as a landmark.

205

Whitsunden. Wicca's woodland pasture (OE *Wiccing denn* → Wichenden 1202 → Wychindenn' 1240 → Wychindenne 1347 → Wissenden 1617). Wicca had another pasture at WISSENDEN.

Whittaker's Wood (Stockbury). It probably derives its name from the local family of de Wetesker' (1270).

Whole Farm (Stone-cum-Ebony). Hollow (OE *hol* → Hole 1254).

Wicham Cottages (Strood). Dwelling place (OE *wīchām* → Wycham 1100 → Wicham 1147).

Wichling (pronounced Witchlin). This place name had the original meaning of 'Wincel's pool' (OE *Winceles mere*) and is recorded as Winchelesmere 1086 → Wincelesmere c.1100 → Whicclesmere 1242. By the side of this form developed that of 'Wincel's people' (OE *Wincelingas*), found as Winchelinge 1220 → Wichelinges 1240 → Wichelinge 1278. Obviously this tribe settled around the spot where Wincel, the leader, had made his home close to a pool. As the settlement grew, the original place name died, leaving the tribal name which has developed to modern Wichling.

Wicken. Recorded as Wickins c.1780, the name may perhaps be derived from that of the family of Henry de Wicombe (1313).

Wickens. (Land) belonging to a farm (OE *wīcing* → Wyking' 1248 → Wykyng 1362 → Wikyng 1510).

Wickham, East (pronounced Wickam). Dwelling place (OE *wīchām* → Wikam 1240 → Wykham 1254 → Est Wycham 1292 → E. Wykham 1610). Called 'East' to distinguish the place from WEST WICKHAM.

Wickham, West. Dwelling place (OE *wīchām* → to wichæma 862 → Wicheham 1086 → Wicham 1231 → W.Wickham 1610). Called 'West' to distinguish the place from EAST WICKHAM.

Wickham Bushes. Dwelling place (OE *wīchām* → Wichā 1226 → Wicham 1242 → Wykham 1311). The affix 'Bushes' is derived from ME *bushoppes*: 'owned by a bishop'.

Wickhambreux (pronounced Wickham-broo). Dwelling place (OE *wīchām* → Wic ham 948 → Wicheham 1086 → Wicham 1087 → Wykham Breuhuse, Wyckham Breuse 1270). During the 13th century the estate passed into the possession of the family of de Brewse, or de Braiose, their name being affixed to that of the place in order to distinguish it from the other Wickhams in the county.

Wick Hill (Headcorn). Together with Wick Farm here, the name is derived from OE *wīc*: farm, and appears as Wyke in 1358, Wike in 1531. Wick Farm, Elham, has the same origin, being recorded as La Wike in 1240. Wick Lane and Wood, Womenswold, is Wike in 1210; and Wick Petty Sewer and Upper Wick Wall, both in Lydd, appear as Wyke in 1323, 'Petty Sewer' meaning a little drain in marshland here.

Wickhurst. Farm wood: wooded hill by a farm (OE *wīc hyrst* → Wykherst 1292 → Wicherst 1313 → Wikherst 1327).

Wickmaryholm Pit (Lydd). The present name appears to have been created by the running-together of two separate names, since in 1552 there are ponds and fisheries here called Wigmore and Holme: Wigmore is probably derived from OE *wīc mere*: farm pool, Holme from OE *holegn*, ME *holm*: holly-tree. The 'Pit' refers to a hollow of some kind in the area, perhaps the remains of the original pool.

Widdick Shave. It is associated with the Kingsnorth family of Withicke, recorded in the parish in 1625.

Widehurst. Wīggȳð's wooded hill (OE *Wīggȳðe hyrst* → Wytheherst 1240 → Wygherst, Wyghethehert 1338 → Wyghetheherst 1340 → Whithurst 1361 → Wytherst 1393). Wīggȳð was a Saxon woman.

Widmore. Withy pool: pool where withy willows grow (OE *wiðig mere* → Withm'e 1226 → Wedemer 1278 → Wythemere 1313 → Wydemere 1334 → Wigmore 1778).

Wierton Place (Boughton Monchelsea). Wīghere's farmstead (OE *Wīghering tūn* → Wyhgherintone c.1225 → Wygherton' 1313 → Wygheruyntone 1327 → Wyghhernton' 1332). The present name is a contraction of these forms.

Wigmore. Broad, or wide, pool (OE *wīd mere* → Wydemere 1275 → Widemere 1327 → Wigmer 1610).

Wildage Farm. See under WOOLWICH.

Wildboars. It takes its name from the family of Thomas Wildebore (1327).

Wilderton, North and **South.** Wilhere's farmstead (OE *Wilhering tūn* → Wilrinton 1050 → Wirentone 1086 → Wilrintuna 1220 → Wilrington' 1226).

Wildmarsh. Wild, uncultivated marshland (OE *wilde mersc* → Weldemersche 1505 → Weldmershe 1538).

Wiles Shaw. The place is associated with the Maidstone family of Willes (1327), also recorded as Wylles (1350).

Wilgate Green. Willow land: wedge-shaped piece of land on which willows grow (OE *wilig gāra* → Wilgare 1235 → Wylgar 1270 → Wyligare 1327 → Wylgare 1332).

Willerd's Hill Wood (Benenden). It takes its name from the family of Thomas Willerd (1348).

Willesborough (pronounced Willsboro). Wifel's mound or tumulus (OE *Wifeles beorg* → Wifeles berge 863 → Wifeles beorge 993 → Wyuellesberg' 1243 → Wyuelesberwe 1254 → Willesborow 1610). Wifel also owned land at WILLSLEY GREEN.

William's Hill (Cobham). It appears to take its name from the family of Willmans, recorded in the Cobham area between 1558 and 1625.

Willington. Wilde's farmstead (OE *Wilding tūn* → Wyldyngton' 1292 → Wylinton' 1332 → Wyldyntone 1344 → Welynton 1407).

Willop Sewer (Burmarsh). Willow land: enclosed marshland where willows grow (OE *wilig hop* → Wylhope 1253 → Willop 1271 → Wylhope 1330 → Willopp 1651). The 'sewer' refers to a drain in this marshy area.

Willow Wood (Ospringe). Self-explanatory (OE *wilig* → Wyleghe 1313). Willow Wood, Tunstall, shares the same origin and is recorded as Wyleghe in 1342.

Willsley Green. Wifel's clearing (OE *Wifeles lēah* → Wiueleslegh' 1226 → Wyuelesle 1240). Wifel also had land at WILLESBOROUGH.

Wilmington. Wīghelm's farmstead (OE *Wīghelming tūn* → Wilmintuna 1089 → Wilmentuna c.1100 → Wilmington' 1226). Wīghelm owned another farmstead at the now lost place of Wilmington in Sellindge, recorded as Wieghelmes tun in 697 (← OE *Wīghelmes tūn*). A third farmstead was on the site of Wilmington Farm, Boughton Aluph, recorded as Wilminton' in 1219, and as Wylmyntone in 1253; though Wīghelm originally owned only land here, since a charter of 858 records his property as Wighelmes land. The farmstead appears to have been built later.

Win Bridge. Meadow bridge: bridge close to a meadow (OE *winn brycg* → Winberegg c.1200 → Wymbregg' 1254). The place lies on the stream which divides Kent from Sussex in this area.

Winburne. Meadow stream: stream flowing through a meadow (OE *winn burna* → Winburn' c.1250).

Wincham Bridge. Corner meadow: water meadow in a nook or corner of land (OE *wince hamm* → Wyncheham 1327 → Wincham 1334). Wincham Bridge lies on a tributary of the Shuttle.

Winchcombe Farm (Crundale). Corner valley (OE *wincel cumb* → Wincel cumbe 825 → Wynchcombe c.1235 → Wynchecumbe 1313). There are two valleys here, divided by a high ridge of land.

Wincheap Street. Wain market: market where wains, or waggons, are loaded (OE *wǣn cēap* → Wenchepe 1226 → Weynchep 1278). The space where this market was held was probably just outside the old Wincheap Gate, one of the gates of Canterbury.

Winchet Hill (Goudhurst). 'Wind land': broad expanse of land where the wind blows (OE *wind scēte* → Wyndschete 1440). This is still an exposed area.

Winch's Plantation (Hawkhurst). It is named after an 18th century worsted-maker, Winch, who ran a prosperous business in Hawkhurst employing about a hundred workers.

Windhill Green. Windy hill (OE *wind hyll* → Windehelle 1278 → Wyndehill 1358). Windinghill Wood, Stalisfield, shares the same origin, being recorded as Windhell in 1262, Wyndhelle in 1334.

Windinghill Wood. See under WIND-HILL GREEN.

Winfield Bank. Recorded as Wenifalle in 1199 and as Wenefalle in

1254, possibly this was a spot at which a wain or waggon (OE *wǣn*) had fallen. Winfield Farm, Wrotham, has the original meaning of 'windy open land' (OE *wind feld*) and appears as Winfeld in 1240.

Winford Bridge. Women's ford (ME *wiuene ford* → Wyneford' 1292 → Wyueneford' 1313). The ford is a shallow one, easily crossed by women.

Wingate Hill (Folkestone). 'Wind gate': gate, or cliff-gap, through which the wind blows (OE *wind geat* → Wyngate 1235 → Wyndgate 1327). .

Wingfield. Wind land: open land over which the wind blows (OE *wind feld* → Winefeld' 1200 → Windefeld' 1242 → Wyndfeld' 1313).

Wingham (pronounced Wingam). Settlement of Wīga's people (OE *Wīginga hām* → Uuigincgga ham 824 → Winganham 941 → Wingheham 1086 → Wyngham 1226 → Wingham 1610). This tribe had a pool at WINGMORE.

Wingham Barton Manor. See under BARTON WOOD.

Wingleton Farm. See under WINK-LANDOAKS.

Wingmore. Pool of Wīga's people (OE *Wīginga mere* → Wengem'e 1240 → Wyngemere 1357). The tribal settlement was at WINGHAM.

Winkhurst Green. It possibly takes its name from that of the local family of Wynkere (1348), the gen-itival form Wynkeres becoming corrupted to Winkhurst: this is not unusual in the development of place names.

Winklandoaks Farm (Ripple). Wineca's land (OE *Winecan land* → Winekelande 1232 → Winkelond' 1343). 'Oaks' is a late affix to this name, the origin of which is shared by Wingleton Farm nearby in Sutton: this was also land originally owned by Wineca, -land being altered at some late date to -ton, perhaps to distinguish the two places from each other.

Winstead Hill (Cobham). Recorded in 1770 as Wincett Hill, the name possibly shares the same original meaning as WINCHET HILL.

Winterage Farm (Elham). Wintra's people (OE *Wintringas* → Wintringe 1240 → Wyntrynge 1292 → Wynterynge 1473). Alternatively, the place may originally have been a spot where early invaders wintered, giving them the nickname of 'the winter people' (OE *winteringas*).

Winterbourne. Winter stream (OE *winter burna* → Wynterburn' 1278 → Wynterbourne 1332). The name is a reference to a stream which only flowed during winter months, swollen by rain and snow.

Winterham Hill (Cobham). Recorded in 1572 as Wyntrame, greatt Wyntram, the name is probably derived from OE *winter hamm*: winter meadow, a meadow on which animals were pastured during winter months.

Winton Farm (Rolvenden). Wīghelm's farmstead (OE *Wīghelming tūn* → Wilmenton' 1334 → Wylmynton' 1338). The present name is a contraction of these forms. The personal name, Wīghelm, is also found in connection with WALMESTONE and WILMINGTON.

Wiselee Gate. It takes its name from the family of Sydney le Wise of Kenardington (1327), -lee probably being a derivation of OE *lǣs*: lea, meadow.

Wissenden. Wicca's woodland pasture (OE *Wiccing denn* → Wychyndenn' 1332 → Wichindē 1334 → Wyssyndenn' 1347). Wicca also owned property at WHITSUNDEN.

Witchling Wood (Westwell). Wychelm clearing: clearing marked by a wych-elm (OE *wice lēah* → Wicheleg', Wichelegh' 1226 → Wychele 1270 → Wecholy 1579). The present name appears to have been influenced by WICHLING.

Witherden Farm (Headcorn). Wiðer's woodland pasture (OE *Wiðering denn* → Wideringdenn 863 → Wytheryndenne 1292). Wiðer, whose name also occurs in WITHERSDANE and WYTHERLING, owned a tract of marshy ground (OE *brōc*) in this neighbourhood, recorded as Wytheringbroc 1226 → Withyngbrok' 1334 → Wytheryngbrok 1350. The place is now lost.

Withersdane. Wiðer's farmstead (OE *Wiðeres tūn* → Wytherestun' 1272 → Wythereston 1307). In the development of this place name, final -ton has been corrupted to -don, producing the modern ending.

Wittersham (pronounced Wittersum). Wihtrīc's water meadow (OE *Wihtrīces hamm* → Wihtriceshamme 1032 → Wittricheshā 1226). The present place name is a contraction of these forms.

Wollage Green. Originally 'wolf heath: heathland where wolves roam' (OE *wulf hǣð*), recorded as Wuleheth' in 1254 and as Wlfethe in 1270, this place name was changed at the end of the 13th century to mean 'wolf hatch' (OE *wulf hǣcc*), probably referring to some kind of trap or snare for the animals. In this form it appears as Wolueche 1292 → Wulfhecch' 1313 → Wollwychwod 1535. The last form refers to Woolwich Wood here.

Wolverton. Wulfhere's farmstead (OE *Wulfhering tūn* → Wulfincton' 1226 → Wolfrynton' 1327 → Wolvrynton 1331).

Womenswold (pronounced Wimmins-wold). Forest of the *Wimelingas*, or active men (OE *Wimelinga weald* → Wimlincga wald 824 → Wymelingewald' 1254 → Wymelingewold' 1265 → Wemelingewold', Wemelyngwalde 1270 → Wymingswold 1610). 'The active men' appears to have been the nickname of a tribe of warriors who held the forest in this area.

Woodchurch. Church within a wood (OE *wudu cirice* → Wudecirce c.1100 → Wodechirche 1235 → Woodchurch 1610). Woodchurch Farm, Acol, has the original meaning of 'a wood' (OE *wudu*) and appears as Wode in 1203, Wod in 1275.

Woodcut. Wood cot: cot, or cottage,

within a wood (OE *wudu cot* → Wodecote 1327 → Wodecot' 1332). Woodcut Hill here has taken its name from the place.

Woodgate (near Addington). Gate on to woodland (OE *wudu geat* → Wudegate 1232 → Wodegate 1270). Woodgate near Langley has the same origin, appearing as Wodegate in 1327. Woodgate House, Borden, has the original meaning of 'wide gate' (OE *wīd geat*), being recorded as Widegate c.1230, Wydegate c.1260.

Woodlands (Gillingham). Self-explanatory (OE *wudu land* → in the Wodelonde 1327). The same meaning is found in the various Woodlands in Kingsdown, Meopham and Stone, and in Woodland, Lyminge.

Woodnesborough (pronounced Winzbra). Woden's mound or barrow (OE *Wōdenes beorg* → Wanesberge 1086 → Wodnesbeorge c.1100 → Wodnesberge 1198 → Wodnesberwe 1247 → Woodnesborough 1610). This was a place of pagan worship, dedicated to the Teutonic god, Woden.

Woods Court (Badlesmere). The place was formerly known as Godislands, being on the site of land owned by an early settler, Godd (ME *Goddes lande*), the name being recorded as Godeslond in 1270, Goddyslands in 1535. After the 16th century the place took the name of the family of Wood, whose ancestor, Robert at Wood, had owned the manor in 1382.

Woodsden. Woodman's pasture (OE *wuderes denn* → Woderesdenne 1291

→ Wadsden 1552).

Woodsell. Recorded in 1535 as Wodsales, the origin of this place name is probably OE *wudu sele*: 'wood building'.

Woodstock. Wood place: place in, or near, a wood (OE *wudu stoc* → Wodestok 1202 → Wodestoke 1332).

Woolpack. It is described in 1545 as The Woolsack: perhaps the place takes its name from an inn sign depicting a woolsack, or woolpack.

Woolton Farm (Littlebourne). Pestilence farmstead (OE *wōl tūn* → Woltun' 1197 → Woltone c.1225). This is a reference to a farmstead which had suffered some kind of disease: there is a pool here which may have caused typhoid in early times.

Woolwich (pronounced Woolidge). Wool farm: farm where wool is produced; a sheep farm (OE *wull wīc* → Uuluuich 918 → Wulewic 1044 → Hvlviz 1086 → Wolewic 1089 → Wulwic' 1226 → Wolwych 1610). Upper and Lower Woolwich near Rolvenden takes its name from that of the Rolvenden family of Waldeys (1278), also recorded as Weldisshe (1327), a surname derived from OE *wealdisc*: 'dweller in the forest'. The surname has also given rise to the name of Wildage Farm, Elham, where the family of John le Weldisse is recorded in 1292.

Woolwich Wood. See under WOLLAGE GREEN.

Wootton (pronounced Wuttun).

211

Wood farmstead: farmstead close to a wood (OE *wudu tūn* → Wudu tun 799 → Wodetone 1210 → Wudeton 1233 → Wotton 1610). Wootton Farm, Petham, has the same origin, being recorded as Wotton' in 1270, Wodetone in 1332. Woottons, Minster, is named after Sir Edward Wotton, who was granted land in the neighbouring parish of Iwade in 1548.

Wormdale. Snakes' valley: valley infested with snakes (OE *wyrma dæl* → Wurmedele 1185 → Wormedale 1195 → Wyrmedale 1313 → Wormedale 1327).

Worms Hill (Goudhurst). Recorded as Wormeshelle in 1327, this may either originally have been 'Wyrm's hill' (OE *Wyrmes hyll*), or 'snake's hill' (OE *wyrmes hyll*) — a hill infested with snakes.

Wormshill. Woden's hill (OE *Wōdenes hyll* → Godeselle 1086 → Godeshelle c.1100 → Wodnesell' 1232 → Wodneshill', Worneshelle, Wormeshille 1270 → Wormshill 1610). Dedicated to Woden, chief of the Teutonic gods, this hill appears to have been known simply as the 'god's hill' by the Christian Normans. The old name returned eventually, however, but changed its form to comply with the established religion during the 13th century.

Worsenden. Weorca's woodland pasture (OE *Weorcing denn* → Worchindenn' 1278 → Orchindene 1313 → Orchynden' 1348). There are no later forms to show how the present name evolved. Weorca — 'the worker' — also owned an enclosure (OE *worð*) at the now lost place of Werchewurda 1194 → Werkewur ð 1201 → Werkeworthe 1375.

Worten Farm (Great Chart). Wierta's people (OE *Wiertingas* → Werting 1202 → Wertinge 1254 → Wertynge 1346 → Wortinge 1621 → Worting 1690).

Worth. Enclosure (OE *worð* → Wurth 1226 → Wurthe 1259 → Worth 1610). Worth Minnis close by was originally land owned by the community (OE *gemǣnnes*) and appears as Mainesse in 1219.

Worthgate. Gate of the Wye people (OE *Wiwara geat* → Uueowera get 845 → Wrtgate 1198 → Wurgate 1240 → Worgate 1254). This is one of the gates of Canterbury, the road from it leading to WYE ten miles away. Evidently the gate was named for the people of Wye who used the road to travel to Canterbury.

Wouldham (pronounced Wold-am). Settlement of the *Wuldas*: the glorious or splendid men (OE *Wulda hām* → Uuldaham 811 → Wulda ham c.960 → Oldeham 1086 → Wuldeham 1089). The *Wuldas* appear to have been a group of victorious warriors who made their home here.

Wraik Hill (Whitstable). Recorded during the 13th century as Rake, the name is probably derived from OE *hraca*: throat, or gulley, a word which has survived in dialect speech as 'rake', meaning a path or tract.

Wren's Hill (Norton). It is described as 'landes in Norton cawled Wrens' in 1509, the name appearing to be a manorial one. Wren's Farm, Borden, is associated with the family of Thomas Wrenne of Borden (1260).

Wrinsted Court (Frinsted). Wren place: place frequented by wrens (OE *wrenna stede* → Wrensted 1111 → Wrenstede 1232).

Wrotham (pronounced Rootum). 'Root settlement': settlement where trees have been uprooted (OE *wrōt hām* → Wrotham c.975 → Broteham 1086 → Wroteham 1177 → Wrotham 1197). Wrotham Wood, Westwell, takes its name from that of John de Wrotham (1295), a native of Wrotham who had settled in Westwell.

Wybournes. The place is associated with the family of Robert and Roger Wybarn (1334).

Wye. Idol, heathen temple (OE *wīg* → Wyth 762 → to Wii 858 → Wit 1086 → Wy, Wi 1226 → Wye 1610). In 724 there is mention in a charter of *Weowera weald*: forest of the dwellers by the heathen temple; and in 858 there is recorded in this area *Wiwarawic*: farm of the dwellers by the heathen temple. These people, the *Wiware*, or people of Wye, gave their name to WORTHGATE.

Wytherling Court (Molash). Wiðer's people (OE *Wiðeringas* → Widerlinge 1174 → Weðerlinga 1177 → Wythering' 1270 → Wytherling 1313). Wiðer himself had property at WITHERDEN and WITHERSDANE.

Y

Yaldham. Ealda's settlement (OE *Ealdan hām* → Ealdeham 1177 → Aldeham 1210 → Eldeham c.1225 → Yaldam 1610). The personal name, meaning 'old man, chieftain', is also found in connection with ALDINGTON, ELLINGTON and YALDING.

Yalding (pronounced Yawldin). Ealda's people (OE *Ealdingas* → Hallinges 1086 → Eldynge 1087 → Ealdinga c.1100 → Ealdynges 1191 → Aldinges 1226 → Yaldyng 1451 → Yalding 1610).

Yardhurst. 'Yard wood': wooded hill where yards, or rods, are gathered (OE *geard hyrst* → Yerdhurst 1240 → Ghardehurst, Yardhurst 1254).

Yaugher. At the old wedge-shaped piece of land (OE *æt þǣm ēaldan gāran* → Eldegar' 1334 → Ealdegare 1343 → Ealdegar 1348). There are no later forms to show how the present name developed.

Yoakes Court (New Romney). Yoke (of land) (OE *geoc* → Yoke 1334). Yoke's Court, Frinsted, shares the same original meaning of a measurement of land, appearing as Jugo 1242 → Le Jug 1277 → Le Zoke 1346 → Yoke 1362. York Farm, Gillingham, was originally a settlement by a yoke (OE *geoc hām*), being recorded as Yocham in 1278. Yotes Court, Mereworth, has the same definition as Yoakes Court, being found as Yoke in 1332, Yates in 1690.

Yockletts Farm (Waltham). Yoklet: measure of land (OE *geoclad* → geocled 805 → Yoklete 1226 → Yoclete 1327). Yorkletts Farm, Hernhill, also takes its name from this old land measurement, appearing as Yoclete in 1254.

Yonsea. Gent's island (OE *Gentes ēg* → Yntesie 1231 → Jenteseye 1334 → Yentesaye 1347). This was once an island of firm ground in marshland, the present name being a contraction of the medieval forms.

Yorkletts Farm. See under YOCKLETTS.

Yotes Court. See under YOAKES COURT.

Addenda

Pluck's Gutter (West Stourmouth). According to local tradition, the River Stour at this point takes its name from a Mr Pluck, a landlord of the Dog and Duck Inn. During the building of the bridge here last century, he is said to have ferried the builders to and fro across the river, and in friendly appreciation of his services they nicknamed this stretch of the Stour 'Pluck's Gutter'.

Shakespeare Cliff (Dover). So named because of its association with William Shakespeare: it is believed to be the cliff described in *King Lear*, Act IV, the setting for the scene between Edgar and the blinded Earl of Gloucester.

Selected Bibliography

F.R. Banks, *Kent* (*The Penguin Guide* series), Penguin Books, Harmondsworth, Middlesex, 1955.

G.M. Boumphrey, *Along the Roman Roads,* George Allen & Unwin, London, 1935.

Kenneth Cameron, *English Place-Names,* Batsford, London, 1961.

G.J. Copley, *English Place Names and their Origins,* David & Charles, Newton Abbot, 1968.

E. Ekwall, *The Concise Oxford Dictionary of English Place Names,* 4th edition, Oxford University Press, 1960.

Roger Higham, *Kent,* Batsford, London, 1974.

A. Mawer and **F.M.** Stenton (ed.), *Introduction to the Survey of English Place-Names,* Cambridge University Press, 1924.

Allen Mawer (ed.), *The Chief Elements used in English Place-Names,* Cambridge University Press, 1924.

Arthur Mee, *Kent* (*The King's England* series), Hodder & Stoughton, London, 1969.

Bruce Mitchell, *A Guide to Old English,* Basil Blackwell, Oxford, 1965.

Murray's *Hand-Book to Kent,* John Murray, London, 1877.

John Newman, *North East and East Kent, West Kent and The Weald* (*The Buildings of England* series, ed. Nikolaus Pevsner), Penguin Books, Harmondsworth, Middlesex, 1969.

R.I. Page, *Life in Anglo-Saxon England,* Batsford, London, 1972.

Margaret Roake and **John Whyman** (ed.), *Essays in Kentish History,* Frank Cass, London, 1973.

Keith Spence, *The Companion Guide to Kent and Sussex,* Collins, London, 1973.

J.K. Wallenberg, *Kentish Place-Names,* Lundequistska Bokhandeln, Uppsala, 1931.

J.K. Wallenberg, *Place-Names of Kent,* Lundequistska Bokhandeln, Uppsala, 1934.

Kent Life magazine.